12 DNA Music of the Spheres Ascension Program from the Cosmic Twins Diary

with Keys to the Universe

by Dr. Angela Barnett

Cosmic Mystery School of the Omniverse
Publications

12 DNA Music of the Spheres Ascension Program from the Cosmic Twins Diary

with Keys to the Universe

by Dr. Angela Barnett

Copyright © 2014 Dr. Angela Barnett
http://crystalmagicorchestra.com

Cosmic Mystery School of the Omniverse Publications

All rights reserved. No part of this book may be reproduced or transmitted in any form or in any means, electronic or mechanical, including photocopying, or retrieval system. If credit is given to the author, Dr. Angela Barnett, content of the book of no more than one paragraph may be shared. For permission to share content of the book with credit given to the author for more than one paragraph, please email krystalaimagic@gmail.com.

This work is solely for personal growth, education and recreation. It is not a therapeutic activity, such as psychotherapy, counseling, or medical advice, and it should not be treated as a substitute for any professional assistance. In the event of physical or mental distress, please consult with appropriate professionals. The application of protocols and information in this book is the choice of each reader, who assumes full responsibility for his or her understandings, interpretations and results. The author and the publisher assume no responsibility for the actions or choices of any reader.

ISBN 978-1505787665

Table of Contents

Importance of Book 6

Prologue My Diary 8

DNA Activation, Violet Orb Stellar Wave
Activation and Infusion by the Cosmic Twins 25

New Jesus and Mary Story 32

Preface The Big Plan 34

The 12 Initiations of the 5th DNA Strand . . . 47

The Keys to Ascension 55

Cosmic Waves of Transformation 60

The Climax of Our Great Adventure 65

Chapter One
Awakening of Cosmic Twins 68

Chapter Two
Cosmic Flame Mission 97

Chapter Three
The Story of My Meeting
with My Starry Brother from Sirius B 133

Chapter Four
The New Jesus and Mary Story 146

Chapter Five
The Near Death Experience 160

Chapter Six
Rebirth into Our Crystal Bodies 170

Chapter Seven
The Promise 185

Chapter Eight
Creating the Stream of Manifestation 208

Chapter Nine
Mathematical Formula
of Christ Consciousness 225

Chapter Ten
Shifting into a New Time 236

Postlog
Making Heaven on Earth 244

Spiritual Healing Technologies
Resulting from Universal Life Force
Stellar Wave Activation 249

Holographic Future Music Created from the
Music of the Spheres 251

The Tower of Babel 285

Moving to Inner Earth 2017 302

Creating Illusions 309

The Truth Shall Set You Free 314

The Ascension Program
of Eternal Life Programming 329

References 408

Index 410

12 DNA
Music of the Spheres
Ascension Program from the
Cosmic Twins Diary
with Keys to the Universe
by Dr. Angela Barnett
Cosmic Mystery School of the Omniverse Publications

Within the covers of this book, the reader will find:

Absolute evidence of the True Divinity and Sovereignty of the Man who has activated 12 DNA sub harmonic strands into each of the 5 DNA. The power of immortality is revealed through the Music of the Spheres raising Man back into His Normal Reality.

This is the Extraordinary, True and Accurate revelation of how the Resurrection was performed by the Elohim Angels through the Holograms they created in the Jesus and Mary Story. This exact same process of Raising the Dead into Eternal Life was revealed once again through the shocking story of one man who had his body completely mutated by three ten ton trucks hitting his body on the freeway and five more cars running over his body before the traffic could be stopped. The body of "aDolphino" had been possessed by three demonic entities called the FAtaLee that the Grey Zeta Rigelians had prepared the interdimensional passage for.

The story of the process of holographic replication, switching the past with the future realities, and time travel to the Sirian Healing Temples in the new Harmonic Universe were parts of the ancient mystery that dated back millions of years. This event is proof that our old reality of Eternal Life is being returned to Earth once again. The story of the Cosmic Twins is what the Elohims told us was their new Jesus and Mary story.

This story, and the Formula for obtaining Eternal Life within it will prepare those Seekers for Truth to understand what has been happening and what will be happening in their own lives as they each go through this process of Resurrection and Re-birth each time they Initiate one of their 12 sub harmonics within their 5 DNA.

This Actual Event occurred to show that everything the Guardians taught as the Keylontic Science of the Music of the Stars is an absolute reality.

Dr. Angela Barnett created The Cosmic Mystery School of the Omniverse many years ago.

Dr. Angela Barnett is and has been for many years the sole founder of and the sole trainer within The Cosmic Mystery School of the Omniverse. So, often the phrase "Teachings of the Cosmic Mystery School of the Omniverse" is often seen on Dr. Angela Barnett's writing, books, articles and recordings.

http://crystalmagicorchestra.com is the home of
"The Cosmic Mystery School of the Omniverse"

Prologue

My Diary

A group of Elohim Angels appeared to me and told me to record the frequencies of all of the Consciousness that is being breathed into the Earth's Morphogenetic Field beginning in the year 2000. The first time the Angels approached me was in 1992-1995 when they taught me how to connect my Consciousness into the Mother Mary Cosmic Consciousness of Transformation. That was the period when the Crystal Magic Orchestra recorded the Base Tone Sub harmonic Frequencies that were required to begin the removal of the 11:11 Frequency Fence that would need to be completely removed by 2017.

In 2000 the Angels told me to write poems that described the Consciousness Flowing through the Universe. When I picked up my pen, the angels wrote the poems through my pen. They told me to write music, record it, listen to it, and then write about it again.

I have been doing this for 14 years now. In 2007 the Angels appeared again and gave me the Divine Formula for bringing the Highest Frequencies to Earth through Music. Once again, they told me to write poetry, draw it in pictures, create the music and then write about it again.

This has been my divine occupation since 1992. What a GRAND MISSION I signed up for. I have been allowed to hear every note, every moment, every frequency of the Grand Transition of an entire Cosmic Time Matrix being shifted into a brand new reality and a brand new time through the harmonic realignment of frequencies within the Music of the Spheres of the Earth's Time Matrix.

I have heard the obvious change in frequencies. Each time I breathe I am recording a brand new reality of time. These recordings will stay in the Hall of Records of the Omniverse as the greatest event that has been known in this Cosmos.

This transformation of an entire Cosmos for the purpose of allowing one Race Line to be set free from the Mortality that was never supposed to be placed upon it has been confirmed.

As the Cosmic Twins wrote and composed the music, they were going through the Keys of their own transformation. During their Initiations they met with different Teams. One of the teams were made of Mother Mary, Mary Magdalene, Zadkiel, Raphael, St. Germain and Merlin.

One team contained the Aquafarian Team of Cinderella, Shajinka, Tinker Bell, Winifred and Ziegfreid. One team contained Taurak and Zaurak and Markus. We were on a team with Kuthumi for awhile. However, that doesn't mean that we utilized the old formulas of Pythagarous. We just learned certain things from these Entities that are here to change reality just as we are. Each team worked with us during one stage of our initiations. These teams were formed between 1992 and 2014. Madamn Blavatsky was on our team in 2008.

You see, each time we travel into the Crystal Caves of the Ascension Vortex by using the Journey in THE COMPLETE ASCENSION PROCESS or the Foundation Meditation, we are met by a Guide who asks us to choose our next mission.

In order to be invited to begin a new mission, we must have our Keys. The Harmonic Keys that contain the Frequency Signatures of all that we have ever been in all ten million life times of this Time Matrix and all other Souls, Over Souls, Avatar and Rishi Selves in the entire Cosmos. Those Key

Signatures are within us, but must be awakened through the use of the Merkaba and the correct alignments into the Spheres where the Information is Stored. The Violet Sphere, that I am holding in the picture on the back cover of this book, contains all of the frequencies of light and sound from all of the Harmonic Keys between myself and the Inner Domains of the Sun. So, this Key or Orb will open all of the 12 Stargates that will lead me back into Attunement with the Music of the Spheres. That Attunement or Alignment Raises the Frequencies into a new level of Consciousness that presents a new reality.

The main purpose of the Individual Eternal Life Album is to connect the Individual to all their Divine Keys, which are frequency signatures.

It is easier to know what the reality is and to be able to imagine it into reality, than just to wait for something to happen. Everything that happens in our lifetime is created by our own thoughts and ideas. We must imagine the new reality or wait until someone else imagines it for us.

The Divine Reality that is presented in the picture is the Truth that the Second Harmonic Universe actually exists within our Sun. That same Sun also exists within the Inner Earth Vortex that is like a Train Station Hub that allows entrance into 12 Universes. When we ascend into the morphogenetic field of Consciousness of Inner Earth, we are aligning with the reality that allows us to live within the Sun.

As in all New Realities, our background knowledge is going to fight very hard to keep this possibility from even becoming imagined. For those who cannot accept the reality that the Second Harmonic Universe is within the Sun, there will be the long, slow route leading into the Fifth Dimension. There will be gradual signs of Inner Earth rising into Earth's Surface as a result of their Accretion Levels becoming identical.

However, those who do not use the Eyes of God, will not be able to see that either. The Masses will be waiting for something that they can see with the Five Senses, and there is nothing in the Fifth Dimension that can be seen with the Five Senses. The Fifth Dimension is beyond the Five Senses, plus the five senses. I have provided the Candle Technique at crystalmagicorchestra.com, to help you see things that you didn't see before with the Five Senses, simply because you didn't know how to.

However, this picture, on the back cover, was given to allow you to see an invisible reality. The Sphere or Orb was invisible to everyone except myself, until I took the picture. There will be more and more people seeing these spheres and orbs of Consciousness Identities every day as our Frequencies Raise into the new Morphogenetic Fields of Consciousness. That reality shows us that we can align into a dimension where we have these harmonic keys that align us directly into the Sun. We can see how there is this oneness between me and the Sun. That Oneness is created through those multitudes of Spheres. We have all seen this reality before. We just didn't know what it meant.

Yes, we are in the Fifth Dimension, and No, most people can't See it or Understand it or even Perceive of the Possibility of Living in the Sun. Only those who Believe in the teachings of Jesus Christ will Ascend. The teachings of Jesus Christ taught how we must align our Consciousness into the Christic Light Patterns of the 12th Dimension that must be activated by the 14th Dimensional Frequencies of Heliotalic Silver Pink Light Waves that attune us into the Mind of God.

Jesus Christ, Avatar 12 went on to say, "If you Believe, you shall do Greater Works than these." We are now entering the Time when we can do Greater Works than what could be done when Jesus and Mary created a Portal that aligned with One of the 12 Stargates. There have been Six Avatars born who carry the 12th Dimensional Frequencies that activate the 12 DNA of the Complete Perfect Template. One of the births in 2008 was the Soul of Sananda returning that stargate once again. The Earth needed these Avatars to open all of the Stargates in order for the True Alignment of all of our Keys to the Universe to return to the Divine Template of our original Root Race.

All of these things can be seen in this one picture. All of these Stellar Wave Infusions and Activations take place through these Harmonic Key Alignments of these Spheres like the one in the Picture. The Waves can also be seen as Aurora Borealis and the dramatic Light Shows that have been seen in 2014. The entire Ascension Program is achieved through Light and Sound. There is no other way to raise frequencies into the attunement with the Sun.

Each time we are ready to begin a new Initiation of another Sub harmonic Key, we must be expanding our Consciousness Reality into a NEW REALITY. When I travel into the Inner Domains, I am given a Guide. The Guide asks me what interest or goal or mission that I want to pursue next. The questions is basically, what is the most important thing that you want to accomplish? Each time I traveled to the Inner Domains I asked to change my mission just a little bit because I grew in my understanding of exactly what it was that I wanted to pursue.

I basically wanted to my mission to be about Healing and Music. That is why my first team contained Kuthumi and Pythagoras. They were just there to guide me to see that the Music Theory that they had introduced on Earth was only their Mission, and my Mission should be to expand what they had already learned into a much Larger Understanding and Teaching.

My Guide placed Mother Mary and Mary Magdalene on my team to help me learn about the complete Cosmaya Team and the Crystal Spheres that Mary used to travel into the heavens. They also taught me the true meaning of Bliss. The Aquafarians taught me how to use the Essence of the Crystal Spheres as tools of Healing and Transfiguration.

In 2012, I was introduced to some new members that would help me expand my perception into knowing where the holograms that are created in my light field come from and how I make them appear. This Mission included Conan Doyle, several Ranthians and Zionites who remain nameless and Light Guardians from the Akashic Records who taught me how to expand into my Coushic Records of the Spiritual Parallel Universe. Just as my 2008 team asked me to read the book explaining Mary Magdalene's Magical Crystal Spheres, in 2012, I was led to these pictures of fairies http://en.wikipedia.org/wiki/Cottingley_Fairies

http://en.wikipedia.org/wiki/File:Cottingley_Fairies_1.jpg

Prologue   My Diary

I was then led to read Conan Doyle's book, that explains exactly why these children could take these pictures. This was obviously to show me two new realities. The first reality was the reason that I could take the pictures of the Violet Spheres, and the second reason was to teach me to learn to see and take pictures of fairies.

Next, I was directed to read Doyle, (1922), The Coming of the Fairies. A more recent team of Zionites directed me to read many Scientific Studies concerning positrons, neutrinos and to understand the chemical make up of hydrolaise (the spiritual water that must be transformed in order for Earth to shift into the Accretion level of Inner Earth).

http://en.wikisource.org/wiki/The_Coming_of_the_Fairies

I am sure that I will have many more journeys to the Cities of Light where my Guides meet me to connect with new teams. I am also traveling into the Inner Domains of the Eighth Sun to meet with Cosmic Light Beings who are connecting me in Consciousness to my original Teams and Family in the Crystalai Council and the Cosmaya Light Realms. They were on the team that came forth when I asked to expand my Healing and Music into a Cosmic School program. They are the ones who took me to the Cosmic Mystery School of the

Omniverse, where all education and creation in the Cosmos takes place.

I hope that this short bio will help the reader realize why I am very well prepared for this next mission of teaching what has been shown to me in the Cosmic Mystery School of the Omniverse. This School will be very different than the Ancient Mystery Schools, because we are now in a Brand New Time Matrix in a Brand New Cosmos.

I was given a dream on December 15, 2014 showing me my body turning into light and disappearing. I have had a string of dreams leading to this one. One dream showed me riding elevators up to space ships, and being at a Universal Airport where I was to choose which Universe I would go to and I had another Cosmic Elevator dream that took me to my Crystal Mansion. I have had dreams like these for three years. However, this one was different because when I woke up there were three Angels waiting to tell me that it is time. They told me that if I want anyone to remember me after 2014, that I need to get my book published.

I have been keeping a diary of the events leading to my Ascension and the Ascension of the Cosmic Twins- my husband and I who came to Earth on a Cosmic Mission. This book is a collection of events from my diary. It is not a book of facts or opinions.

Prologue   My Diary

It is just a diary of the events in my life that led me to this departure event.

I hope it will help others find their personal paths of Ascension in the times following this closing of the Time Matrix called the 9/9/9 in 2014.

The meeting of the Cosmic Twins began long before our marriage. We had actually known each other for millions of years and we had been on many missions from the Inner Cosmic Domains into Earth's Outer Domains during the First and Second Seedings of the Human Angelic Raceline about 5 million years ago and 250,000 years ago.

Each time a Soul floats through the Cosmic Etheric, the Starry Streams and the Plasma Waves into the Earth's Portals, there is a plan made in the Heavens, long before that Soul departs from the Universal Planning Stations. The Cosmic Twins created a plan long before they began their departure to Earth.

Many of you will learn these same types of events happened to you after you grow beyond your Akashic Records into your Eternal Life Records of the EKA-Veka Music of the Spheres.

We were required to consider many things before our plan from the Crystalai Council could begin. We were to consider the actual time line of events that would lead us to remembering the exact things that needed to be done during our mission on Earth.

We knew that in order for a Star to be reborn on Earth as a Soul, we would need to break our frequencies apart into the Electro and the Magnetic or the Male and the Female. We knew that we would need a complex plan of finding each other again on Earth when we were old enough to remember.

We were to remember our past lifetimes on Earth, and the millions of family members that were taken away by demons and Phantom Matrix Fallen Angelic Races, in order to create a path to bring them home.

First, we needed to discover the exact date that would place us in the exact timeline of our Ascension back to the Inner Realms even before we began our mission. We were to be born in 1954, six months apart. We were to be aligned with the Christic Consciousness that connected to the Crystalai Council and the Elohim Angels on the Jesus and Mary Mission. We were to be connected to entities such as Mary Baker Eddy and Joel Goldsmith because they were also a part of this Cosmic Council before they completed their missions on Earth.

I chose to be born into a family where my Father was the youngest son of a family of 12. His father was Amish and his mother was a fanatic about Christian Science, Unity and the Infinite Way. My grandmother was the beloved who over saw my project on Earth after she died. She was one of those original women who fought for her rights of freedom of religion. My grandfather was Amish and did not agree with the Christian Science Sunday School, but allowed it for awhile. So, all of my Aunts and Uncles attended the Christian Science Sunday School, but were at the same time advised against it by my Amish Grandfather.

This exact Consciousness within my family was a very important guiding influence all of my life in finding my way. My mother was introduced to the Infinite Way teachings of Joel Goldsmith by my Aunt, and she was very dedicated to those teachings all of my childhood. My mother and father were not Christian Scientists, however, they both agreed that their children should be raised exactly the same way that my Father's family was raised. So, as my plan had shown me, before I chose my parents, I was taken to Sunday School every Sunday from the moment I was old enough until the day I was too old to attend.

Joe chose a family who would guide him into these teachings in a very different way. He also had two Aunts who were fanatics about Christian

Science, and a mother who hated Christian Science because she was forced to live with a Christian Science Aunt when she was a child.

Joe had a Great Grandmother who was an American Indian who was his beloved guardian from her Soul level. Joe was mostly guided to find me as a result of his great love for music. We found each other the first day of a Jazz Band Practice. Paul the Venetian was one of Joe's Beloved's who guided him in his music. He was one of the greatest composers of all times that we have never heard about because he too, was on Earth creating music from the Music of the Spheres.

Four years before we met, a Psychic had told me that I had already met my husband in a hallway of the music department at Chico State University. She told me that we would meet again at a Junior College near my original home.

I did not believe this Psychic because I was already in my third year of college. I was attending UC Davis as a Russian Studies Major. I had attended Chico State University for one semester to pursue both Russian and Music. I was studying accompaniment at that time and so I was the piano accompanist for brass groups, string groups, soloists, orchestras and individual singers.

I especially like to work with trumpet players. I had a good friend that played the trumpet who kept trying to introduce me to a friend of his who also played trumpet and trombone, and his brother who also played trumpet. The introduction never took place, because his friend was married at that time.

That person that my friend tried to introduce me to was my future husband. I guess that friend of mine was also a messenger from one of my beloved guides.

I had a dream that I did meet my husband at that University, at that time, and that we had a baby on a space ship. I was actually pregnant at that time, and did not know how, except through that dream. I was pregnant for three months and then the baby disappeared.

That is not an uncommon story between women who have been taken on space ships to give birth to the new hybrid race of Earth. There are many of us who have been told that we are the Mothers.

It wasn't until a year after I finished five years of undergraduate study in music in college in Illinois, that I returned to California. For some strange reason, I decided that I wanted to go to a local Junior College to play with a Jazz Band. I was working on my Masters Degree in Music at the

University and I wanted the experience of playing with a Jazz Band.

My future husband had also completed his B.A. in music a year earlier. He signed up to play in the same Jazz band at the same time in the same place. He was just doing it for fun.

This time when we met, he was no longer married. So, it was the first day in Jazz Band Rehearsal at the Junior College near my original home that the Cosmic Twins found each other. The Psychic was EXACTLY CORRECT.

These are the things that my husband and I experienced beginning in 1992, when the Guardians Promised our Ascension would take place in 2017. This was the beginning of removing the 11:11 Frequency Fence that was keeping our sub harmonic DNA strands from braiding together the over tones from our Over Souls into our DNA.

We also had events in our lives that corresponded to the exact date of the Harmonic Convergence in 1985. That was when we were first told to MAKE GOD's MOVIE, and when we discovered that we were staying in a village in Turkey where Mary Magdalene once stayed.

Most of the diary was written between 2000 and 2012. During this same period of time when the Stellar Wave Activations that were designed to bring in the Consciousness that was removed from us, the Crystal Magic Orchestra recorded the frequencies of each and every Infusion and Activation of this Consciousness that was restored in the Earth's Morphogenetic Consciousness Field.

We would like to share with you this picture, on the back cover because it contains a truth about each one of us within it. Each of us was Cosmic at one time. We Involved from Cosmic Plasma into Universal Stardust, into Galactic Creators, into Solar expressions, and finally into the Planetary manifestations of all that we once were. We have complete our Involution from the Cosmos, and now we are beginning our Evolution back into the Stardust that will transform our bodies to begin the new Version of ourselves.

The picture was taken in June 2008 which shows the portal of our Harmonic Keys that lead back to the Violet Sun that we came from. This was the Ascension Portal that we created in 2008. We watched thousands of dolphins and whales ascend to the second and third harmonic universe through that portal. This was the portal given to me , that allowed me to bring my Cosmic Twin back to Earth after he died while he used his body to export several Demonic Groups to the healing stations in Sirius B.

DNA Activation, Violet Orb Stellar Wave Activation and Infusion by the Cosmic Twins

This is the story about the Violet Sphere or Orb that I'm holding in my hands, (picture on back cover)which was created by the D-6 Stellar Wave Activation of Sirius and the completion of the D-5 Violet Wave Infusion from the Pleiadian Alcyone Spiral. This was the day the miracle of Stellar Wave Activation and Infusion took place simultaneously on Earth. And this is the picture that the Sirian Council wanted me to take. This was also the day that the Fifth Dimensional Dolphins Ascended into the Cloud Cities to prepare the path home to the Violet Sun.

That was the date we created the Ultra Violet Blue Sun Album.

The Electric Over Tones of the Sub harmonics were returned to Earth through the Stellar Wave Activations and Infusions. Over tones are frequencies of Consciousness from our Starry Families of our Higher Selves Original Creation, and Base Magnetic Tones are from our original Root Race Families. Our DNA is made from Over tones and Base tones in the 12 Sub harmonic strands. Those overtones and base tones were disconnected from specific chakras to remove the immortality from our race line.

The picture was taken the day the Cosmic Twins were involved in the process of the Stellar Wave Activation and Infusion of the Violet Wave. The Stellar Waves brought in the electromagnetic activation of the Earth's 12 Crystal Star Grids.

This is a true story of how DNA Activation actually takes place through the Universal Plan of Stellar Wave Activations and Infusions, followed by DNA strand Initiation and Consummation. The races of Earth are finally reclaiming their reality of their 12 strand DNA construction and returning to the heavenly land of Terra Firma. The prerequisite for this reality is activation of the 5th DNA Strand.

Our Guardians have sent Universal Life Force Currents of Light and Sound Consciousness Waves called Stellar Wave Activations and Infusions for the purpose of activating the DNA. There is no other way to activate the DNA than to participate in these Activations and Infusions of the 12 dimensional frequencies which are inherent in the Stellar Waves.

Stellar Wave Infusions and Activations create the time acceleration shift that is needed to advance the evolutionary blueprint through consciously assimilating these energies into the body. Yes, the wave infusions and activations did take place. No, not everyone consciously assimilated these activations into their blue print that would begin to create better health, vitality, multidimensional awareness, access to knowledge of all lifetimes in all dimensions and immortality.

If the stellar wave frequencies are not assimilated into the body, the time acceleration would create degeneration of the body rather than the re-birth process into immortality.

Those who are on the Ascension Path will accelerate their ability to communicate with the Guardians until complete telepathic communication with the over soul is reached. Communicating with dolphins is one step in the process.

There were Six Waves of Infusion and Six Waves of Activation.

The Waves and Infusions came from fields of Consciousness. The D-4 Solar Activation in 2000-

2004 together with the Blue Wave Infusion of 2002-2006 caused the Solar Spiral to align with Earth's Merkaba fields. That caused the frequencies of the Earth's Consciousness Field to rise exponentially.

Next, the D-5 Pleiades Activation of 2004-6/2008 and the Violet Wave Infusion of 2006-2010 increased the Earth's frequencies exponentially again by adding the consciousness of the Pleiades-Alcyone Spiral to align with the Solar Spiral Merkaba Fields.

The third activation took place 6/2008 and ended in 2012. The third activation was the D-6 Sirian Activation. This activation followed by the Gold Wave Infusion allowed the Sirian Spiral to align with the Pleiadian-Alcyone Spiral Merkaba Fields.

This Third Activation that took place in June 2008 is the time that this picture was taken for the purpose of showing the Violet Wave Infusion and the Sirian Activation simultaneously taking place.

The picture is showing the completion of the Violet Wave Infusion. The Violet Wave Infusion was completing at the same time in June, 2008, that the D-6 Sirian Activation began. I was asked by a representative of the Sirian Council to move to Monterey, in order to be there at this exact moment in history.

The Cosmic Twins were living in Redwood Shores, and had wonderful, well-paying jobs when Zaurak, my Starry Brother from Sirius B, came to our living room in April, 2008, and asked us to be completely moved to Monterey by May, 2008. We immediately gave our resignations and began packing, and started searching for the correct apartment to move into in Monterey.

This is the reason that the Violet Frequency was activated within me as I connected my consciousness into the Elohim of Hearing in Gaia to bring the highest frequencies to Earth through music. When I exhaled this Violet Wave, the 5th DNA completed its activation, which is called DNA consummation. At the same time, the D-6 Sirian Activation began.

This Stellar Wave Activation was required to begin the activation of the 6th DNA strand. The 5th DNA consummation could not complete until the 6th DNA initiation had begun. This is the process of DNA activation.

This process of DNA activation is a huge Universal and Cosmic plan which required the Consciousness of the entire Solar System, the Pleiadian Consciousness, the Sirian Consciousness, Arcturian, Orion and Andromeda Consciousness. These streams of consciousness brought in the Over Tones of the Sub harmonics into the DNA.

These problems of Broken Consciousness could only be restored by bringing the Frequencies of Consciousness in through the Stellar Activations, which brought in one dimensional layer of Consciousness at a time. First, the D-4 Solar Spiral, next the D-5 Pleiadian-Alcyone Spiral, followed by D-6 Sirian, D-7 Arcturian, D-8 Orion and D-9 Andromeda.

The original plan was to bring in D-10 Lyra-Vega, D-11 Lyra Aveyon, and the D-12 Lyra Aramatena Activations in May 2017. That plan was changed. These Activations were brought to Earth in 2012 to insure Earth's separation from the Phantom Matrix and guarantee the Bridge Zone Project's Victory. The Bridge Zone would give Earth enough time to merge into oneness with the Ascension Earth.

The final Activation of the D-12 Aramatena brought the Pre-matter Hydroplasmic Liquid Light "Christos Divine Blueprint" of the Earth-Tara-Gaia and the Universal Divine Blueprint for all intergalactic systems in the 12 dimensions of our Time Matrix. This took place in December of 2012. These 12 Star Gates of Earth's templar will remain open through Eternity from this moment on.

(Original information obtained from the Guardian's original plan that was given in THE VOYAGER'S 2 (Deane,2002). However, many of these dates were changed in Deane's workshops. In my experience, the dates did not change.

New Jesus and Mary Story

THE DIARY OF THE
NEW JESUS AND MARY STORY

Hopefully, this record of my existence will be of help to future races who pass through this plane of existence, or a situation that is similar to the one that happened to Earth.

Since this is my private diary, I will be speaking of my self, to my self and in relation to myself. This diary will be very educational in nature, and will be used in future classes of The Cosmic Mystery School of the Omniverse.

Since it is my diary, my view of and understanding of reality shifted daily. I will not be editing my spelling or grammar. Since it is my diary, I will not be quoting others, because this is my diary of my life with my Cosmic Twin. Those who are still using Low Context Rules of Communication where every little word must be placed in context and must not disagree with any other idea or thought within the book, will only find themselves disagreeing with me. In Normal Reality, things shift and change every nano second. My reality, my versions of understanding, my understanding growing because of new entities joining my creation teams are all a part of new realities forming and growing continuously. And, since this is my diary, I will be giving my opinion about many things that should be known about that have been kept secret to the world.

I know all that I know because I am always talking to my Angelic Consciousness, which is mostly at the Cosmic Level and the Primal Life Consciousness Field where the first ideas of Source are created and re-manifest within each breath of Source. I raise my consciousness into the highest frequency of Source. That causes a wave of consciousness to come into the atmosphere around me. The thoughts that come to me in those sound waves are always filtered so the ideas that come to me come on the Waves of Love which is the highest frequency in the Universe. When the Sound and Light fields weave into a vortex, a new idea is formed and it is retrieved by my pineal gland in my mid brain. All ideas that are retrieved from God's Mind.

Preface

The Big Plan

I am going to begin this story with the eleventh initiation in 2007, because that is the CLIMAX of the story and the entire point of the story. Everything else that occurred in the lives of the Cosmic Twins was obviously a part of the BIG PLAN of remembering who we are.

First, a short memory journey of the Cosmic Twins normal life. We were married 35 years ago. We chose the paths of being musicians from the time we were very young. That was no coincidence. We chose to be in the exact same place at the same time in order to find each other. That was no coincidence.

We recently learned that we both landed in a spaceship at the Sutter Buttes, Yolo County, California, 60 years ago. We were both born in the same year, six months apart. The towns we were born in were about thirty miles apart. We didn't find each other until after we had graduated from college. We had each traveled far from the place where we were born and then returned again.

We each made a simultaneous decision to join the Jazz band at Butte College for no obvious reason. The first day of band practice we decided to go to a Jazz Concert in San Francisco together, and we have been together since that moment on. Love at First Sight - not really - we had known each other for millions of years. We were actually one Star light years ago. And it won't be long, until we become that Star again.

There is only one way to become a Star. It is always accomplished through the Music of the Spheres spinning faster and faster, creating new Symphonies of Love, until a new Star is born. We had no idea that we were about to begin an Ascension Journey back to the Stars until about five years ago.

We chose to continue our experience with music on a multitude of levels including classical, jazz, pop, rock and roll, world, and healing music, and then to travel all over the world learning about many other forms of music, and then finally to learn the music of the angels. We had been prepared through the study of the physics of music to better understand the music of the spheres. I was a concert pianist and accompanist for various singers and orchestras before becoming interested in Jazz. My Cosmic Twin was a master composer and Jazz musician who chose the trumpet and trombone as his major instruments, followed by the guitar.

We were being prepared all of our married lives to understand languages, education, communication and music on an international level, obviously for the preparation of Multi Dimensional Communication, which is in fact Authentic Encounter or Telepathic Communication. We both achieved University Degrees in Music and Inter Cultural and Multi National Communication, as well as Authentic Communication and Ethnic Studies.

We became International Communication Consultants in Multi National Corporations as a result of my study of Education, Multi National Communication, Culture, Ethnic Studies, Intercultural Sociology, Russian Studies, Asian Studies, Neuro Linguistics, Language and Culture, and Music, that resulted in a Doctorate that combined research from multiple Master's Theses and Degrees into a Dissertation that took a microscopic look at Multi National Education, and resulted in the Dissertation Multi National Communication in International Business.

My true objective of combining these areas of study and working in Multi-National Corporations was to show that every thing that is learned and taught on Planet Earth was designed by a Control Group that was so powerful with their hypnotism, that the entire world would believe that what they were being taught was actually increasing their intelligence, when in fact, the true purpose of all education was to prepare the multitudes to become military warriors at a moment's notice. In fact, I was poisoned to remove the possibility of the Illuminati's control being discovered.

My Cosmic Twin mastered the art of Authentic Encounter in every country that we lived in. The true communication of Oneness replaced the need for any language in any country. We both learned the communication of raising our Frequencies of Consciousness to a Realm so far above the illusions of the world, that we could know what was really being communicated in each situation.

Asian cultures responded to this type of communication as the natural means of life because they are a high context culture that continues to use telepathic communication and communication from the heart. High Context Communication is needed to understand the God Language and the Star Language that always includes a meaning that is as big as the Cosmos. There is nothing to consider at any level of Dimensional Reality that doesn't exist in all other dimensional realities. Everything is always being considered by the Mind of One.

These parts of our lives that led us to live and work on almost every continent on the planet were obviously preparing us for Multi Dimensional Communication, because that is what we were finally taught when we learned how to use the Three Crystal Spheres of Crystal Liquid Light, Crystal Dust and Crystal Gel to form the Key that connects all realities into the original moment of creation at the state of Pre Plasma- pre light and sound- which is the Highest Frequency. The Angels taught me how to bring the Highest Frequency to Earth through Music. This formula allowed the Voice of the Angels to appear each time I exhaled.

Please note that this book was originally a diary. It was written to record day to day events. I tried to compile all of those events. Some of the events might not be in the exact order that they happened in. Since I was writing this over a long period of time there may be some present tense situations that are now past tense situations.

This book was begun in 2007, first published as a pdf in 2011, and then edited in 2014. It is taken from my diary of the past 30 years. The book began as THE MATRIX OF ILLUSIONS, QUANTUM JOURNEY 1-7, QUANTUM SCIENCE OF MANIFESTATION AND ASCENSION, FUTURE

GLOBAL MANAGEMENT and the COSMIC TWINS. All of these books are still available for purchase as pdf's and books.

I had been given a warning early in 2014 to have this book finished by my birthday in November. I didn't meet that deadline. Finally, on December 15, 2014, I had a dream where I saw my body turn into light and disappear. When I woke up there were three angels standing in front of me. They told me that if I did not publish a book before this year ended, there would be no trace of me left on this Earth. They told me that I would disappear, and I would not be remembered by any one.

I will simply apologize that my second edition did not get finished in time, and my third edition did not get finished in time. I will also apologize for any and all typos and misuse of the grammar that was created by the controllers of our cultures, because I have no respect for anything created in the holograms of world cultural beliefs. If you don't understand the words in their Low Context form, just use your High Context KNOWINGNESS.

The real names of the authors are Dr. Angela Barnett and Joe Barnett. Crystalai is the name of my highest self, who is a pre light and pre sound Cosmic Entity of Light who guides and directs my writing, teaching and singing. aDolphino was the name that Joe chose to best connect him to his original family and friends from the Oraphim Braharama Cetacean Family, when he was a Dolphin. However, he was told that he was Atoni, who was actually the Second Seeding Seres Race who became the Egyptians.

The Twins have been together for millions of years. They were a Star that was formed from the Violet Suns Ha and La. Sun Ha is the Sixth Sun, where the Cetacean Family lives and Sun La is the Seventh Sun, the home of the Oraphim Raceline that were the original creators of Gaia.

Crystalai and aDolphino began their study of music long before they met. Crystalai began speaking to Angels when she was five. Her name was Angela. She began the study of Christian Science at age 5, and also studied the Infinite Way teachings most of her life. In 2000, she was told to find a new teaching that would tell her everything she needs to know. After searching for two years, she found Keylontic Science, which she believes, is the completion of Christian Science and the Infinite Way.

aDolphino had always had a thirst for spiritual teachings, and found them on the counter next to Angela's bed when they first met. He found writings by Joel Goldsmith and Mary Baker Eddy. Those were the teachings that Angela was raised with. aDolphino became a Christian Science fanatic, and soon became a Christian Science Practitioner.

The International Life of the Cosmic Twins began in 1981, only two years after they met and got married. It was all, obviously, a designed life that led them to all of the places that they needed to be to remember who they really were. After being dismissed from the Air Force for Religious reasons before their first year of service was completed, the Cosmic Twins found themselves working on Communication programs in Korea. This began their journey of Intercultural Studies in South Korea, continued their Asian Cross Cultural and Communication Studies at University of Hawaii and completed special Communication Masters Degrees in Authentic Encounter, Neurolinguistics, Cross Cultural Education, before continuing research abroad while working on Doctorate Degrees.

The twins had already spent six years working on their B.A. and M.A. in Music before leaving to Korea. They had adventures in Universities around the world and living in South Korea, Hawaii, Turkey, Puerto Rico, Japan, Switzerland, Belgium, Taiwan, Cyprus, Boston, San Francisco, Los Angeles (Beverly Hills, Marina del Rey, Dana Point, Temecula, Visalia, Redwood Shores, Monterey), and finally back home to Chico and then Paradise, California.

We worked with Multi National Corporations around the world doing Communication Audits, designing International Communication Programs, designing JIT Management Programs, and teaching in Universities.

These were just a few of the places we have lived. Most of our homes were only for a year or two. We stayed in Japan the longest, and we identify with Japan and Korea more than any other country we have lived in. Every adventure was a critical part of a Divine Plan. There are more details of these international events in THE MATRIX OF ILLUSIONS.

LINK to PURCHASE Book is
http://crystalmagicorchestra.com/buy-books

We lived in Paradise, California, during the first year of our marriage; and, it never was a plan to return here. Our return to Paradise has been a big surprise for us.

We worked on our Masters Degrees at California State University, Chico in 1984, following our studies in University of Hawaii. Most of my research for my dissertation was done abroad, with a short return to Southern California to complete my doctorate in 1995. We returned to Chico in 2010.

Our life has completed its circle from Paradise to Korea, and then finally from Japan back to Chico and then finally to Paradise once again. In 2008, the Angels told me that it would be much easier for them to reconstruct our minds and bodies and reconnect our neuronets into the Grand Consciousness if we were to return to a place that we had spent a great deal of time in earlier in our life.

We never thought we would be returning to our original home base in 2010. Each and every moment in our lives together has been preparing us for this BIG EVENT of Ascension. We were told that 2014 will be the last year that there is a record of us on Earth. I do not know the meaning of that yet.

The times in Korea allowed us to remember our relationship to Ursa Major, M31, and the landings of our space ships from Ursa millions of years ago when I was a part of Zauraks Star Fleet.

We learned more about our relationships with Arcturians when we lived in Japan. We lived close to where we had landed on Space Ships near Beppu, Japan, thousands of years before and again after World Wars to take bodies upon our ships.

We lived in Puerto Rico and in Monterey to help us remember very ancient times and to remember our Oraphim Braharama Dolphin families and our families in the Cities of Lights. We lived in Cyprus to remember the times when the true Christians escaped into the Crystal Caves from the Roman Empire.

In the study of Cultural Travel, we learned that each time we change from one cultural reality to another, we go through CULTURE SHOCK. This shock actually transforms our DNA into creating a new reality. Our consciousness, and the way we perceive the world completely changes. Each time we go through a huge transition such as Culture Shock we actually INITIATE another subharmonic strand of our DNA.

We went through Culture Shock over and over again as we completely shifted our minds through Authentic Encounter and complete telepathic communication. In 1967 I went through an Initiation that was actually a Walk In of a higher Soul into my body when I died as a result of being thrown from my horse onto a very hard red dirt.

My Soul was switched to another Version of myself in 1985 when I was given Lethal Poison at a Five Star Hotel in South Korea. This was also my first meeting with Zaurak, my Starry Brother from Sirius B. This was when I learned that I was on Zaurak's Star Fleet Mission to create Mt. Sorak in South Korea millions of years before.

This was the event that changed my life forever. Zaurak was with me when the Zeta's arranged to have me poisoned. He was there to warn me and to arrange for my re-birth after ward. The event was staged to look like I was was being removed by the Korean Management who was at war with the American Take Over Process going on in Korea. However, it was always the Zeta's who were arranging the take overs, the wars, the murders on all levels. In 1982 I was a teacher for the Blue House Security Guards (Korea's Blue House is like America's White House). My students were the men who guarded the Korean President. I was informed by this powerful group that I was in great danger working as a Communication Investigation Consultant at this Hotel because the Entities who were in charge of this Hotel were much more powerful than any human being. Interesting fact to know is this Hotel is where the Secretary of Defense always stayed during visits to South Korea.

To make a very long story short, I had been warned several times that I was in grave danger, and by grave they meant I would go to my grave if I did not leave this job. So, one day, after my class at the hotel, many of my students bowed deeply and said they were sorry.

Hours later, when I was sipping on my coffee, Zaurak arrived in front of me, and told me to run for my life. I walked as fast as I could to the hotel door and jumped in the first taxi. My directions home were easy. I just said I live at the taxi apartments. In fact, the apartment that we lived in was called the taxi drivers apartments. So, all taxi drivers knew this place. Those were the last words that I said. The taxi driver got me safely to my apartment.

I was unconscious. When my husband came home that night he consulted a pharmacist about my condition. The pharmacist said that I had been given Love Poison, a Lethal Poison that was used to Kill the Little Wife in the old dynasties of Korea and China. He said that the poison was Lethal and that it was absolutely impossible for me to be alive.

I had in fact died and been reborn into a new version of the same body with a new level of Soul. This is what is called an Initiation that builds a new DNA strand in the body. This was the second time that this happened to me. When 2008 came, I was to learn that these deaths and rebirths would be very necessary for what was to happen next.

It is the Eleventh Initiation that was the most important, because it was the beginning of our True Mission on Earth. We were beginning the process of knowing that we were here to remove the Tower of Babel and return to the voice of the Angels.

The 12 Initiations of the 5th DNA Strand

There are 12 initiations required to activate each of the 12 sub-harmonics in a DNA Strand. We were completing these 12 initiations of the 5th DNA, so that the 5th Strand would Consummate in June 2008. This was the moment when the 6th DNA strand began it's first sub-harmonic strand initiation. Now, it is 2014, and we are half way through our 6th DNA strand initiations. The 6th DNA cannot Consummate until the 7th Strand begins initiation.

Our 11th initiation began in 2007 when we met our Elohim Angel Team and received our three spheres of crystal light, crystal dust and crystal gel. In 2008 Markus and Zaurak directed us to purchase a book by William Henry, titled Mary Magdalene: The Illuminator (2006). I will be mentioning this book in other chapters of this book. One of the main points that Markus wanted me realize is there is a very good reason he is telling us that we are the new Jesus and Mary project.

I was directed to page 84 in William Henry's book, Mary Magdalene: The Illuminator, (2006), to learn that Job had brought three bands or spheres of shimmering light with bright sparks, like the rays of the Sun, home with him after his travels into the stairway to heaven. Job gave those spheres to each of his daughters, including Mary.

This was the Key to understanding my relationship with Mary Magdalene. In 2007, in my apartment in Redwood Shores, Mary, Raphael and Zadkiel stood before me, and said, "We will show you how to bring the highest frequencies to Earth through Music." Next, three Knights of the Templar knelt before me and handed me three spheres. One sphere was crystal liquid light, one was crystal dust and one was crystal gel. Just as Job had handed Mary and his other daughters the three spheres of shimmering light with bright sparks like the rays of the sun. Henry also mentions that the Knights of the Templar wore those same three bands or spheres on their belts, and they were taken captive by the Roman Church because the power was to only belong to the Church.

So, I was given the same gifts that Mary Magdalene was given. It was the Knights who handed them to me. So, this was obviously a continuation of the story that had been stopped when the Roman Church arrested and tortured the Knights, and everyone who was related to Mary and Jesus were silenced and killed.

The story of Job, in the Bible, said that Mary and her sisters could use these bands of spheres of plasmic energy to live in the heavens in eternal bliss. The sisters never had any desire for any thing of the world from that day on. They lived in Bliss and knew they had the kingdom of heaven within them. Henry also says that when each of the sisters was given the spheres, they began to SING IN THE LANGUAGE OF THE ANGELS. These events are also documented in the book of Job in the Bible. These events were to be continued through Crystalai and aDolphino. This was the mission that needed to be accomplished before we were given our next two missions.

That is exactly what happened to me when the Angels taught me how to use the three spheres of cosmic energy - I began to sing in the language of the Angels. That was when I learned to connect the spheres of crystal liquid light (the light stream that connects to the mind of God) the crystal dust (the energy of healing) and the crystal gel (the energy of transformation).

I learned to see and feel and hold those three spheres in my crystal heart and then inhale up into the fourteenth dimension to the Elohim of Hearing and then exhale the Language of the Angels into the Crystal Spheres that I held in my hands. The spheres in my hands acted like a cosmic microphone that recorded these wonderful angelic languages and frequencies.

When Mary, Raphael, Zadkiel, and hundreds of other angels stood before us, they made it very clear that they were speaking to BOTH OF US. They told us that we were One and everything we do must be done as ONE. We always recorded our frequencies together. aDolphino always participated in the arrangements, the recordings, the technology, and he was the one who transformed all other frequencies with the Breath of Source. Again, this sounds exactly like the relationship of Mary and Jesus. We will speak of that in detail in later chapters that explain the Adonai, Adonis, Atoni and Adoni principles.

I later learned that this cosmic substance in these spheres is the plasma, the gamma rays, the heliotalic silver pink pastel energy of the fourteenth dimension. That is the energy of Transformation. That is what was called Prana, and the bread of Life. The frequency of light and sound that connects into the full spectrum of light energy of Source at the pre light and sound energy level. That is the frequency that transforms us into the Blue Body of Multi Dimensionality and Eternal Life.

The frequencies of crystal light, crystal dust and crystal gel are the transformational substance of the stardust and the gelaisic substance that transforms the body from within. The spheres are made of light, but they are also made of sound. They are made of the breath of Source igniting the flame that creates the stars and the suns. This transformational energy is extremely powerful, and when the mind is connected to the Elohim of Hearing a divine frequency carrying the language of the Angels and the Language of the gods of the eighth dimension.

The language is a frequency. Different entities have different Frequency Signatures. We learn to know each other through these signatures that carry frequencies that each sound a little different from one another. We are not talking about notes of a scale. We are talking about frequencies that each carry a different FEELING.

The Knights of the Templar bowed before me because it was time to bring the spheres back to Earth so that the mission of Mary and Jesus could be completed.

The gift we share is the ability to bring the Highest Frequencies to Earth through Music.

The 12 Initiations of the 5th DNA Strand

Our Elohim Angel Initiation Team included Mary, Raphael, Zadkiel, St. Germain, Melchizedeks, and thousands of other Orbing Entities. Our team connected us personally to the Elohim of Hearing. Next three knights handed us three crystal spheres of light, dust and gel. This is the exact technology used to bring the highest frequencies that are breathed from Source into the Ears of the Elohim of Hearing. Our angelic family translate these Keys to Eternity into the breaths that we create our music from. This is the Gift of the Highest Frequencies brought to Earth through our Music. These highest frequencies are the keys to heaven.

One of our initiations was in August of 1987 when we were living in Antalya, Turkey. We later learned that Mary and Jesus had visited this city many times. We were woken at 2 a.m. by an Etheric Entity clothed in a white garment of light. He had one simple message for us. He said, "Do It. Make God's Movie. Do It Now."

Another initiation took place in 1993 in Beppu, Japan. Again we were woken up at 2 a.m. by a different Etheric Entity who said, "Make God's Movie Now." That same night, aDolphino was given the music and song named No More War, Crystalai was given the song, Greater Works the next day. aDolphino was given a screen play to go with the music within the next few weeks. The album and the screenplay were complete within a few months. This was THE TRILOGY. In 1994 we completed the "Promise" album, which we later realized was the complete story of the Promise of the 11:11 ascension, when we will all return to the moment "before the world began."

Another initiation began in 1998 when we were again directed to "Make God's Movie." This was the year we were directed to Hollywood, California to begin creating the visual movie of "The Promise." In 2004 we won the Hollywood Spiritual Music and Film Festival Award for "The Promise." In 2000, aDolphino began working for Steve Oedekerk and Tom Shadyac, writers / directors / producers of Evan Almighty, Nutty Professor, Bruce Almighty, Ace Ventura - Pet Detective, Ace Ventura: When Nature Calls, Patch Adams, Accepted, Kung Pow, and many other award winning movies. aDolphino was an animator for several of the Thumb Movies, including Thumb Wars and Thumbtanic, at these Producer's O Entertainment Studio.

What is interesting about Joe working with Tom Shadyak for a short time, is that Tom had a near death experience about the same time that Joe did. Shadyak is now producing movies that reflect his new awakening, such as I AM and DRAGONFLY.

We are hoping to cross paths with Shadkyak some day soon and hope him to visualize our story of Making God's Movie into a movie.

That was the initiation that allowed us to realize that Making God's Movie is not something that is done in Hollywood (read our book "Quantum Science of Instant Manifestation" - LINK to PURCHASE Book is http://crystalmagicorchestra.com/buy-books

Making God's Movie is the Divine Gift of manifesting our actual desired reality every moment of every day. It is the art and science that is directly related to the three spheres.

The Keys to Ascension

The Keys to Ascension are always these Spheres created of Crystal Star Dust of the most Etheric Form. During Involution and Evolution we leave behind these Harmonic Spheres that include our Frequency Signatures. We can only return or ascend back to the places that we came from. The Human Angelic Race had their KEYS removed so that we could not Ascend back to where we came from. Ascension requires the re attunement back into these Keys of Universal Life Force Currents that strand together like a Rainbow Bridge between the place where we exist and the places from which we came. This was the same Science that Jesus and Mary were teaching when they were on Earth about 2000 years ago.

The Angels, including Mary, said we will show you how to bring the highest frequencies to Earth through Music. Next, three Knights of the Templar kneeled before me and handed me three spheres. One sphere was crystal liquid light, one was crystal dust and one was crystal gel. Just as Job had handed Mary Magdalene, and his other daughters, the three spheres of shimmering light with bright sparks like the rays of the sun. The Crystal Liquid Light was also what was called the Blood of Christ in the Bible. It is the 12th dimensional Liquid Star Dust that turns the Blood into the new Blood Crystals that transform the body. The Crystal Star Dust was the Healing Powder and the Crystal Gel was the Atomic Radiation Gelasic Substance that Transforms and Creates new Reality. The Spheres have a specific Resonance and Harmonic Structure that continuously pulsate and echo through out the Universe. The Spheres contain the Frequencies of the Music of the Spheres.

Henry (2008) also mentions that the Knights of the Templar wore those same three bands or spheres on their belts, and they were taken captive by the Roman Church because the power was to only belong to the Church.

So, I was given the same gifts that Mary Magdalene was given. And it was said that Mary and her sisters could use these bands to live in the heavens in eternal bliss. The sisters never had any desire for any thing of the world from that day on. They lived in Bliss and knew they had the kingdom of heaven within them. Henry also says that when each of the sisters was given the spheres, they began to SING IN THE LANGUAGE OF THE ANGELS.

That is exactly what happened to me when the Angels taught me how to use the three spheres of cosmic energy. That was when I learned to connect the spheres of crystal liquid light, the light that connects to the mind of god, the crystal dust, the energy of healing and the crystal gel, the energy of transformation. I learned to see and feel and hold those three spheres in my crystal heart and then inhale up into the fourteenth dimension to the Elohim of Hearing and then exhale the Language of the Angels into the Crystal Spheres that I held in my hands. The spheres in my hands acted like a cosmic microphone that recorded these wonderful angelic languages and frequencies.

The Knights of the Templar bowed before me because it was time to bring the spheres back to Earth so that the mission of Mary and Jesus could be completed.

Our twelfth initiation began in 2008 when aDolphino disappeared right before my eyes. Markus appeared before me and told me that aDolphino was gone, and that thousands of Angels had tried to bring him back into his body, but they couldn't find him. They told me that the only way to bring him back would be to arrange a hologram of his body to be killed, so that he would be horizontal long enough for them create a new version of him. They told me that if they didn't do this that I would never see my husband again.

Two days later I received a call from Mercy Hospital in Redding. I learned that my husband was hit by three trucks and five cars. When he woke up four months later, three angels appeared to him and said, turn over and thank Crystalai for saving your life. They said, "We could not save you. Only she could save you."

This was the moment when we both knew that we had now created God's movie. We had become the Quantum Observers of the reality that we could make as our Frequencies aligned into the Infinite Unknown of Source Consciousness. The angels told us that our names were written across the skies of heaven and that all angels have heard our music, because they are the ones who have made our music.

In an earlier initiation, in 2010, where we were working with a team of Aqua Crystal Light Fairies from the fourteenth dimensional liquid light rebirth chambers of Inner Earth, the Oraphim Angels and Elohim Angels who were aligning our frequency chambers through our breaths into the crystal pillars of Aqua Crystal Light Fairies Reality. We were told that we are the Lightning Rods on Earth connecting the Sound Frequencies from Inner Earth into the Light Frequencies of Sirius B in the Aquarius Galaxy. Our frequencies connect the rainbow bridge between the atmosphere of Earth into the birthing chambers of Inner Earth and out into the Star Dust of Sirius B.

There were many other events between these dates. The Masses completed the hardest part of the ascension journey in 2012 that prepared us for our mass transformation in 2014. Now we are in 2014, and this is the year of the 9/9/9, meaning we are completing the Cosmic Clock of this Time Matrix. There will be some Avatars on Earth who are completing the initiation of their 8 DNA strand. The completion of the 6th Strand harmonizes us into the Second Harmonic Universe. The eighth is the octave connecting us into the new harmonic universe three. 2014 is the beginning and the end of a brand new reality.

Cosmic Waves of Transformation

We are each created from sphere upon sphere upon sphere as the music of the spheres. Each one of these spheres is one of our selves incarnate. In our original template there are 144 spheres containing selves. In the larger cosmic template there are 144,000 of these spheres containing selves. In the complete Cosmaya template of our Oneness with all, there are uncountable selves. All of these selves are now being separated by a mucus membrane lining which we have called KARMA. This karma is simply the frequency film that is separating us from our oneness with all that we are.

We can think of these spheres of selves as the petals of the lotus blossom. As we connect our frequency signatures into each one of these petals, we open that petal into oneness with our frequencies. Our consciousness is unfolding as each of the petals opens and unfolds. When we finish weaving our frequency signature into each petal in the lotus blossom and all blossoms are opened, this means there is one brand new frequency of oneness with all of the SELVES or the petals.

I was trained by a group of Elohim angels to use three crystal spheres, which together activate all of the spheres of our 144,000 selves. Each activation is like connecting notes into one chord or frequency and then connecting into more notes to create a new tone or frequency. Until all frequencies align into one brand new frequency.

If we were actually trying to do this with notes on a musical instrument, there would be a limited number of notes that would align so harmonically. However, when I do this process by first activating my breath through the alignment of the three crystal spheres through my soul into Source and then back through my breath, the 144,000 breaths align in a beautiful new frequency.

Many of you have heard these frequencies at crystalmagicorchestra.com. I've aligned the music of the spheres through these spheres out into the breath of Source, that is the point beyond the Cosmaya Template of 12 Cosmos. Next, I align my consciousness into that same activation of Source through the Cosmaya frequencies.

Next I breathe these frequencies into Sun Alcyone's frequencies, and then I exhale these frequencies into our Solar Sun. And the I align those frequencies into the Heart of Mother Earth. Now, that I have these same frequencies that will be used for our transformation, I exhale them into my own 144,000 selves or spheres within spheres.

This is how I activate the removal of all karma that is creating separation between all the VERSIONS of my selves. When all of this karma is removed, the more I can meet personally with each of my selves and gain their unique qualities and powers as my own. I have spoken many times before of my family of consciousness to include Cinderella, Shajinka, Winifred, Zaurak, Zeena and many others from Aquafaria.

This is my Aquafarian Family who were the original creators of the StarDust Foundation of the Earth. They are Elementals who connect our Sixth Dimensional Selves into our Complete Cosmic Template. They are in fact Cosmic Entities including the Cosmic Dolphins. I meet a few new members each time I initiate a new activation. My relationships with these family members is what increases my wisdom, my knowing of what is happening in the future, and my manifestation abilities.

This same activation will take place naturally for those of you who align your consciousness into the Stellar Waves of Universal Life Force Currents, that will be used to activate the Consciousness of Earth and all who are upon Earth. It is by understanding how to use these Currents of Consciousness to open your spheres into your selves, that you allow more and more Versions of yourself to appear.

Each time one of these bursts of gamma waves comes to Earth between 2000 and 2017, along with the Cosmic Blanket of Plasma Energy activated by the breath of Source, we will have an opportunity to allow another layer of karma to be melted away from the spheres that make up our templates. Each one of these spheres is one of our incarnate selves who has had personal experiences on this plane and many other planes. Some of our incarnate selves could be a part of the 10 million years of reincarnations on earth. They could also be selves who never fell into this system at all. They could be selves from Aquarius, Aquafaria, Orion, Sirius, Pleiades or any of the million systems. Some of our incarnate selves may even be a Star or a Sun.

As we realign into Oneness with all of these selves, we gain the ability to know and do everything they have done. That means if one of our selves has been a sun, we can also be a sun one day. If one of our selves is from Aquafaria, then we are also able to return to Aquafaria. If we have opened access to a self who has been buried in the fear of death from torture, then that self will bring that karma of fear into our lives until the karma is melted away. Removing karma can only be done by raising ones frequencies completely into the frequencies of the cosmaya flame as it is penetrating the Earth.

The Cosmaya Flames have already come to Earth two times. Each time there has been a great stir of may levels of karma that might include fear, confusion, intimidation, and even images of those selves coming forward.

The reason that we must not try to remove those selves is because they are a part of who we are. They each contain diverse parts of our self that we have not had access to before. It is the oneness with these other selves that will make us able to have instant manifestation. As each of these selves may have been either a genius, very wealthy, a sun, a moon, a star, an entity of great cosmic wisdom, etc. etc., once we obtain oneness with all that we are, we also contain those abilities. We will also begin to see each of our selves and choose to take on qualities and appearances of other selves. We will eventually gain the ability to morph into any or all of these selves. This doesn't mean any one of them ceases to exist. We all exist individually and collectively.

The Climax of
Our Great Adventure

About four months after his body was lain on the hospital bed, the new aDolphino arrived on Earth for the first time. He turned to me and he said the angels were sitting on the bed talking to me. They told me to turn around and thank you for saving my life.

Later, Markus and Zaurak told us many other things about our adventure. They told us that they actually pulled aDolphinos real body through his past self up into a space ship and replaced it with a hologram when the three trucks hit the body and the five cars ran over the body. That would explain why his body appeared almost untouched in comparison to such a catastrophic impact on his body.

The Climax of Our Great Adventure

His body was retrieved by a helicopter after a report of a ten ton truck throwing his body out in the middle of a freeway after another ten ton truck and thrown him in front of that truck, and there was a third truck that brushed his body as it was flying across the freeway. After the body landed on the freeway five more cars ran right over the top of it without stopping or even knowing it was there.

So, imagine what a body would look like after that happened. His body did have a huge scar on the forehead where he had broken the headlights of the truck with his head and his hips and spine were broken from the fall after flying through the air. The only damage from the cars was a broken off leg.

Zaurak and Markus actually told me that they were hoping this would become their new Jesus and Mary story because they are really tired of hearing the "Jesus was nailed to the cross" story. And the fact was that they made up that story. They said they were on the team that chose Arihabi to be nailed to the cross and then created the hologram of his resurrection. They said they didn't know that their story would be such a long lasting dogma that would keep people mesmerized for so many years. They told me that they thought this would make a much better story, and some time in the future enough people will understand this story and how important what we did was.

The Climax of Our Great Adventure

They told me that there would be much more to be known about the portal and the saving of many of the Whale People who were our original family of creation – the Oraphims from Gaia.

The reason I wanted to tell you about Zaurak is because he is back again with his star fleet from Sirius B, the Blue Maharaji. They will be the second E.T. race that the masses will meet. I have already met one of them.

The Sirian Council worked together with the Ra Confederation, Eieyani, Azurites, Ranthions, Zionites and the Majaraji on the project of Comet Ison. Project Ison was actually the completion of what the scientists discovered in 2005, when they saw the explosion in the Ursa Major, 550 million light years away.

This flow of Cosmic Rays is the flow of the frequencies that are needed to re-awaken the mid brain in a way that will allow the seventh seal to melt away and the accretions of the magical crystal gel of transformation will begin to flow through our bodies.

Chapter One

Awakening of Cosmic Twins

aDolphino and Crystalai (I am Crystalai and aDolphino is my husband) came to Earth to find each other after leaving a Standing Wave Hologram of themselves in the Cosmic Aquafaria. We return and reconnect with our twin selves in Aquafaria every day.

aDolphino faces his Dolphin hologram and reunites in oneness as Crystalai faces her Mermaid hologram and enters into oneness. When we were in Aquafaria we agreed on this Cosmic Mission to leave our standing wave patterns of our full frequency signature so that we could reconnect and return at any time. We can return to Aquafaria and transform back into Dolphins or Mermaids and bring that complete Cosmic Frequency Signature back to Earth.

Chapter One   Awakening of Cosmic Twins

That Cosmic Bi-location ability allows us to open doorways and star gates that allow many others to pass through physically unharmed into the higher dimensions. Most on Earth will ardoah out of this Earth Plane by stepping into their Blue Body and Light Body and then receiving a new body of Mass that is not as dense as this present physical body. Those will be the ones who did not keep their physical body - or what has been formally called death. This is no longer death. This is the needed evolutionary process into our new reality.

There were originally many of those of us who came from the Cosmic Realms to open the doors at this time. Most of us got destroyed by the Grey Ones and other Dark Entities who know that our power must be eliminated in order for their drama to prevail.

Crystalai has died twice and aDolphino has died once. The Zeta Greys found Crystalai when she was working at the Five Star Hotel in Korea. The Greys have complete control of all governments and all banks and all wealthy institutions in the world. So, it was natural that they would be in control of this hotel that was used for frequent Department of Defense meetings. The Greys arranged for lethal poisoning of Dr. Angela Barnett at that time. She went through the planes into the plane of Bliss and was met by her starry families including the Elohim,

Zaurak from Sirius, and her Aquafarian mother, Cinderella.

This was the moment when Angela became Crystalai. Crystalai was reunited into her hologram or standing wave pattern of her complete frequencies of Aquafaria and then returned to her body that had already died. That happened in 1985 at the very beginning of the harmonic convergence. This was the beginning of the preparation for the complete opening of the doors and stargates in and out of the Earth Matrix.

Crystalai and aDolphino were asked by Zaurak to move to Monterey, California in 2008 to prepare another Evac scenario and to begin the Cosmic Mystery School of the Omniverse. We were directed to live in an apartment that was on top of one of the deadliest Zeta Grey stations on Earth.

The Monterey Naval Academy contained a stairway down to an underground city that provided a safe place for officers and politicians and an experimental lab where many terrible processes allowing the Zeta Greys to experiment on our Cetacean families.

This city was located in a parallel inter-dimensional area. There was also a Black Hole Funnel a few hundred feet out in the Bay directly in front of our apartment. Many Marine Divers had attempted to explore that Funnel. Most of them died, and none of them ever returned--declared missing.

I had a friend named Tinker Bell, who was a Seal who lived in that area. She asked me many times to go swimming with her into that Funnel. She told me it would take me to the Cities of Light. I told her that I was excited that she thought I could make it. I told her that I would like to wait. The angels told me that I should wait until after 2014.

We met our Cosmic Cetacean families in Monterey. Cinderella, Shajinka, Winnifred and Tinkerbell as well as hundreds of other whales, orcas and dolphins, as well as seals frequently tried to meet us on the beach. Every time we saw them coming toward us, we also saw a military marine ship take off toward them and shoot them. We ran frequencies through the underground base that was capturing our family members and created an ascension portal through Monterey.

We saw our family being lifted into the sky through the doors that we opened back into the Cloud cities and up into Urtha and all the way back to Aquafaria. We also saw our Orca friends escape the tanks by disappearing from the tanks and reappearing in the ocean.

The Zeta military knew that there were extreme beings at work in the area and began to hunt us down. One day, while aDolphino was walking on the beach, the Greys captured him and took his Soul. They chose not to kill him, but to take his Soul. They knew that he loved Crystalai so much that he would do any thing to save her, including risking his own life.

First, aDolphino told Crystalai that he was like the walking dead. He told her that they said if we would both leave Monterey forever that they would promise to not do to Crystalai what they had done to aDolphino. They told aDolphino that they could only stay together if they would leave. aDolphino was being ordered around by the Greys and terrified just as they had done to Adolph Hitler, and many other leaders that had their souls taken by the Greys. The difference was that Hitler sold his soul for power and technology of the deadliest war machine, while aDolphino was being held in exchange for Love.

Crystalai worked day and night running frequencies that would transmute the darkness out of Monterey and out of aDolphino and to create an Ascension Portal that would free aDolphino. The oversoul and starry families and hundreds of angelic councils appeared before us and told us that there was nothing that they could do. They told us that there were thousands of angels trying to save aDolphino's Soul. They said there was nothing that they could do. While I was creating the Violet Portal, aDolphino disappeared. Marcus--aDolphino's Higher Self, appeared and told me that aDolphino was gone forever. He said that thousands of angels had tried to bring him back to his body, but they couldn't find him. They said he went some place that even they could not go.

Crystalai continued to send her frequencies into Aquafaria and searched for the hologram of aDolphino in Aquafaria and tried to reunite with his hologram. Before aDolphino became more and more possessed by the Zeta Greys, he had been directed moment by moment by Marcus. He had been told weeks before that there were three Demons who wanted to possess his body. He had been practicing staying in complete communication with his higher self during those weeks. Moments before he disappeared, he stood in the center of the living room like a zombie with his arms stretched out as if he were nailed to the Cross.

He was completely unconscious and could no longer be contacted. Next, he laid across the floor of our music studio and ordered Crystalai to stay away from the music and to never touch the equipment again. It was definitely a different demon entity possessing his body at this time.
 The Greys were showing that they were afraid of two things. The first was Christ being nailed to

the cross which would result in the resurrection of mankind. The second thing they were afraid of was our music studio which was able to bring the music of the spheres to earth. Later that day, an angel appeared and told Crystalai to leave because she was in great danger, because the Greys had decided to destroy both of them.

Crystalai left the apartment and stayed in a hotel that night. Crystalai had left her home without her purse or any money. A divine angel, Adriana, who was a student in the Cosmic Mystery School of the Omniverse, offered to help Crystalai pay for her room in the hotel. Crystalai stayed gone two nights to make sure it would be safe when she returned.

When she returned, she learned that there was a part of aDolphino's consciousness still attached to her and that both wanted to return to her and yet protect her at the same time. The new version of aDolphino drove hundreds of miles away and then commissioned a jet plane to bring him back to Monterey and then immediately got back on the plane and flew away again. He was going back and forth from wanting to remember who he was and then wanting to forget.

Crystalai worked together with a trained psychic who had technology from Ashtar Command who were able to help Crystalai locate the direction that aDolphino was traveling. I actually wasn't sure that

I believed the facts that I was being given because aDolphino had left from Monterey and the psychic said he had traveled south and then East. That meant that he was going back to where we lived before in Visalia (near Bakersfield) and then inland toward our home in Temecula, which is on the way to the Four Corners, where he would reach Arizona. The next day, I got news through radar that he had traveled back to Monterey again. I was sure that he must be on a space ship.

The angels directed me to call my credit card company to find out where he had used the card. I learned that he had in fact driven to Bakersfield, and then to Arizona and back to Bakersfield. After that, he had rented an Airplane and flew to Monterey. Then he got back on the plane about one hour later and returned to Bakersfield. (My heart knew that there was still something inside of him that was remembering me as his home, but then something else that was making him forget).

The fourth night, Markus, Zaurak, the Elohims and the Aquafarians visited Crystalai at her bedside and told her that the only way that aDolphino would be able to return to his body would be through death. They told her that his soul would be lost forever unless he was stopped by some tragic accident. They told her that she would need to be prepared for a long journey with aDOLPHINO to bring him back.

The next morning Crystalai received a phone call from Mercy Hospital near Mt. Shasta. Crystalai was told that aDolphino was in the emergency care center. She was told that he was basically a corpse when they scraped him off of the freeway. They said that he was dead on arrival; but, there were signs of life, so they assumed he was in a coma.

However, they didn't really believe that there was any hope of him coming out of the coma. The neurologist asked permission to drain the blood out of his head, and, there would be a very high risk of mortality.

Crystalai's presence was requested as soon as possible. Crystalai immediately went to the airport and arrived at the hospital as soon as possible.

Crystalai was told by the neurologist that aDolphino would remain unconscious for unknown amounts of time and that it would be absolutely impossible for him to return because of his condition and his age. The doctor said that only a healthy twenty year old could possible survive the condition.

The other doctors told Crystalai that her husband was trying to commit suicide by standing out in the center of the freeway. Another 911 caller reported that there was a person laying in the middle of the freeway trying to get run over.

Chapter One

The truck driver that did hit aDolphino called me at the hospital and told me what actually happened. He said that it looked like another truck had just pulled into the truck gas station on the freeway, and as he was pulling in, he must have pushed the body out into the freeway. He said that when he struck aDolphino it appeared as if he were falling out into the road. The truck was traveling at 50 mph and dodged the body only to strike it with the left front light. He said the light was cracked and had blood on it. That was the only fact that was left in the police report. It said there was blood on the front left light of the ten ton truck.

The truck driver shared the story that was also recorded on the police records. There was a recording of when the truck driver pulled over and called the police. During the phone call I could hear all of the cars driving by and people screaming and the truck driver saying the body is laying in the middle of the freeway and the cars just keep driving over the top of it. He said at least five cars already drove over the top of the body. He said he couldn't see clearly because there was another truck that pulled in to the station to miss hitting the body.

The truck driver said someone has to stop the traffic. They just keep coming and driving over the body. There were many screams in the recording.

Chapter One — Awakening of Cosmic Twins

This is the story that Markus and Zaurak told me later to explain what had actually happened on the Freeway that night.

aDolphino's car was stopped on the freeway right outside of Mt. Shasta. His body was lifted up into the Mother Ship through a torsion field. He went through the process that we think of as dying. But it was actually much more than that. It was a journey to the place where others have had their souls taken away and replaced by the dark illuminati.

aDolphino opened a door for himself to return to Earth and a door for those who were trapped in the mirror to move on through.

Joe's body reappeared on Earth in the center of a highway. Three truck drivers who hit his body each testified the same thing. They said his body appeared in the middle of the road out of no where and they don't know how he got there. Joe was hit by three trucks and then five cars ran over his body. He was very dead, and yet his oversoul self, Markus entered his soul into Joe while he was on his journey up to Aquafaria and into the Plane of the Bliss. Markus waited until Joe was ready to return to his body. Crystalai watched the oversoul fly out of the back of Joe's body and join together with another light body coming into aDolphino's body. It was like watching death and rebirth happen at the same time.

Back at the hospital, Crystalai told the doctor to keep his opinion to himself and was not given any permission to pursue operations on aDolphino. Crystalai did this because she knew that the Greys would be able to attach themselves easily to aDolphino once again during a medical operation.

Crystalai stayed at the bedside of aDolphino and kept playing the Ascension Kit music that they had created together which contained a combination of both of their frequencies of them together as Cosmic Flames in Aquafaria as well as the complete Cosmic Frequency Signatures of the Elohim Council, Mother Mary, the Elohim of Hearing and an entire Ascension Portal that would unlock all doors on all planes between Earth and Aquafaria.

aDolphino's condition improved dramatically each day. His one thousand broken bones healed dramatically to the point that he could stand up. The tumor in his brain disappeared. Crystalai coached aDolphino daily to remember who he was and to repaint his memory of his life in Aquafaria. aDolphino was able to remember his holographic standing wave pattern of himself as a dolphin long before he could remember his family on Earth.

It was four months later when aDolphino got up from bed and turned to Crystalai and said there are three angels sitting on the bed talking to me, and they told me to turn to you and say thank you. They told me that they were unable to save me, but it was you, Crystalai who brought me back.

It wasn't until December of 2010 that Crystalai finally understood what happened, why it happened and how it happened. The journey that aDolphino took included a trip to the dark place where Lucifer had been wandering around in for eons. aDolphino spoke to Lucifer to find out what he was doing there. Lucifer told aDolphino that he didn't know how to get out. aDolphino showed Lucifer the light and told him how to go home.

Something that is very unique about our NEAR DEATH experience is that because we are Cosmic Twins, meaning the same entity originally, I could experience everything that he experienced. I was able to talk to Markus through aDolphino's body. I was able to hear aDolphino's journey into the home of Lucifer and his entire Aekashic records coming out of his mouth. I was able to create a portal into the Cosmic Realms where there is still a hologram of the Star that we were as ONE. I could reconnect myself into that Star in order to return aDolphino back to Earth.

The essence and consciousness of aDolphino is an entirely different person than the husband that I had before. He doesn't seem like any one that I have ever met from Earth. He acts like a Sirian, not an Earth Being. He is completely oblivious of our ways of thinking. I try not to force him into our sociological patterns, and I protect him from being labeled crazy at the same time.

The adventure that aDolphino took was a completion of opening portal doors that would free all other Indigos and Crystal Beings from the demonic possessions that were planned to occur on Earth over the next few years. There had to be one set of Cosmic Twins to set a pattern where our Maharaji Sirian Families could free all of the other Demonic Possessions.

We were the ones who did this for the Earth. We also completed the task of Freeing our Oraphim Family, who would had been pulled into the Phantom Matrix and had their raceline removed forever.

The Demons were actually Green Dragons. The Red Dragons took over the Oraphim raceline through possession techniques exactly like the ones described here. The Red Dragons set the formula of taking over the female body in order to capture the cosmic twin templates. The Oraphims became Blue Dragons and then got so angry that they decided to become Green Dragons and then demonic beings. When they lowered themselves to that frequency level they could then possess one of their own origin in order to be set free from the hell they were pulled in to.

So, you see, the demons were actually originally our Creation Family, the Oraphims. They were fallen because they were taken prisoner by the Red Draconians. They used the pattern of knowing that they would need to possess a female Indigo in order to get the cosmic template.

What we didn't realize until later, is because Zaurak and Markus had set the stage for this entire event to happen in Monterey, part of the trick was to have me spinning my Merkaba counter clockwise instead of clockwise, and to have aDolphino spinning his merkaba correctly. This caused the Demons to believe that aDolphino was the FEMALE.

But, after he was taken, they told him that they would take my body as well. That is why he fled from Monterey. He was being directed by Markus to get as far away from me as possible because the demons knew that they had taken the wrong partner and they still needed my body.

That is why aDolphino's subconscious - his Higher Self, Markus, told him that he had to follow directions very carefully in order to save us both. And then I had to make the final choice of allowing the accident, appearing at the hospital and then creating the cosmic portal. I was told that I was the only one who could do that. I was told by Markus that thousands of angels had tried to save aDolphino, and they couldn't get him to return to his body.

That was the beginning of opening the stargates and doors that will allow all on Earth to travel out of the planes that have been blocked from the light for eons.

Now, we realize what has happened and how we are now prepared to complete our contract of opening the doorways to Deity Planes. This last shift is bringing us into alignment with what we need to do to fulfill our deification process and fulfill the contract we came with to Earth before we began searching for each other. Now we can begin helping the rest of the host mission here by opening the doorways for others to pass through.

Our first mission on Earth was to find each other. Our second mission on Earth is to open the doors for all back to the Cosmic Planes of our full reality. This will be the beginning of all Cosmic records from the Halls of records of our past, present and future realities. We will soon know ourselves from all millions of lifetimes on this matrix and beyond into all universal realities.

Only moments before completing this book, the angels reminded me of a few more events in my life that I had never considered before. They told me that when I was knocked unconscious from falling off of my horse in 1969, that I also had a Death Experience. They told me that my Soul was switched to a new walk in Entity that connected me to the portal that I would need later in my life. They said that portal of my rebirth was also needed in creating the 11:11 Fence that saved the Earth from Solar Implosion in 1972-74. They told me that was the reason why the Magnetic Base Tones were distributed through our Promise Album in 1992-94. They told me that the Cosmic Twins have been a central part of the entire Harmonic Convergence Process. This rebirth in 1969 was the connection to the Rishi Soul Essence of Crystalai, the most powerful being of ONENESS in the Cosmos.

We were creating portals of rebirth into the Earth's Morphogenetic Field during each of our Near Death (which were actually Death's and RE-births). This happened in 1969, 1985 in Korea, and it happened to me a third time when I was called to the hospital. These portals needed to be created before the demonic possession event of 2008.

I'd like to review our first Christic activation journey that happened right before aDolphino was taken by the Fata Lee (who we originally thought were the Greys) in Monterey. We had just spent five full days and nights having our Christ Body activated in the Mother Ships. A Cosmic Team, plus Zaurak and Markus, came to guide us through this process and to keep reminding us to stay awake and to focus. Unfortunately we fell asleep a couple of times. We were guided by many great Entities during the process who asked questions to test us on our sincerity toward healing. It was a very long, gloriously painful process. We were told we were being used to cut a path for others if this process completed successfully. We had to remained completely inside Aquafaria day and night to make the activation complete.

We were given all of the meditations needed to help others through this process. It was much like entering the pearly gates where there is a board of Angels judging constantly.

We were told that the frequencies were high enough and it was possible for the complete Ascension to take place. Before we can slide back and forth between Earth and Aquafaria we will be pulled through a funnel into the ultra violet blue frequencies of our Mother Star Ships of co-creativity.

We will be completely transformed into our 12 Original Blue Print of our original Divine Selfhood. At this time we can live on Earth and sleep in Aquafaria. We have already committed to living on Earth for doing the Cosmic Mystery School of the Omniverse. We made the commitment for this assignment.

Chapter One

We have been given greater explanation of this responsibility to bring forth at this time. We were told that this is necessary for completion of the Full Christed Being. We were told that we must enter into the Earth herself in order to ascend with her. As we enter into the Christic domain of Earth's Crust and become the lightning rods to connect the 12th dimensional Christ Grids in Earths Crust up into the Christ Grids 10,000 feet above the Earth and to connect through consciousness into the Cosmic Domain of Earth within her Crystalline Core - her Heart. Mother Mary told us that ascension is always completed through the Heart of the Planet. This is because our heartbeat changes as Mother Earth's frequencies change. We were told it is our responsibility, as the leaders of the ascension process, to continue in the frequencies that we have been given in our recordings and to do the meditations that align all frequencies into attunement.

We each have this option now available. We must state this desire with unshakable conviction. To become the fully Christed Being we must take a slightly different path to the New Earth. We must connect to the highest frequencies of all of the Sun's in the Galaxy as Mother Earth has done. Our complete Multi-Lifetime Records become available all of the Frequencies of the Suns or the Frequencies of our Consciousness aligned through the Crystal Heart into these Frequencies are allowed to penetrate our crystal cells in our hearts and our bodies.

When this complete activation of the body is known and understood we become the original immortal selves who can return to this Earth to teach others how to Ascend into this perfect state of being. The physical body is now realigning into a new chemical structure that turns the density structure that has been flowing inward into a new reality that flows outward and upward.

This is what is causing the bursts of pain in the body. It is being transformed. The body will feel less and less dense as the process becomes fully activated. We become more and more airy feeling. The new structure of the body is a silica based form that transforms into a healed alignment as the source of crystal light is called upon. Each of the healing energies or elementals of alignment have names that we call on for these activations.

The names and codes that were placed in this music call on these entities of crystal dust, crystal gel and crystal light to realign the body toward the process of ascension.

The first stage to returning to the Christed State is to glide, bi-locate and slide to New Earth. We have gone through these processes of gliding in consciousness, bi-locating our bodies, and finally being taken aboard the Star ship where several Entities worked on our bodies using light frequencies. When the body is completely aligned by the Sirian Healers through light frequencies our bodies are in a new chemical make up that allows transformation into crystal dust energy for sliding into our Aquafarian Home.

The eye of the Cosmos connects to every smaller structure of Spirit and light and matter that are within the body of the Cosmos so from the core of the cosmos there is now coming in a light and a wave as it enters into our system. It is actually making the air run like water. The air is taking on a texture. A hydrolaise infusion is coming in.

There will be sparkles on the skin where the skin crystals interact with the hydrolaise. The texture in the air is some where between air and water and it is substance you can both swim in and breathe. It is a natural substance on Urtha and on Ascension Earth.

These are the tones of the Crystal Light Energy. There is a set of tones for each of the transfiguration points. Each body has a set of corresponding tones that are unique to itself. The braids of energy coming in from the five spheres frequencies are aligning Mother Earth's Body and our body into a new density alignment. This is activated by bringing together the frequencies of the higher spheres into our bodies and then calling on the Entities for help in aligning these energies into our bodies. This awakens the crystal cells in the body to remember their Akashic Records of who we really are.

The base pulse rhythm of the original out breath from God Source is the One more tone is needed in this process. It is layered in frequencies of Source Energy, Crystal Light Energy, Etheric Self Energy, and Oneness Energy. This is the activation code for Prana and for the Aqualene Sun Activation aligning us through Oneness to the Ascension Earth, and to all dimensional realities. Re a Vea Ru Christalo Hydrolaise is the final element required to unite Earth into the complete frequency and crystal light alignment of Aquafaria. Aquafaria is the original home of many of us on Earth at this time. Hydrolaise is the blood of the Christ - the Lava Flows from the Eye of God - the Eye of Alure - the always opened eye of Source – the Cosmic Eye that forever keeps the Cosmos in Balance.

Hydrolaise is created by millions of elementals on the co-creation team. The entities of light and gelaisic form, and vapor form and millions of entities who are dedicated to the actual ascension of individuals work together to create a substance that allows us to actually slide across into the world of Aquafaria from our home.

The hydrolaise mist becomes a light water vapor. It gently comes down from ceiling as a mist on the body It is pale green and aqua colors. It has a twinkling or sparkling in the air. It has veins full of multi-colored heliotalic iridescent sparkling light of pastel shades.

The eye of the Cosmos connects to every smaller structure of Spirit and light and matter that are within the body of the Cosmos so from the core of the cosmos there is now coming in a light and a wave as it enters into our system. It is actually making the air run like water. The air is taking on a texture. A hydrolaise infusion is coming in. This is the heliotalic silver pastel liquid light energy from the fourteenth dimension. The energy was brought in by comet Ison combined with the Frequencies from the Photon Belt of Sun Alcyone, which carried our original Divine Templates of our creation in our original Aquarius Star System.

The transformation energy of the silver pink energy will cause sparkles on the skin where the skin crystals interact with the hydrolaise. Hydrolaise is the Spiritual Water that is being transformed through this process of the Positrons spraying onto and into Earth.

The scientists have already identified these positrons and the neutrinos that are completely altering the physical structure into matter and anti matter becoming one in saturation. The texture in the air is some where between air and water and it is substance you can both swim in and breathe. It is a natural substance on Urtha and on Ascension Earth.

Our Starry families will create a Crystalline Magnetic Shield around Mother Earth. That Magnetic Shield will be created by what many have called the Mother Ship. The Mother Ship is the connection and collection of all of the Frequency Signatures and Light Bodies of all of our Universal or Christic Families. These Frequency signatures are woven into the Sun of Aquarius to allow the entire Cosmic Flame from the Breath of Source to ignite a new reality.

THIS IS THE STORY THAT WAS THE PLAN OF THE FALLEN ANGELIC NATIONS -- THIS STORY WAS CHANGED (However there are still rumors of this reality taking place).

THERE WERE TWO PROBABLE FUTURES in the consciousness of our Galaxy up until 2009, when that reality was changed to a new HEROIC FUTURE. One probable future said the Death Star would saturate the Earth with asteroids that kill millions of people. The other probable future said the Earth would become wrapped in a Plasma Blanket that will make those asteroids bounce off and we will be unharmed. The Plasma Blanket created by the Mother Ships of the Guardian Races created by the Ra Confederacy would saturate the Earth and transform her back into her original consciousness.

So, there was this war going on of the two probable futures. One reality was being created by Fallen Angelic Races and the other by Angelic Races.

Finally, those two realities split apart. The Negative Future fell into the Phantom Matrix and left this reality. How did that happen. Earth was moved into the 8th reality. Earth was being shifted each year from 2000-2012. She was being shifted from the first, to the second, to the third and finally to the eighth reality by 2012. In that eighth reality, she was able to be pulled free from the wormhole that would pull her into the phantom matrix. She was pulled back into the alignment with the Original 12 Star alignment. She was pulled out of alignment with Nibiru and into alignment with Aramantena.

THIS IS THE OLD REALITY AND HOW IT WAS CHANGED

This will happen (that was the plan) simultaneously as the Death Star is aiming dead center for the Earth. However, much has already been achieved in the last war in heaven that began September 2011 and ended on Christmas. That war in heaven was all of our starry brothers fleets removing millions of fleets of dark entities from our planes who were planning on preparing the way for Nibiru. So, the Death Star plan has already been dismantled. That doesn't mean that Nibiru won't come. That just means the plan won't work.

The Frequencies of this Huge Cosmic Flame will transmute all lower frequencies into Christic Frequencies. The Earth will be wrapped within this Cosmic Cocoon which is like a Mirror Ball. The Mirror is the mirror image of our Christ Consciousness.

Most of you haven't seen your hologram of your Christ Self standing in front of you yet. This takes place as a result of Trancing out of the Neo Cortex part of the Brain and tuning into the Frequency Specific Mid Brain where the pineal gland and pituitary gland become activated and allow the mind of God (in the lower cerebellum) to project through the third eye.

That still doesn't mean you don't need to do anything to get ready for this event. We will all be experiencing this drama. This Cosmic Cocoon will look like a blast of light of twenty billion suns encompassing the earth in a 360 degree sphere. The light will be so bright and so powerful that no person will be able to look at it. It will be light of all of our Christ Families with the power of the Cosmic Elemental families sending the transmutation frequencies that open the star gates from this dimensional reality into all fifteen dimensions of Cosmic Consciousness.

We are surrounded by the Cosmic Cocoon, however the appearance wasn't as dramatic down here as it is when you view it from above. The light is the light from a million Star Ships surrounding the Earth. The ships are not what was known as the Ashtar Command. The ships are made of Plasma. That means they are the pre light and pre sound stage of creation. They are the original Guardian Races called the Yani (Eieyani) or Grand Yanas, and also called the Yanel.

The higher frequencies must always proceed the lower frequencies. We already learned that we must enter into the FULL SPECTRUM of light to transform into the Blue Body of multidimensionality. The Silver pink heliotalic must connect with the plasma and the white light to create the diamond door. We must walk into the full spectrum of light and then return from the Mirror Ball as the Blue Body.

This transformation takes place in the brain. If we stare at the candle until the thinking brain is TRANCED out, we then move into the Mid Brain that is Frequency Specific. We must remain Frequency Specific. That is why I create the Eternal Life Albums for those individuals who want to remain FREQUENCY SPECIFIC.

This light of the billions of suns will be so intense that it will frighten many people to death. The light will continue for twelve days and twelve nights. Those who do not know what is happening will become terrified simply from their own not knowing. The only reason that many will die is because they are not prepared and they do not know.

Well, that version of the story DID NOT happen. The new version is the positrons and neutrinos have replaced the electrons and protons. The polarization of matter and anti matter was replaced by a new substance where the sub harmonics of the DNA are being saturated with the spiritual substance of immortality.

If the Death Star was planning on hitting the Earth full force, it would be causing a pole shift that would flip the Earth so quickly that many would die from that shock and from the tides and waves and earthquakes. That drama is NOT going to happen. What is happening is a good thing. However, those who are not in the knowing will not be ready.

That is the reason that aDolphino and Crystalai have just received their final activation and awakening of their twin contract to prepare for the planetary evac situation. Our contracts have been commissioned here to get ourselves and who ever we can host into the Deity planes, the Aurora Fields and the Temples of Aquafaria.

We will be brought into alignment with what we need to do to fulfill our deification process and fulfilling the contract we came with as far as helping the rest of the host mission here. We were given the contract to complete the Violet Flame Mission. That mission was completed March, 2014 when the Violet Aurora Flame appeared and the Violet Flame holder activated the seventh strand DNA.

Chapter Two

Cosmic Flame Mission

We are a Cosmic Flame. We came to Earth as a ray - a crystal light vehicle - from Sun La. We were a part of the Cosmic Shield of our Oraphim Race from La. We came from the original Oraphim Cosmic family of the 7 Suns. The Oraphims were the creators of the original dolphin and whales on Earth. Only a few of the original ones are left on Earth today.

We were here on Earth to create a shield that would allow the ascension of the original Oraphims. The Oraphims were the original Angelic Race that was on Gaia before it fell into Tara. The Tara Race was the second Angelic Race also created from the Oraphim line of consciousness.

The original Electric War, millions of years ago destroyed the Oraphim Race. They were completely destroyed. They were taken down by some of the worst Fallen Angelic Races and Demonic Races in the Universe. When a race is taken or fallen, it means the demons took their Souls away and use their energy as their own. However , the original Oraphim, that was created by Source as the perfect image and likeness of God – the divine Blue Print still exists in the Frequency Shield of the Sun La.

Crystalai and aDolphino are the carriers of this shield of La on Earth. The way the Oraphims were taken by the demons millions of years ago, and the way the demons have caused the fall of millions of races is always the same. The demons find the pair that forms the Cosmic Flame - such as Crystalai and aDolphino.

They know that together we form the 12 DNA template of the Sun La. We each brought a part of the DNA template to Earth because 12 DNA could not enter through a normal birth. Crystalai went through three near death experiences to bring in more of her template. When our light quotient was high enough to hold the Solomon Shield – the light shield of Christ Consciousness on Earth - the demons spotted us.

We were warned by Markus and our other Higher Selves that there were three demons that would try to take us down and that we had to listen very carefully to what our higher selves guided us in doing or we would be taken - fallen. We both remembered that this had happened to us before, millions of years ago.

This all happened in Monterey, California in 2008. We were taught by our Maharaji family from Sun Ra that the demonic take overs that have created the fallen angelic races always occur when entities are in their prime light quotient. When the light body and etheric body are just about to align into the plasma body or the cosmic field, is when the demons spot the cosmic flame and attempt to take it over.

If the demons were successful in possessing the body that held the light, they could take down the entire Solomon Shield and turn it into a demonic shield. This would had allowed the pole shift and take over of the Earth by the Zetas and Draconians to be fulfilled by 2011.

Markus told me that there was a war being fought in heaven and the fallen races were planning on blaming it all on us - the holders of the Cosmic Flame. They could do that by making the Shield become a demonic shield while it was actually being held by the Solomon Shield - the Christic 12DNA family of consciousness.

The Oraphim Race had already been taken over by Fallen races millions of years ago. They are a race that became darker than any of the other fallen races in order to get even with them for the terrible thing they did to their race. However, the Oraphim Race has always wanted to return to the emerald covenant and to be restored back into their divine template and become one with Source.

You see, fallen angelics were not always fallen. They were taken over in consciousness by demons.

I watched this process take place right before my eyes. Even though we did everything Markus directed us to do to survive the demonic take over - the take over did happen. I watched aDolphino's Soul be removed from his body right before my eyes. We were in a very unique situation that none of the previous times of Earth Shifts have had available.

We had training in light activation. We knew how to stay in our Merkaba spinning into oneness with Source Consciousness. We knew how to stay in this protective field. I knew how, as the other half of the Cosmic Flame to reunite with my Cosmic Shield on the other side and bring it back. These are the reasons we survived.

Markus announced to me that aDolphino was gone from his body and there was nothing that they could do. He told me that millions of angels were working to keep aDolphino from leaving his body, but the only one that could save him was me, because I was in fact his other half.

When a Cosmic Flame comes to Earth as the representative of the Sun they represent, the female holds the magnetic half of the field and the male holds the electromagnetic half. It is always the female who can pull the male back when he rises into light at death.

aDolphino was already gone as he stood before me in our Monterey condo. That was the same weekend that the angels had planned our workshop in creating an Ascension Portal. We were commissioned to come to Earth and create an Ascension Portal for the Oraphim Race in Monterey. We had already seen many Dolphins appear to us in the Cloud Cities above the ocean as they helped us create this shield of liquid light energy above the oceans.

The demons who had taken our Oraphim Race down millions of years ago were watching us as our light grew in Monterey. As aDolphino was walking on the beach one morning before our Ascension Portal workshop, a chemtrails was aimed directly at him. The chemtrails were created for exactly this purpose. To create spontaneous mind control of those individuals containing the codes and light quota that the demons needed for their take over of the Solomon Shield.

So, there was this perfectly laid out plan of demonic take over of the planet. The 25,000 year plan of the phantom take over would be fulfilled right before our eyes in Monterey. Isn't it nice how the world is allowed to carry on in its inorganic bliss as these events take place?

aDolphino didn't know who he really was any more. However, Markus remained attached to his consciousness. Because Markus is a part of our Cosmic Shield that connects us to the Maharaji Consciousness of Ra. The Cosmic Consciousness of the Oraphim Dolphin Race was to be restored on Earth and the team of Consciousness that was on this team was enormous. I was connected through the Crystalai Council to stream the light of Aquafaria into La. aDolphino was from the Sun of La and Markus from the same Sun with his connection as a Maharaji that could contain the Soul of aDolphino even though he was removed from his body. I was the anchor - the magnetic part of the merkaba shield that could anchor aDolphino back into Earth.

All of these parts of the divine formula were needed to make this experiment work. After 500 million years of practicing this event over and over with future role forward time machine practice movies, we finally got it to work.

aDolphino didn't die immediately. He was still being directed continuously through our Maharaji family of Ra. He was mostly maintaining his memory from eons ago that told him that he must save Crystalai. The demons told him that if he didn't do what they told him to do that they would take over Crystalai as well. He didn't want that to happen to me. He wanted to sacrifice his life for mine. That is a part of the divine commission of a Cosmic Flame. The demons can't really get control of the Earth unless they get the female. They can't get the female until they take down the male.

He was told that if he would leave Monterey, then they would leave Crystalai alone. They told him that he must separate from Crystalai to save her life. This was all true on two levels. The demons couldn't take over a Cosmic Flame unless they could take down the female. Markus told me that they were using aDolphino as a veil to hide my true identity.

They told me that they had been directing me to spin my magnetic shield clockwise in order to confuse the demons. They actually thought aDolphino was the magnetic shield and I was the electromagnetic shield. We tricked them into taking down the wrong half of the cosmic flame.

Chapter Two

The female can always save the male. But the male cannot save the female.

So, aDolphino was taken. He drove away into the sunset. I had no idea where he went. He removed all possibility of locating himself through the help of the demons. Before he left Earth he stood in the middle of the room with his arms out as if he were nailed to a cross. Next, he was lying on the floor, as if to guard the music room. There was another entity inside of him making sure Crystalai could not get near the music. They knew the music was very powerful and that their mission would be destroyed if I could access the music.

A voice came out and said leave the apartment now and never come back. You are in great danger. Leave and never come back. I left the apartment and moved into a hotel for two nights. I had a friend locate aDolphino through a star fleet Command tracking device. Later I learned that a star fleet Command was actually on the Fallen Angelic Team that was trying to kill aDolphino. That was the only reason they were helping. They were using my friend as access to aDolphino's body. She had no idea that she was being used. And she wouldn't believe me.

During the time aDolphino was absent I took walks on the beach where I had met Zaurak the first time. Zaurak guided me to the restaurant where he had led when we first came to Monterey.

That is when the fun began. After I was given the privilege of watching a Starfleet land right in front of me, I was directed to this restaurant, that I assumed was Chinese or Japanese - it was Asian in nature. The waitress sat me down right in front of a picture that covered the wall of Mt. Sorak. This is a mountain in Korea that is considered sacred. It is like many of the other sacred Mountains in the World. Zaurak, my Starry brother from Sirius B started talking to me through that picture. He told me that I had created that mountain with him millions of years ago.

I lived in Korea for seven years. That culture fascinates me because I really believe that they were able to hold on to more of what the gods who came from Ursa Major brought to the country than most other cultures. I worked at a University called Dankook University. Dankook means the Bear Children from Ursa Major.

This is an entire culture and raceline of people who still remember being children of the Ursa Major Raceline. I could always feel something was very familiar to me when I lived in Korea 1981-87, but I didn't figure it out until 2008, when my Starry Brother, Zaurak told me that I needed to move to Monterey.

When I lived in Korea, I was a communication consultant for a Five Star Hotel. After I had received hundreds of warnings to quit my job and leave the hotel, and after I had one hundred students bow before me saying I am sorry for what is about to happen, I sat down to have a cup of coffee.

Even though I was still not considering any of the warnings others had given me, I clearly heard a voice in my head, saying run for your life. I began to feel quite dizzy and realized it was the coffee. I knew there was poison in the coffee, and the reason I was being warned to leave, was that those dark ones who wanted me dead would most likely wait for me to pass out, take me through the back door and dump my body in the Hahn River.

So, I walked as quickly as my feet would carry me to the door where the taxis stop. The door man already knew where I lived so he already told the taxi driver. I don't remember anything else. When I was awake again, my husband had arrived home and taken me to a pharmacist. I was diagnosed to have a lethal poison in me called Love Poison (a drug used in ancient times in Korea - and not legally allowed in the country). The poison had been used in the good old days to poison the little wife, after she had the baby for kings.

Those were the kings that we are just learning about at this time. They were the Annunaki who would rape Leviathan Women who carried the fifth strand DNA. They wanted the blue star dust essence from the women when she died, and they wanted the child with the 12 sub harmonics that would soon be the new Leviathan Cable or Puppet for the reign of the Annunaki.

Yes, you are correct. These events actually took place in Egypt. So, they say. However, there is all of this evidence in Korea, if you travel to Cheju do Island, that the mermaids who were reassembling ISIS who was broken into many pieces and separated from his greatest sexual mechanism, has statues of this penis myth all over the island. That is the Isis that I remember. The one on Cheju do Island. These are recorded MEMORIES of the events that happened in the Stars. There have been bits and pieces of this memory in all races because we were originally one race with One Mind.

The truth is, the myths and records of our history were completely obliterated by the Annunaki ten thousand years ago. They created the Tower of Babel that would erase our memory forever, and they conveniently re-wrote history in a way that would serve them best. The only truthful memory that could exist was anything that was left in the cellular memory. And that would have to be retrieved from the Spiritiual Parallel Matrix.

And, how is it that a Cosmic Event that caused an entire Consciousness of a Star to blow up and scatter all over the Universe be located in one tiny little geographic location? The event took place in consciousness, and the event took place all over the Seas, and the event had much to do with the Aquafarians, the Dolphins, the Cetacean Nation, the Mermaids, and the Mother Mary Story is another Cosmic Event involving the entire FEMALE or Magnetic Half of the Merkaba, and how all of these sacred technologies got twisted, turned around and blew up in our face.

We now know that Mary means a Female Christ and Jesus Christ actually meant the male Christ. When we put Jesus and Mary back together we get the complete star that they came from before they were separated into frequencies that could be accepted into the Earth's portal. So, the story of the Cosmic Twins is repeating itself.

So, the Leviathans were the prime Ascension Race Line that had been created through hybrid projects of the Elohim and Sirians. It was the first time after millions of years that we had some people with 5DNA on Earth. The Annunaki took advantage of these entities, and turned them into a Fallen Race Line that would be used by them as their cable or puppet slaves. We call them the Illuminati. There really aren't very many of them on Earth - less than one thousand. Most of the government are just slaves of the slaves.

Well, I had just met up with the Illuminati carrier of the Annunaki gene, the Greys who worked interdimensionally with them, and my long forgotten past of thirty thousand years ago.

The Leviathan race is a group of Beings who became 5th dimensional on Earth, who have been bred here on this planet. They were the result of an experiment that went wrong. The experiment was the Guardian races had allowed in the fallen angelic collectives and what is called bio-regenesis which is regeneration of their DNA template so they could evolve to get their Christos potential back. They entered a Christos Covenant which was a Christos coevolution agreement. Certain groups of the fallen races agreed to be a part of the Emerald Covenant. They waited to evolve back into the 12 D Christos pattern. They wanted to get their DNA back to hold the Christic frequency. There were a small group of them who were permitted to get back into human form.

There was a very specific way that the DNA template had to be blended in order to create this evolutionary option of what was called a hybrid race. Unfortunately, the hybrid race worked well and it blended well with the angelic human template, but, certain groups of them motivated by their fallen angelic kin from other places decided to take over our planet.

They had an In to Earth once they got into human light bodies, and progressively they raided the human races and mutated our DNA to the point where we have nothing left of our memory of who we really are. We have had our light switch turned off.

We are dealing with a huge history of problems and a huge solution. There is the history of the Leviathan Races, along with the history of the fall of Atlantis. There were 550 million years of problems before those more recent ones.

What is happening now is a part of what is called the Luciferian Covenant that was an agreement of the anti-Christic races and their Leviathan hybrids that were here to take over this planet when the next stellar activation cycle occurred. We are now in that stellar activation cycle that is happening from 2000-2017. This cycle is happening now.

If we participate in this activation cycle consciously by knowing it is happening, we can become the new Christic race, reborn on Earth once more. This time matrix began billions of years ago. The matrix was caused by metatronic science that allowed the gods to create and mis create realities that were not in tune with the Source Frequencies.

There is a huge connection between metatronic science and what became the Greek Olympian Gods and Roman gods. Both mythologies were based on truths that were taking place in Atlantis. Mythology is a way of taking history and consolidating it in fairy tales with a mean sense of humor. Turn a collective of people into one person and then having this person marry that person - when in fact, they were actually talking about Race Lines of people.

Roman mythology contains known history of Atlantis that has to do with Metatron, Lemurians planets in Wesadrak Matrix.

BACK TO THE STORY

Markus and Zaurak were there with me. Markus was there because he is my higher self. Zaurak was there because he is my Starry Brother. We were both in Korea on a mission together millions of years ago and again thousands of years ago. How did the Grey ones and Dark Cable find me? It is my FREQUENCIES. I finally found out why I seem to always be located by these deeper level people in the government and I am always loosing jobs about every six months. It has always been a part of the run for your life plan, and the reason I loose jobs is to get me out of those places where someone is planning on killing me.

  When my husband went to the hotel to give my resignation to the American Manager, he said that he was about to send a crew to check the Hahn River for bodies. He knew that something was up. The Hotel was being taken over by an American Management team who would own the hotel in partnership with the Koreans. There was a lot of American domination going on in Korea at that time, and a lot of corporate take overs. The American Manager had already told his wife to get on a plane that morning after he heard what happened to me.

  So, this incident was related to international take overs, the hotel was the place all Security Meetings of International importance took place, and my friend, who was the body guard for the President of Korea had told me that he didn't even have jurisdiction in that hotel. He had also told me that I was in grave danger because who ever had jurisdiction of that hotel was far above top security clearance, beyond the government itself. So, who do you think that might be? Let's see, it could be the Greys, the Illuminati, the Draconians, the Cable or it was just a figment of my imagination?

And yes, I had been killed before, and I had guns placed to my head before. I will get to that story later.

BACK to 2008

So, the third day I return home and aDolphino's body is gone. The fifth day I get a call from the Mercy Hospital in Redding telling me that they have aDolphino's body. His body had been hit by three big rig trucks and five cars ran over his legs. The neurologist thought his brain would never become active. I told the doctors to leave him alone. I refused to give any permission to operate. I knew that there were some demons running the show. My friend was there being directed by a star fleet calling themselves the Ashtar Command. I ordered the hospital staff to not allow anyone near his body except me.

I was told by my higher selves that the reason that aDolphino and I had been directed to create the frequency music of our frequencies together - our breaths together was because that is how a cosmic flame returns the other half back home. I placed earphones on his unconscious body and worked on the alignments we had learned into the universal and cosmic and realms of Source, and using the alignments of the Earth's Heart into the Heart of

Sun Ra to create the perfect portal and shield to return us into our original harmonic attunement.

When aDolphino woke from his demonic take over, the angels first spoke to him and said welcome back. Please turn to Crystalai and thank her. We could not had brought you back. Only she could do it. Your mission was completed successfully.

Congratulations. That was the completion of our mission at that time.

The rest of our time here is to hold that Solomon Shield open, the Cosmic Shield blending the Seventh Sun La into the Second Sun Ra and then grounding into the First Sun Ka. This allowed our frequencies to keep us anchored into the Heart of Mother Earth into Shamballa and up into the heart of the Sun to bring us back into Tara and Gaia and restore the race of the Oraphim Angels and the Oraphim Dolphins on Earth.

I have recently reconnected with my higher self from Sun La. Interesting my Earthly given name Angela easily translates to my higher self Anshala. Shala is the Universal stargate that connects us into Andromeda M31. My connection to my Starry Brother Zaurak from Ursa and Sirius B came much earlier than my Starry Sister Anshala – from Shala Star Gate. It turns out that my Starry family has many High Connections.

The mission of Crystalai and aDolphino on Earth at this time was a very critical one and a very dangerous one. The reason we have stopped interacting and giving workshops at this time is because it is more important for us to just stay alive and keep bringing in the Aquafarian Shield, than to allow the possibility of any more demonic take overs.

We are a Cosmic Flame. We came to Earth as a ray - a crystal light vehicle - from Sun La. We were a part of the Cosmic Shield of our Oraphim Race from La. We came from the original Oraphim family of Consciousness. The Oraphims were the creators of the original dolphin and whales on Earth. Only a few of the original ones are left on Earth today.

We were here on Earth to create a shield that would allow the ascension of the original Oraphims. The Oraphims were the original Angelic Race that was on Gaia before it fell into Tara. The Tara Race was the second Angelic Race also created from the Oraphim line of consciousness.

The original Electric War, millions of years ago destroyed the Oraphim Race. They were completely destroyed. They were taken down by some of the worst Fallen Angelic Races and Demonic Races in the Universe. When a race is taken of fallen, it means the demons took their Souls away and use their energy as their own. However , the original

Oraphim, that was created by Source as the perfect image and likeness of God - the divine Blue Print still exists in the Frequency Shield of the Sun La.

Crystalai and aDolphino are the carriers of this shield of La on Earth. The way the Oraphims were taken by the demons millions of years ago, and the way the demons have caused the fall of millions of races is always the same. The demons found the pair Cosmic Twin that forms the Cosmic Flame.

They know that together we form the 12 DNA template of the Sun La. We each brought a part of the DNA template to Earth because 12 DNA could not enter through a normal birth. Crystalai went through three near death experiences to bring in more of her template. When our light quotient was high enough to hold the Solomon Shield – the light shield of Christ Consciousness on Earth - the demons spotted us.

We were warned by Markus and our other Higher Selves that there were three demons that would try to take us down and that we had to listen very carefully to what our higher selves guided us in doing or we would be taken - fallen. We both remembered that this had happened to us before, millions of years ago.

This all happened in Monterey, California in 2008. We were taught by our Maharaji family from Sun

Ra that the demonic take overs that have created the fallen angelic races always occur when entities are in their prime light quotient. When the light body and etheric body are just about to align into the plasma body or the cosmic field, is when the demons spot the cosmic flame and attempt to take it over.

If the demons were successful in possessing the body that held the light, they could take down the entire Solomon Shield and turn it into a demonic shield. This would had allowed the pole shift and take over of the Earth by the Zetas and Draconians to be fulfilled by 2011.

Markus told me that there was a war being fought in heaven and the fallen races were planning on blaming it all on us - the holders of the Cosmic Flame. They could do that by making the Shield become a demonic shield while it was actually being held by the Solomon Shield- the Christic 12 DNA family of consciousness.

The Oraphim Race had already been taken over by Fallen races millions of years ago. They are a race that became darker than any of the other fallen races in order to get even with them for the terrible thing they did to their race. However, the Oraphim Race has always wanted to return to the emerald covenant and to be restored back into their divine template and become one with Source.

You see, fallen angelics were not always fallen. They were taken over in consciousness by demons. I watched this process take place right before my eyes. Even thought we did everything Markus directed us to do to survive the demonic take over - the take over did happen. I watched aDolphino's Soul be removed from his body right before my eyes. We were in a very unique situation that none of the previous times of Earth Shifts have had available.

We had training in light activation. We knew how to stay in our Merkaba spinning into oneness with Source Consciousness. We knew how to stay in this protective field. I knew how, as the other half of the Cosmic Flame to reunite with my Cosmic Shield on the other side and bring it back. These are the reasons we survived.

Markus announced to me that aDolphino was gone from his body and there was nothing that they could do. He told me that millions of angels were working to keep aDolphino from leaving his body, but the only one that could save him was me, because I was in fact his other half.

When a Cosmic Flame comes to Earth as the representative of the Sun they represent, the female holds the magnetic half of the field and the male holds the electromagnetic half. It is always the female who can pull the male back when he rises into light at death.

aDolphino was already gone as he stood before me in our Monterey condo. That was the same weekend as the angels had planned our workshop in creating an Ascension Portal. We were commissioned to come to Earth and create an Ascension Portal for the Oraphim Race in Monterey. We had already seen many Dolphins appear to us in the Cloud Cities above the ocean as they helped us create this shield of liquid light energy above the oceans.

The demons who had taken our Oraphim Race down millions of years ago were watching us as our light grew in Monterey. As aDolphino was walking on the beach one morning before our Ascension Portal workshop, a chemtrail was aimed directly at him. The chemtrails were created for exactly this purpose. To create spontaneous mind control of those individuals containing the codes and light quota that the demons needed for their take over of the Solomon Shield.

So, there is was, perfectly laid out plan of demonic take over of the planet. The 25,000 (give or take several thousand years) year plan of the phantom take over was to be fulfilled right before our eyes in Monterey. Isn't it nice how the world is allowed to carry on in its inorganic bliss as these events take place?

aDolphino didn't know who he really was any more. However, Markus remained attached to his consciousness. Because Markus is a part of our Cosmic Shield that connects us to the Maharaji Consciousness of Ra. The Cosmic Consciousness of the Oraphim Dolphin Race was to be restored on Earth and the team of Consciousness that was on this team was enormous. I was connected through the Crystalai Council to stream the light of Aquafaria into La. aDolphino was from the Sun of La and Markus from the same Sun with his connection as a Maharaji that could contain the Soul of aDolphino even though he was removed from his body. I was the anchor - the magnetic part of the merkaba shield that could anchor aDolphino back into Earth.

All of these parts of the divine formula were needed to make this experiment work. After 500 million years of practicing this event over and over with future role forward time machine practice movies, we finally got it to work.

aDolphino didn't die immediately. He was still being directed continuously through our Maharaji family of Ra. He was mostly maintaining his memory from eons ago that told him that he must save Crystalai. The demons told him that if he didn't do what they told him to do that they would take over Crystalai as well. He didn't want that to happen to me. He wanted to sacrifice his life for mine. That is a part of the divine commission of a Cosmic Flame. The demons can't really get control of the Earth unless they get the female. They can't get the female until they take down the male.

He was told that if he would leave Monterey, then they would leave Crystalai alone. They told him that he must separate from Crystalai to save her life. This was all true on two levels. The demons couldn't take over a Cosmic Flame unless they could take down the female. Markus told me that they were using aDolphino as a veil to hide my true identity.

They told me that they had been directing me to spin my magnetic shield clockwise in order to confuse the demons. They actually thought aDolphino was the magnetic shield and I was the electromagnetic shield. We tricked them into taking down the wrong half of the cosmic flame. The female can always save the male. But the male cannot save the female.

So, aDolphino was taken. He drove away into the sunset. I had no idea where he went. He removed all possibility of locating himself through the help of the demons. Before he left Earth he stood in the middle of the room with his arms out as if he were nailed to a cross. Next, he laid on the floor, as if to guard the music room. There was another entity inside of him making sure Crystalai could not get near the music. They knew the music was very powerful and that their mission would be destroyed if I could access the music.

A voice came out and said leave the apartment now and never come back. You are in great danger. Leave and never come back. I left the apartment and moved into a hotel for two nights. I had a friend locate aDolphino through an star fleet Command tracking device. Later I learned that the star fleet Command was actually on the Fallen Angelic Team that was trying to kill aDolphino.

That was the only reason they were helping. They were using my friend as access to aDolphino's body. She had no idea that she was being used. And she wouldn't believe me. Nobody will believe the true story of how the Ashtar Command is a completely Fallen Angelic group until after 2017.

So, the third day I return home and aDolphino's body is gone. The fifth day I get a call from the Mercy Hospital in Redding telling me that they have aDolphino's body. His body had been hit by three big rig trucks and five cars ran over his legs. The neurologist through his brain would never become active. I told the doctors to leave him alone. I refused to give any permission to operate. I knew that there were some demons running the show. My friend was there being directed by the star fleet Ashtar Command. I ordered the hospital staff to not allow anyone near his body except me.

The rest of our time here is to hold that Solomon Shield open, the Cosmic Shield into La and Ra and to keep us anchored into the Heart of Mother Earth into Shamballa and up into the heart of the Sun to bring us back into Tara and Gaia and restore the race of the Oraphim Angels and the Oraphim Dolphins on Earth.

I have recently reconnected with my higher self from Sun La. Interesting my Earthly given name Angela easily translates to my higher self Anshala. Shala is the Universal stargate 3 that connects us into Andromeda M31. My connection to my Starry Brother Zaurak from Ursa and Sirius B came much earlier than my Starry Sister Anshala – from Shala Star Gate.

HUMAN ANGELICS and INVADER RACES

Humans were a race of Angels that were put here on this planet to guard this planet and to protect the Earth's shields and to help restore them and heal them because they have been damaged by a group of fallen angelic races.

The fallen angels were originally a part of the normal creation, but they made decisions and choices that created a fate for themselves that was very unfortunate.

They created a situation by rebelling against Source. They genetically altered themselves in a way that they could no longer hold the higher frequencies of consciousness that connect us all to Source.

So, they decided to become masters of the Universe themselves. They tried to take over other universes and to feed off of them. For many eons this planet has been under siege and there has been a time that was waited for. It was a time when the planetary star gates - the portions of the planetary templar stargate that opens between this space time place and other space time places in the higher heavens. This is that time.

A stellar activation cycle is 26,556 years. Ever since Atlantis, it was known that this is when the next one was going to occur. There were plans made in Atlantis - on both sides - fallen and unfallen sides.

Now, all of those forces are back on this planet - the Christic and the anti-Christic. Both sides are here. Most people are asleep. They don't remember the Atlantian times. They don't remember the agreements they chose to be a part of. They don't know what forces are moving them or moving with them or moving through them. This makes the people and the planet very vulnerable because there are things here we don't see unless we use our inner eyes. There are things going on that we need to know if we are going to maintain the integrity of our own Divine Blue Print and help the planet do that as well.

Those who do light work correctly because they have the genetic codlings of the Angelic Human and the Indigo Races are assisting in running the Christic frequencies back into the planet in order to open the Star Gates. Angelic Humans are the keepers of the Star Gates. We are the only ones with the genetic codlings that can open the star gates.

That is why we were placed in a state of amnesia by the Annunaki races. The original teachings of the Founders Races used the 15 dimensional structures to align our consciousness to the best understanding needed at this time. This represents the structure of the way creation is in this Universe. The D12 is the twelfth dimension where the Christos frequencies of pre-matter of the Divine Blue Print exist.

There is a Christos life line that links us all in the higher god worlds and to Source. That is why translations come down through the Bible that Christ is your savior and your link to God. It was referring to the fact that the Inner Christos frequencies align us through the pre matter template. We all have the ability to carry those frequencies in our bodies.

It is our Divine Blue Print that links us to Source. The planet has a Christos frequency potential and so does the Solar and galactic. But, things have happened to the scalar templates on this planet over the 25,500 years so that the planet could not run 12 D frequencies, which made it very vulnerable to infiltration from lower angelic kingdoms. We are here to restore those Christos frequencies that were removed from our planet. Our bodies are the conduits that allow these frequencies to be restored.

The type of energy we carry will depend on how much we know about our anatomy. If we don't know that we have chakras that have a scalar template, and we don't know about auric levels and how to keep them clear we are not going to know what to do with ourselves. We will become easy pray for those living in the D4 astral plane. They might be using your fields for something that you don't ever know they are using you for. We use frequency shields created from Cosmic and Source fields to protect us.

The Eieyani Races are the founders races who are in Inner earth at this time. When we use the codes and frequencies given to us by our Founder races, we are reactivating the mathematical programs that are a part of the planetary divine Blue Print within ourselves.

When we use sound and light technology combining the frequency signature and code or symbol of the idea to be manifest, we collect frequencies by oscillating consciousness into the domains or the dimensions of Christic and Cosmic and Source and then bringing those tones of transformation into our templates.

The more we use the light and sound to activate our bodies, the sooner we awaken to our 12D templates and our fifth dimensional selves that allow our multidimensionality of all times in no time. There are things happening in this 15th dimensional system that have been things done by our guardian races to keep these chaotic things from happening.

The fallen angels have never fully agreed to work with the guardians for our recovery of our Christic Template. There have been many fallen angelics that have come back on board and then retaliated again and again to the dark side. The light and sound technologies are the beginning of remembering how our body and souls work and how to begin to recreate the Christos civilization on this planet.

The Christos frequencies have not been on this planet for 208,000 years except for the reactivation brought by Jeshua 12 two thousand years ago. There was a stellar activation 25,000 years ago when the frequencies almost reactivated shortly. Our entire history has been about wars and wars over land. The land that was fought over contained star gates on this planet and portals that go with them. The fallen angelics have taken these star gates and blocked them with metatronic radiation that would reverse them and spin away from source fields.

The blockage of those star gates has been blocking our bodies and our brains from the Christic Templates that were once placed within the Earth. Stargates were always on this planet. Fallen angelics have been fighting with each other for eons. They chose to make us into their foot soldiers.

The Leviathan race is a group of fallen angelics who have been bred here on this planet. They were the result of an experiment that went wrong. The experiment was the Guardian races had allowed in the fallen angelic collectives and what is called bioregenesis which is regeneration of their DNA template so they could evolve to get their Christos potential back. They entered a Christos Covenant which was a Christos coevolution agreement. Certain groups of the fallen races agreed to be a part of the emerald covenant. They waited to evolve back into the 12 D Christos pattern. They wanted to get their DNA back to hold the Christic frequency. There were a small group of them who were permitted to get back into human form.

There was a very specific way that the DNA template had to be blended in order to create this evolutionary option of what was called a hybrid race. Unfortunately, the hybrid race worked well and it blended well with the angelic human template, but, certain groups of them motivated by their fallen angelic kin from other places decided to take over our planet.

They had an In to Earth once they got into human light bodies, and progressively they raided the human races and mutated our DNA to the point where we have nothing left of our memory of who we really are. We have had our light switch turned off. We are dealing with a huge history of problems and a huge solution. There is the history of the Leviathan Races , the history of the fall of Atlantis.

What is happening now is a part of what is called the Luciferian Covenant that was an agreement of the anti-Christic races and their Leviathan hybrids here to take over this planet when the next stellar activation cycle occurred.

We are now in that stellar activation cycle that is happening from 2000-2017. This cycle is happening now.

If we participate in this activation cycle consciously by knowing it is happening, we can become the new Christic race, reborn on Earth once more. This time matrix began 950 billion years ago. The matrix was caused by metatronic science that allowed the gods to create and mis create realities that were not in tune with the Source Frequencies.

There is a huge connection between metatronic science and what became the Greek Olympian gods and Roman gods. Both mythologies were based on truths that were taking place in Atlantis.

Mythology is a way of taking history and consolidating it in fairy tales with a mean sense of humor. Turn a collective of people into one person and then having this person marry that person - when in fact, they were actually talking about Race Lines of people. Roman mythology contains known history of Atlantis that has to do with Metatron, Lumarian planets in Wesedrek Matrix.

Scalar Grid mechanics is the substance God creates with. This was knowledge that belonged to the guardians of the planet. The human angelics are these guardians. We were denied this info since Atlantis when a few people came in and took what didn't belong to them. The whole planet lost its memory. The science of the shields – the planet has a scalar template and every being on the planet has a scalar template that is connected to the planets templates. These templates circulate primal life force currents.

They circulate the energy of god through the templates. The templates on the Earth are dependent on the Earth's template. The damage to the Earth's template erased our memory.

There were things done here to block the planetary scalar shields. They were twisted in ways that are abnormal. That shut off certain frequencies that carried cognition. They carried higher frequency information. They carried our identities.

If our DNA was working the right way, we would know our selves as Christic beings – as Avatars. Our bodies wouldn't die. We would not get sick. We could manifest instantly.

There were things done to the electromagnetic field of the planet to block our DNA. Working with the Light and Sound technology is to help bring back the D12 frequencies. The Divine Blueprint has the ability to reset all of those misalignments of frequencies in the planetary grid.

We can now bring through these frequencies for the first time since 208,216 B.C. This planet can run 12 D frequencies. That was way before 25,500 B.C. when it began to get really messy here. There were a series of cataclysmic events that have happened here during our history.

We have these higher parts of ourselves that never lost connection to god. Those carrying the Christos message are carrying the same message they have carried for the past 500 million years. It has been on every planet. They carried the truth about our connection to Source. They promise the ones in certain races, who incarnated as the human angelic race, to heal this time matrix.

There was a Universal Distortion that happened 250 billion years ago in Earth time between races that were the Christos Founders races. There was a time of Lyran Elohim Wars. Certain groups of Elohims fell from grace. They went through code convolution. Meaning their DNA templates became distorted because of inbreeding. That created distortions in consciousness and they started warring with founder races.

This was a place that was supposed to be based on freedom and co-evolution. It was not supposed to be a warring matrix. The problem began billions of years ago. The original sin was when the entire time matrix almost imploded down into a black hole.

Chapter Three

The Story of My Meeting with My Starry Brother from Sirius B

I first met Zaurak when I was in Redwood Shores - near the S.F. Airport. My husband first was told by his Guide, Markus, that someone wanted to talk to me. I listened, and soon Zaurak started talking to me. Because we are related as a Soul Family, much of the communication is just in knowing, but sometimes it seems like spoken words.

What Zaurak wanted to tell me in March, 2008, was that he needed me to move to Monterey, California. He said he needed me to be there by May.

So, at that point in time, my husband, who had a glorious, high paying job in a wonderful company on the glorious island called Redwood Shores, agreed to start packing, making arrangements to leave the company, and we made our first trip to Monterey that week to find our new home.

Everytime we went to Monterey there were very clear messages given to us in the sky through the clouds. We clearly watched Zaurak's space ship land. It first looked like a spaceship within a cloud, and then several blue orbs separated out and we could see their faces looking at us through the trees.

We were guided around Monterey to several places that Zaurak told us were possible, but not exactly the right place. Finally an add appeared for a Condo that sat right on the Beach and was way out of our price range. I felt like I just had to live in that Condo. We went there, and Zaurak said yes. This is the place that you used to live when you were Mary.

It took me a long time to figure out the meaning of that statement. I assumed that he meant Mary Magdalene. Later he told us that we were the new Jesus and Mary story and that Markus and Zaurak had been working on this Jesus and Mary project for millions of years before the world knew of their (Jesus and Mary) existence.

They were talking about the Soul Families of Jesus and Mary, and those who originated the plans of bringing the Christic 12D frequencies back to Earth. They were showing me that I was once an original

Soul of the Elohim Family and I was forever on this team of re-creating the Elohim Family from Gaia.

This place on the shores of Monterey was at one time a place where I had been when the Earth flipped into the anti particle phase during her Eiugo cycle. I was there for the preparation of the Spiritual and Physical planes to reunite.

They were referring to the Cosmic Mary streaming cosmic liquid light energy into the other Mary's, the Mary was the Female Christ. She was not so much a person with a name, but a frequency signature that held entire omniverses of energy. Mary Magdalene and Mother Mary hold that frequency of consciousness.

I was there because a new ascension portal needed to be established. I was there because a fleet from Sirius B was there. I was there because we were in the process of ascending a million dolphins and whales out of the oceans back into the Cloud Cities. My husband and I moved to that Condo on the Shores of Monterey, and we watched many glorious things happen in the ocean and in the skies. We watched the dolphins and whales actually rise into the skies and become clouds.

We watched many space ships from Sirius B fly above us. We did create an Ascension Portal there. And we did create Ascension Formula Frequencies

Chapter Three — Meeting My Starry Brother

together there. We were being taught by the Elohim Angels and the Grand Yanis to create pre light and sound frequencies and we learned to communicate with the whales and dolphins through frequencies.

And we created the Cosmic Mystery School of the Omniverse. We were told we would be having an experiential class in creating an Ascension Portal.

In July, Markus approached aDolphino and told him that we were in grave danger. He said there were three demons who were following us and planning to take over our souls. We were very careful and listened to every word Markus said to try to keep us safe. He told us that in order to save us we would have to do exactly as we were told.

And then it happened. One morning aDolphino was no longer in his body. Markus spoke through his body and said thousands of angels tried to get him to come back to his body, but he would not return. aDolphino went through stages of going crazy and demonic type behavior and he told me to pack up every thing in the house and leave.

I did pack the house, but I was listening to Markus and Zaurak's directions. They told me to pull all of the money out of the bank. They told me put all passports, bankbooks, identity records of all important types in a case and in the trunk of the car.

Chapter Three — Meeting My Starry Brother

They told me to pack everything and leave it in the garage.

I did these things. And then a voice from within aDolphino told me to get out of the house and to not come back. He said you are in danger. If you don't leave, they will do the same thing to you that they did to me.

I was very frightened and I moved into a room at the hotel where we were having the Cosmic Mystery School of the Omniverse classes. I was too scared to go back home the next day, so I stayed at the hotel a second night. The next morning I did go back.

The car was gone. The place was locked up.

I went to the manager to have it opened. There was no one there. The car was gone. But, I noticed that whoever was living in my husband's body didn't take any suitcases or change of clothes of any kind.

The car was gone with all of the important records that I had put in the trunk.

That night I was walking out side and he came back. I say he because I didn't know who he was anymore. He just kept saying I've come back to save you. You have to leave with me. If I don't leave they will kill me. If you stay here they will kill you too. They said that if we leave or if we stay apart they will leave us alone. And then he said start running with me. He made me run clear to the end of the beach and back which was about five miles. He was dragging me most of the time. It was the strangest behavior. Almost boiling with fear.

He scared me so much that I knew I could not go with him. I knew he was possessed even though the real aDolphino was still trying to save me.

I tried to trace his where abouts by following expenditures on the credit card. I called in every hour to find out if he had used the card. The second day I learned that he had rented an airplane in Bakersfield and flown back to Monterey. He left Monterey again about an hour later. The behavior appeared as if the old aDolphino wanted to come home, but the demon within wasn't going to let him. OR, later it seemed more like the reverse was true. The demon wanted to posses both of us, but my husband was trying to keep me safe.

Much later - two or three years later, I learned that the demons were FAtaLEE. They did come to posses my body. That is the way all demonic wars are fought and won. They take posession of the female body. The reason why is a true Christic Being who is Female can always bring the Male back when his soul has been taken. However, If the Female is taken, the male cannot bring the female back. Entire Planets were over taken by demons in this manner. And there was a very good reason why they wanted my Soul.

I was, in fact, at one time a very, very important Soul from the Elohim Family in Gaia. When we first arrived in Monterey, Zaurak had guided me to a restaurant - it was a Korean Restaurant that sat right on the ocean. When I was seated I looked up and saw a picture of Mt. Sorak (pronounced Zorak in Korean), covering the wall. Zaurak told me that he had created that mountain with me millions of years ago.

When my husband was gone Zaurak directed me back to the restaurant and he told me to remember the time when I was poisoned at the hotel in Seoul Korea by the Illuminati demons.

He told me that I did, in fact die, as the pharmacist had said. He asked me to remember how there were voices directing me during that time. How I was directed to get up and walk out of the hotel as fast as I could and get in a taxi and go straight home. He told me that was him talking to me. He told me that he is always with me. He is a Soul Mate from another time. He told me he was from Sirius B, but also an Eieyani from Inner Earth.

He told me that he had been with me as long as the Aquafarians, and that we were related as the Whale Family, and that is why we were there together. We were preventing another slaughter of Whales and dolphins by sending them home to the Cloud Cities. He told me that I was one of the original Dolphins from the Oraphim Cetacean Family that they were trying to kill and possess.

The demons were once Oraphim Dolphins themselves. They were taken over by the Red Dragons - the Draconians, using this manner of possesing the Female in order to take down the Males as well. They turned all of the females into Red Dragons. The Oraphims only escape was to become as bad as the Red Dragons and to become demons so that they could return quickly to Source as Space Dust in time to be born again into the new kingdom.

This was the reality that was taking place. aDolphino had actually volunteered for this mission before coming to Earth. He said,"both of you knew what your lives were really for."

The next day, I got a phone call from a hospital in Redding, California - near Mt. Shasta. They told me my husband was dead.

Zaurak and Markus and the Elohim Angels directed me to re-create the Ascension Portal and bring aDolphino back. I followed their instructions and the music that we made together with our frequencies recorded side by side. I prepared the portal to carry his soul which was actually our soul. I learned that we were at one time one star that was broken in half in order to lower our frequencies so that we could enter Earth's realm.

What I was doing with the portal was recombining our souls as one. I sent my frequencies of the female magnetic spin up to the Cosmic Realm to connect with aDolphino's electric spin and created a merkaba that would spin together and bring him back down.

Two hours later I got another phone call and the hospital told me that my husband was alive, but in a coma.

I immediately went to the airport and took the first flight to Redding. Zauarak, Markus and the Angels continued to direct me every moment that I was with my husband in the hospital. They told me that the demons were still trying to take him again. They told me that I needed to keep everyone away from him because there were other people involved in this possession, who didn't know that they were being used.

I kept everyone away. I stayed in the hospital most of the night every night and made sure the earphones stayed on his ears playing the frequency music that we had created together.

Zaurak told me that our mission was a success. We did create the Ascension Portal. It did bring aDolphino's Soul back into his body. I actually watched this event take place. I watched an Orb that was Blue go directly into aDolphino's back, right around the heart chakra area.

About two months later, the new aDolphino arrived on Earth for the first time. He turned to me and he said the angels were sitting on the bed talking to me. They told me to turn around and thank you for saving my life.

Later, Markus and Zaurak told us many other things about our adventure. They told us that they actually pulled aDolphinos real body through his past self up into a space ship and replaced it with a hologram when the three trucks hit the body and the five cars ran over the body. That would explain why his body appeared almost untouched in comparison to such a grand event.

His body was retrieved by a helicopter after a report of a ten ton truck throwing his body out in the middle of a freeway after another ten ton truck and thrown him in front of that truck, and there was a third truck that brushed his body as it was flying accross the freeway. After the body landed on the freeway five more cars ran right over the top of it without stopping or even knowing it was there.

So, imagine what a body would look like after that happened. His body did have a huge scar on the forehead where he had broken the headlights of the truck with his head and his hips and spine were broken from the fall after flying through the air. The only damage from the cars was a broken leg.

Zaurak and Markus actually told me that they were hoping this would be come the new Jesus and Mary story because they are really tired of hearing the "Jesus was nailed to the cross" story. And the fact was that they made up that story. They said they were on the team that chose Arihabi to be nailed to the cross and then created the hologram of his resurrection. They said they didn't know that their story would be such a long lasting dogma that would keep people mesmerized for so many years. They told me that they thought this would make a much better story, and some time in the future enough people will understand this story and how important what we did was.

They told me that there would be much more to be known about the portal and the saving of many of the Whale People who were our original family of creation – the Oraphims from Gaia.

The reason I wanted to tell you about Zaurak is because he is back again with his star fleet from Sirius B, the Blue Eieyani. They will be the first E.T. race that we will meet. I have already met one of them.

The Sirians worked together with the Ra Confederation, Eieyani, Azurites, Ranthions, Zionites and the Majaraji on the project of Comet Ison. Project Ison was actually the completion of what the scientists discovered in 2005, when they saw the explosion in the Ursa Major, 550 million light years away.

This flow of Cosmic Rays is the flow of the frequencies that are needed to re-awaken the mid brain in a way that will allow the seventh seal to melt away and the accretions of the magical crystal gel of transformation will begin to flow through our bodies.

The project that was begun millions of years ago, that would restore the 12 Dimensional Krystic Consciousness was begun by the Ra Confederation, and now must be completed by Sun Ra. Our original Founders Race Line will continue to activate harmonic universe two with Cosmic Rays until all of the Error or Miasms of Frozen Crystals are melted away through the Liquid Light Streams Ionizing and Transforming us by combining the physical back into the spiritual.

Zaurak was also a part of the group that activated the Grids in Earth a few months ago. That was the completion of the Great White Lion Grid project.

We were all here together thousands of years ago and millions of years ago working on all of these projects of ascension that are finally going to be completed in a few more years.

Even though this is not the beginning. It is the end of 500 million years of hard work by entities such as Zaurak and Markus who would never give up on their plan to save us.

The stories of the countless wars in the heavens that they have fought for us will soon become bedtime stories for the Indigos who will be awakening in the near future.

Chapter Four

The New Jesus and Mary Story

The Crystalai Cosmic Councils visit me every night at about 4 a.m. and ask me to read something or direct me to listen to them. I always write down what they tell me afterward.

This time, I also hooked a golden sphere up above my head 36 inches and into my mid brain and asked to be taken into the reality of what will happen in the next three months, before going back to dreamland.

First, I will tell you about the bi-location experience that many still call dreaming or astral projection. This was a bi-location dream into the future - the very near future.

The dream was pure vivid color lucid 3D blue ray quality reality. First, I was standing in a field looking up and seeing two suns unite as one, next I saw spaceships that could easily appear to be a comet. There were many space ships. Suddenly they burst into the Earth's atmosphere and could easily be seen, and then in an instant they were landing on the ground around the area I was standing. When they touched the ground, they took on the appearance of helicopters.

I was so excited and happy that I ran up to the spaceships and started banging on the outside of the ships and screaming Welcome, We love you. I was crying so hard with joy that I woke up drenched in tears. Scientifically speaking - in the Science of the Stars, this is what is taking place at this time. I was bi-locating into the experience that is happening right here, right now, in this second harmonic universe. The reality is invisible to those who don't have the keys that allow them to walk through the doors into multiple realities.

What NASA is calling Comet Ison is in fact a space ship. The entities are members of the Crystalai Cosmic Council including Ra Confederation, Azurite Council, Eieyani from Sirius B.

The Space Ship is guarding and guiding the Holographic Beam of Morphogenetic Frequencies from the Photon Belt of Sun Alcyone, which are, in fact, the frequency signatures of the original Tara before the explosion 550 million light years ago.

We even have scientific evidence of all of these events happening. January, 2005, New Scientist magazine reported Ultra High Energy Cosmic Rays appearing to originate from the Ursa Major area of space 550 million light years from earth. Glennys Farrar, a physicist at New York University discovered this celestial spring of mysterious particles slamming into Earth in 2005.

Ancient people had discovered that the Earth acts as a mirror to the energies of the cosmos. Very recently we have learned that the Plasma Ships are the Cosmic Mirror that will reflect the frequencies of the Cosmic Rays into our bodies. These revelations came to me from Zaurak this morning, March 28, 2014. Yesterday, as I was adding the paragraphs to my book about the Koreans who taught me that they were the Bear People from Ursa Major, I asked Zaurak if any one else knew about this.

This morning, Zaurak told me to go get the book, Mary Magdalene: The Illuminator by William Henry. I picked the book up and opened directly to the page that said the Bear People were from Ursa Major. Later on, in the book, the clarification came that M82 is the Starburst Galaxy that is called Great Bear. (W.Henry, 2006. Pg 12)

Zaurak just informed me that he was the creator of one of those Stars in that system. He also informed me that Mt. Szorak, in Korea is the portal that allows him to travel inter-dimensional from M82 into the Earth's Core. The top of the mountain is the eighth dimensional octave that creates the vortex between dimensions, and the same vortex exists deep within the Etheric Inner Core of the Earth's Core. These are vortexes that allow inter dimensional arks into other dimensions, must like walking through the doors of the faces of the merkaba.

I was given the same explanation about Mt. Shasta. The top of Mt. Shasta is at 10,000 feet. That is the location of the Cloud Cities, and the area where the Halo Effect is also seen. That is the Harmonic Convergence Zone or the Octave between dimensions. I was told that about one thousand years ago, those of us who arrived on Earth through one of those portals in Mt. Shasta used a rock as a communication device to those extra terrestrials who used that portal.

When I was in Monterey, I was told to use a Rock that sat on the shoreline between Asilamar and Monterey, right above Lover's Point. That was the rock that Zaurak used to communicate with me. When we arrived at Mercy Hospital in Redding, there was a picture of that Rock in Monterey covering the wall in the Waiting Room. Zaurak had planned all of these events to take place in order to connect the Islands of Light between all areas in Northern California. The Islands of light are in the Cloud Cities at the locations above the mountains. The Halo point at Mt. Sorak is also one of the connecting points for this massive Island of Light where the consciousness that transforms us will be carried.

So, we had starburst in 2005, the Sirian Fleet arrived in 2008.

I purchased this book in 2008, the week before aDolphino had his episode with the Sirians and the FAtaLE. I think it was Markus who told us to purchase that book.

It was during that same week that Markus and Zaurak told us that we were the new Jesus and Mary story. In 2006, we were told that I was Crystalai and my husband was Atoni. My husband kept listening to make sure he was hearing correctly. He wasn't sure if he was being told Atoni or Adoni or Adonai. It sounded like a mixture of these. And then we have the help of this definition - Adonai is referred to God but Adonis to human superiors.

Now, we have more clarification from Keylontic Science which says the Atonis female must reunite with the Adoni Male. The Atonis would be the physical female and the Adoni would be the spiritual male. This combination of Soul Mates is only found on the Cosmic Twin level, and these mates have a very hard time finding each other.

At that time, in 2006, we went to Google and tried to learn more about Atoni and Adoni. We learned that these names were associated with Isis when he was blown up and his penis was blown off. The story goes that Osiris put Isis back together again. This is the story that reminds me of Cheju do Island in Korea. The Island has phallic symbols all over it. South Korea has phallic symbols scattered around it as well. This is why the idea of the Koreans being from Ursa Major, the Isis Story, and the Cosmic Mary stories make me realize that these events were Cosmic rather than in specific locations like Egypt.

So, it is very possible that the Cosmic Mary and the Universal Mary - the Female Christ, might had sent cosmic rays directly to Monterey, or it may had more to do with the Oraphim Dolphins and Whales who lived there.

Monterey, and the ocean in front of Big Sur are well known for having a Crystal City under water. I have bi-located there many times and met many old friends from Aquafaria. We watched the Crystal Cities rise in June and July of 2008.

There is another clue about this location being connected to a Vortex that would reconnect us to all extra terrestrial races connected with Earth. There was a wormhole directly in front of our condo. The Marine Base has a full time training activity for divers to attempt to travel into that wormhole. Thousands of divers died trying. I think one diver got out alive.

I also know that my friend, who was a Seal named Tinker Bell, tried to convince me to swim with her into that wormhole several times. Apparently it was a common trip for her to take. But, I had to explain over and over again, that I was not ready yet and it would be too dangerous. I was told that I could travel through this vortex after 2015.

In 2008, we were guided to this book by William Henry that says we take the spiritual consciousness from ATON (the Lord). Two pages later, the book handed to me says Jesus was called Adon or Adonoi, and he transmitted the Holy Spirit to his disciples by breathing upon them.

This book talks about Mary Magdalene being the Illuminated one who was illuminated by the light of glory, meaning the light of love and spiritual consciousness from Aton.

It was Mary Magdalene who knew the secrets of releasing the secretions from the pineal that raised the illumination of consciousness. She was the one who knew the stairway to heaven was achieved through the stairway to heaven, which was the bliss of the seventh heaven. The transformations that Mary and Jesus spoke of were the exact science of bringing in the cosmic rays that created liquid light energy within the mid brain. That cosmic frequency ignited the cells and the skin would glow.

These secrets have all been returned to Earth. I know and understand all of the science that Mary and Jesus taught. This science activated a new strain of humans in the blink of an eye. Now, once again this science is activating a new strain of humans in the blink of an eye. Mary and Jesus both used this spiritual substance called atoni, and Jesus was named Adoni, meaning Lord.

There was also a race line named Atoni. They were later known as the Seres and the Egyptians. When Joe asked for his spiritual name, he was told that he was Atoni. He was given that information in 2006, and we did not know what it meant at that time.

However, the name Lord actually meant Christ, and the name Mary also meant female Christ. The spiritual substance was called Atoni, meaning the anti-particle or spiritual substance on the parallel spiritual universe side must be reconnected to the particle female magnetic substance. This is basically how the sub harmonics within the DNA are becoming activated.

Their science was showing the uniting of an extraterrestrial consciousness into the human consciousness. The extraterrestrial consciousness was the cosmic rays from the seven stars of Ursa Major. The hybrid strain of humans included this transformational frequency of the twelfth dimensional energy.

Now, we have all of the spiritual tools and science that Jesus and Mary used to Breathe the Cosmic Consciousness back into the humans who are already a hybrid strain that was created from the original template of the Oraphims from Gaia, the Tarans from Tara, the Sirians from Ursa Major. The hybrid human is returning to Earth as a result of the Cosmic Rays from Ursa Major in 2005 along with the other 12 Stellar Wave Activations.

This time the DNA activations are happening on a Mass Level through the biosphere of Earth. The frequencies are being saturated within Earth's Core and her Cosmic Heart and then flowing out through her Veins or Christ Grids. It is the human template on Earth that acts as a conduit for these frequencies to rise into our atmosphere. And the activation takes place through our breath.

The Bliss that is associated with Mary as she climbed the stairway to heaven is the Breath that is used to activate the Merkaba. The keys that unlock the doors to the higher dimensions are the frequencies created by spinning the Merkabas at the speed of light energy of Love. It is the activation through spinning of the Merkabas within Merkabas within Merkabas that unlocks the doors.

What are the doors? Every cube of the upper and lower face of the Merkaba contains four sides. Each of those sides or faces is actually a door into four more faces and four more and four more. The sides of the cube are the doors into infinity. When the entire Merkaba mechanism is studied in its entire complexity, and then understood at a level where it can be visualized while the breathing is taken place, the entire structure of the carbon based body is unlocked into the silica based, star based structure of the original body.

When the star body is turned on, it glows. First the skin glows, then the bones turn into tones or frequencies, and the blood turns into crystal energy with a blue hue. The entire body takes on a blue hue. The body becomes the fifth dimensional body which is multi dimensional in consciousness. That body can learn to become an orb and to transport itself into other galaxies, other universes, and even inter-dimensional realities.

That is the science that Mary and Jesus taught two thousand years ago, and it is being taught again at the Cosmic Mystery School of the Omniverse. That Mystery School is not on Planet Earth. It is in the

14th Dimension where all Creation takes place. It is the place where we Ascend into a new reality after being transformed through the needed educational experiences in each dimension. It is where we learn all that is needed to Initiate each of our Sub harmonic Strands of Consciousness into our DNA

The plasma ships are creating a Magnetic Mirror around the Earth. It is just like the mirror that we walk through when we merge our consciousness into the full spectrum of light within the candle flame, as explained in the Candle Technique on the Home Page crystalmagicorchestra.com.

We walk into the full spectrum of light by standing within the candle flame. We absorb all of the frequencies up to the silver pink frequency, which is fourteenth dimensional heliotalic silver pink pastel, and then we absorb the white light of the pre light and sound or Source Frequencies and that is the diamond door that we move through, turn around and return as the Blue Body. Once you take your consciousness into the Full Spectrum of light, the Blue Hue is Created. That is the only way the blue hue is created. That is the only way to become the Fifth Dimensional Blue body.

The Plasma Ships are the Magnetic Bubble that will transform us into the Harmonic Universe Two fifth dimensional blue body raceline. That field of energy is called a morphogenetic wave that carries the consciousness of all of those spiritual ones who came before us.

The morphogenetic frequency field held within the holographic beam is putting Tara back together again. The frequencies of the original consciousness of Tara, which was originally a star created by Sun Alcyone, are being woven back into all of the 12 planets in the Milky Way Galaxy.

When Tara exploded, she was divided into 12 pieces - 12 stars. One of the stars is our Sun. Inside of our Sun is a Golden Crystal Core that holds all 12 pieces of Tara. Now, the morphogenetic frequency field of Sun Alcyone's Photon Belt, where the original frequencies of Tara have been stored are re-uniting with the Sun and the 11 planets within the golden crystal core of the Sun.

In NASA's eyes, the 3D science can only see the planets as separate. That is because the angle of rotation at this density creates a distance in reality that isn't really there.

So, we saw Comet Ison. We saw Comet Ison hitting or coming very close to Mars, Jupiter, Saturn, and then see Comet Ison heading for the Sun.

Comet Ison was supposed to go into the Sun on November 28, 2013. In reality, the holographic beam guided by the Space ship went into the golden crystal core of our Sun to re-unite the Photon Belt of Sun Alcyone with the Planets within the Sun.

Once that happens, the new morphogenetic frequency field that is created is the re-birth of the 12 dimensional frequencies of the original Tara, which is called the Sphere of Amenti. That Sphere of Amenti will enter Earth's Core to IGNITE the Cosmic Frequencies within the Iron Core. The D1 level of Earth will be filled with D15 frequencies. This will re-ignite the complete Divine Consciousness of the Earth into At One Ment with all 12 pieces of Tara, including the Sun. This blast of frequencies will TURN ON the 5 DNA within Earth and it will flow into our bioenergetics fields.

When I created the Parallel Universe Album, I was uniting my consciousness with the Holographic Beam as it was making its portal directly from Sun Alcyone's Photon Belt under the direction of the Guardian Councils.

The alignment with our Parallel Universe was one of the necessary steps in allowing the Councils to enter our Frequency Field. They can remain in the Cosmic Frequencies as they blend the D1 of Harmonic Universe One - Earth Density with D15 of the Earth's Matrix including the Cosmic Fifth Sphere.

That alignment was completed in order for the Comet to complete its journey into our Solar System. Once the Holographic Beam is activated within our Sun, which will be rebirth of the total morphogenetic field of Tara, that Morphogenetic Field can penetrate Earth and wrap around Earth.

That is what NASA sees as the Comet's tail wrapping around the Earth. Once that happens, the NEW BEGINNING HAS BEGUN!!!

Share the ride of the HOLOGRAPHIC BEAM through the Frequencies on the Parallel Universe Album. I will continue to collect the frequencies of the completed project including the connection of the Sun Alcyone into our Sun, the rebirth of the golden crystal core and the activation of the Sphere of Amenti in the Core of Earth. The final frequency signature that will be born from this Atonement will be 5 DNA.

Chapter Five

The Near Death Experience

By 2004, our starry families from the Sirian Council, Pleiadian Star League, Sirian Arcturian Coalition for Interplanetary defense and the Andromeda Federation of Planets created the bridge zone to save the human populations from the final scene of their drama. So, here we are in the final scene of planet Earth's movie. I've been listening to my higher self direct in making sure that I leave planet Earth harmoniously, making sure I never engage contact with fallen angels through my Soul Family's protection and here I am surrounded by these people who call themselves light workers who are eagerly awaiting their next misguided dialog with the very fallen angels who are planning to destroy the entire human population.

Chapter Five — Near Death Experience

In order to make sure I was paying close attention to what is going on, I got to personally witness my own husband have his soul taken by these demonic angels to make sure I knew that I was more powerful than all of them and an entire host of millions of angels who could not save him.

It was my Soul Families ability to connect me into the harp strings of my cosmic consciousness where I frequently visited my light families of the Braharama Dolphins and Whales of the 13th Dimension that allowed me to create the Cosmic Flame where my Cosmic Twin, aDolphino could be brought back to Earth.

I watched his old Soul leave and I watched his new highly upgraded oversoul morphogenetic family of consciousness enter in through his back door. I watched the disconnect and the reconnect. I watched it transpose through the frequencies I engaged from the highest frequency of Source Consciousness allowing a brand new idea to be born on Earth through my husband. I know now that everyone on this Earth has a Soul family and Cosmic Family that will reassemble our DNA, realign our soul families into oneness with all we once were. The transition is exactly what has been called a near death experience - (NDE).

NDE is basically our souls watching us make the decision to leave our bodies. Allowing the soul to reunite with the soul families of past lives, transmuting agendas that should no longer be a part of the new reality, creating a new reality through the light of Source - making a new mission and ascending into a new experience.

This time that new experience for most will be moving into Tara. A few of us will go as high as Gaia. The frequency fence is an electromagnetic sonic pulse holograph machine that will create illusions in the consciousness that manifest as that reality. That frequency fence has transmitted metatronic holograms to create false fields of reality that have been used to control us and to kill us. One frequency fence sonic pulse hologram machine was 9/11. One was the Philadelphia Experiment. One was Montauk. One was the AIDS virus. One was the swine flu, and several other virus manifestations that seemed to occur over night.

These holograms are illusions keeping the human angelics from realizing that they are the creators of the wealth, healing and peace. The higher frequencies of Cosmic and Source Consciousness allow everyone to connect their higher self into the Mind of God for instant manifestation of any reality that they wish to manifest. It is time to rise above the holographic realities that are being created around us into our own manifest realities. That frequency fence was put there to trap the human race in the same way the Fallen Zetas did where they took people up in their space ships to obtain coding and even souls for their own resurrection.

Fallen Zetas and Draconians will go into the phantom matrix and we will say good bye forever. Not all Zetas are fallen. Many of them have been here on Earth helping us. Those will also receive healing. The Annunaki and Illuminati will be taken to Sirius Star System for healing. The guardian races always see all of us as Children of God – it doesn't matter how fallen the entity has become. They always love them and try their best to help.

December 21, 2012 was the day the fallen angels had planned to destroy the human population by drawing us into their wormhole and using us for food and energy until our planet was completely destroyed. The Annunaki from Death Star Nibiru have also planned on destroying our race because they see us as a cosmic disease. That reality will not exist any longer. We will ascend to become the seventh root race. In the third dimensional story of Nostradamus many are destroyed and disappear and the Earth ends in mass destruction. We will be removed from that third dimensional reality.

The Earth was moved to a new time line where that probability no longer exists.

We are not in that dream any longer. Soon we will learn that this isn't our reality at all. We will soon see what the reality of the human angelic race looks like, what our Inner Earth families look like, what we really look like, what our Taran families and our Gaia families look like. We will be meeting them all very soon.

THE PROCESS OF OUR RE-BIRTH

The Fallen Angelics and Illuminati races will be escorted to quarantined healing facilities in the Sirius star system. This is not as black and white as it might sound.

Almost everyone on Planet Earth has been contaminated by Fallen Angelic Raceline breeding and Illuminati breeding. There have been hybrids created in Sirius that reconnect the human who lost his sub harmonic connection with his higher selves, into that original divine template of the original Elohim Angel Raceline. There are other raceline involved in this hybrid activation including the Oraphims, Eieyani, Maharaji, Zionites, Ranthians and the future Essene Race.

For many of us, this stage has already taken place and is taken place. My husband and I have both been taken to Sirius B for transformational healing. Remember, that we all came from the Oraphim raceline, which is the Cosmic Creation family of the Elohims on Gaia. That Raceline was destroyed and then created through the hybrid raceline of the Sirians and Elohim re-creation team.

Now, most people on Earth, except those few Indigo Children who were born as hybrid children, need some type of restructuring. The way this is done, is the template of the soul from the Past self is taken forward in time to the future self for healing. The Present self isn't aware of exactly what is taking place.

However, sometimes there are dreams that actually cover up the surgery that is taking place to remove the pain. Sometimes these events take place during sleeping time and sometimes we are just told to take a nap during the day. The transformation is realized within the following week. The body begins to feel brand new, realities that were invisible start becoming more tangible.

The same process is used when we are moved into the Inner Domains of Inner Earth for our complete 12 Christic Coding. The Inner Domains are the place where our original perfect self still remains.

Activations will continue until 2017 when full mass landing of Emerald Covenant Races occurs. Then the second wave of healing will begin, to prepare the second wave into the Consciousness of Tara by 2022. Earth and Tara will merge gradually over the five year period. The entire Earth will already become Inner Earth by 2017. That will allow all Friendly Race Lines to enter Earth's Consciousness Fields. By 2017, Earth will begin to morph into Inner Earth (what many know as Agartha). At this time many Angelic Humans and the races of Earth will be prepared for visits with the Inner Earth Eieyani, Sirius B Maharaji, Azurite, Aethien and Serres Emerald Covenant Races. They will make contact through our Founders Races and will invite Earth races to join the Emerald Covenant.

The physical mass contact of the Emerald Covenant Nations is scheduled for 2017. Entering the Covenant is like being given an multidimensional passport.

The first contacts will be made individually and privately, as early as 2013. I've already had many interactions with all of these Races and many more. First, most star seeds will meet with Eieyani races because they look the most like us - only they are blue. After star seeds become familiar with the Eieyani, we will be met by Azurites and Maharaji.

These are all Guardian Races. The Priests of Ur, who have been the Intervention Team who has over seen the entire process of Earth's escape from complete annihilation during this process will also meet us. The Zionites, who created the Inner Time Portals allowing us to regain our 12 DNA Divine

Blue Print that existed in Tara. The Ranthians, who are the water people who share our accretion level, and yet have the highest level of inter stellar and inter dimensional time travel ability of any one in the Universe. The Zionites and Ranthians talk to me continuously about their plans.

Blue Flame keepers will become 9th level avatars, as the blue flame spirals down from Sun Alcyone on March 20, 2013. Flame Holders who carry a rare recessive gene will have this gene activated. These holders contain a specific magnetic base tone in their DNA that allows them to become very magnetic and are able to hold this activation on Earth. We are from the Oraphim Cetacean Braharama Raceline who hold the Biosphere of the Omniverse, and continuously align with the Dolphins and Whales that we created to be our lightning rods on Earth. We are the holders of the Frequencies of the Divine Biosphere of 12 Coded Divine Blue Print. We were the grandfathers of the Elohim of Gaia.

Once the D 5 flame holder holds the frequencies of Sun Alcyone and pulls the frequencies into her Flame Keepers fourth heart chakra an intense infusion of harmonic universe two frequencies spread through the Amenti morphogenetic field and through the Earths Grid. This will allow rapid acceleration of fifth and sixth DNA strand assembly to occur throughout the populations. The seventh strand will begin assembly in those who already hold fifth and sixth. This activation will create a huge multidimensional awareness to occur on Earth.

When the halls of Amenti merge Tara and Earth together, those who have assembled the fifth strand and are eligible for ascension to Tara will be guided (in consciousness) to inter-dimensional transportation locations to Tara. Those who have sixth and seventh strands may be eligible for transport to Gaia. There may be others who will be transported to Aquarius, Aquafaria and a few who will go play in the heavens with the gods. This will happen in 2017.

First, we will shift into a different chemical make up. We will leave behind our carbon based bodies. We will become less dense. Our bodies and our environment will change. Those who move on to Tara will have an entirely different type of body than those who stay in Inner Earth. Those who move on to Gaia are almost invisible. Those who are of higher densities can see the lower densities; but those who remain 3D will not be able to see any of the new realities. It might seem like things are disappearing because the higher particle shifts will pull some in one direction and the lower will pull those in another direction. There are infinite density levels.

Earth's elemental particle base will rise to 5 and the Earth's atmospheric particle base will rise to 6. This accretion level will allow the atmosphere and elementals from Inner Earth to appear on Earth. This will be our first vision of our New Earth. We will begin to see the atmosphere of Inner Earth forming around us and then we will notice more and more new species and inner earth gardens will appear. All of the animals and plants in Inner Earth sing continuously. We will notice this difference in Earth immediately.

Chapter Six

Rebirth into Our Crystal Bodies

In a Normal Planetary System, a baby is born into the Divine Template that has its perfect formula that is connected through the silver seed atom that will blossom and bloom into the perfect Christ Body by age 33. In our present Earth Matrix, all of the stages of a baby's birth from the stage of the sperm and ovum have been distorted through activations placed within our bodies. There was a finite, anti Krystic 666 creation code placed in our Tail Bone that would place an invisibility cloak around our true Divine Template. The normal body has a crystallized standing wave radiation field of pure Source Consciousness placed around the Silver Seed Crystal at the time of conception.

There was a distortion carried through the Ghi ring in the sperm which would cause the Chi in the sperm and the Ki in the ovum to interrupt the natural organic process of the spark of Source being released into the baby's body by day six of conception.

The Spark of Source that would create the Violet Flame of Transmutation into the Multidimensional Consciousness of a true Christic baby was harnessed by a frequency signature that magnetizes into it the elements from the elemental base field in the surrounding environment - meaning the world's consciousness field at the first chakra of density or the hertzian field of light. At that moment, the child becomes locked into the hertzian field of reality and cannot expand into the 15 dimensions of the normal reality. This membrane or cloak that blocks the reality of Source Consciousness from entering in was placed in the tailbone.

This Cloak or Seal that was placed in our tailbone will be removed by the violet flame of transmutation when the Cosmic Template is placed into full activation. This will begin the restoration of our Frequency of Source Consciousness connecting eternally into our Divine Template. This will begin the release of and activation of our Silver Seed Crystal and allow our normal eternal life flow currents to flow into our innate intelligence and consciousness of the normal body.

The cloaking causes an inorganic birth to result by placing a metatronic electro magnetic harness around the Spirit Body which creates the carbon body which is inorganically polarized into a Tube Torus vortex spin, forming the distorted Yin Yang flow. This causes the body to become a carbon based body which is blocked from its Spirit Body through the twisted Ghi Force. The normal body becomes an organic Crystal Based Body rather than a Carbon Based Body when that metatronic twist is removed and the Living Conscious Spirit returns to the body. This is how our bodies will be transformed as we use the Stellar Wave Frequencies. This is when the real Christ Man will begin walking on Earth.

How did we stop being Normal? Invader Races, including Jehovian and Annunaki lines placed metatronic flows in our bodies and in our planet to block the flow of Source Consciousness and the Music of the Spheres breathing process. This was for the purpose of controlling the Human Angelic Race, taking control of the Blue Flame carrying the Divine Template of Co-creation, and taking control of the star gates. The Invader Race story was changed to make it sound like there was one individual named Jehovah causing all of the problems. The Jehovians and Annunaki and many other Invader Races created these stories.

The long story is this:

When we were in the Galactic Level of Consciousness we were all known as gods. A god is a normal entity who can create his own reality. Each of the gods in the Andromeda Galaxy was creating their own realities. When an entity from another Galaxy joined a creation group in the Andromeda Galaxy, an experiment went wrong and the Star they were creating blew up. We can think of it like children in a chemistry lab trying to learn to create a star, but the wrong amount of substances interacted incorrectly.

The piece of that star from the Andromeda Galaxy flew out into the Milky Way Galaxy. There were gods in the Milky Way Galaxy who were also creating their own realities out of the fallen stars from other Galaxies. One of those gods, whose name was Jehovah from Nibiru, came to this planet Earth and saw that there were many other gods creating their realities here. Jehovah was a jealous god and he wanted to be the only god on the block. Jehovah knew how the Normal Body is created from the formula given above, as all gods know. So, he went to his own experimental lab and formulated a plan that would cause the Normal Body to self destruct because it was blocked off from the reality of Source Consciousness. Jehovah was the god who created a man made template that would allow only the elemental part of the Normal

Man to remain, and that Normal Man would never be allowed to know himself.

Jehovah knew that as long as man could connect his consciousness from his Soul into the Mind of God and instantly manifest his reality, that there would be gods many and Jehovah would not be able to control the world. Jehovah was so jealous that he wanted to make sure that he was the only god. So, he thought of a way to hide the Soul of Man in a place where he would never find it. He hid our Soul from us in this invisibility cloak which resulted in this carbon based body. Our transformation back into the normal mangod that we are in our Normal Form is simply changing the carbon body back into the crystal body. Jehovah continued his plan of control and destruction by implanting radiation fields within the Earth's crust that would also block or cloak the Christ Fields of Frequencies and the Source Fields of Frequencies from entering our Consciousness as we tune into the Earth's Frequencies.

Now, that we know the truth about what made us this way and how we got here, we can begin to correct it. That entire reality or movie that was created by Jehovah will be ending on this Earth in the year 2012. Each of us will remember that a god is an entity who creates their own reality, and our reality is ours. We are not within the reality of another being. We have simply been trapped within the hologram of the creation made by Jehovah. It certainly wasn't the real movie made by our One Source, or the real gods of our creation in Andromeda, Aquarius, Aquafaria, as well as all of the gods who were on Earth creating this reality before Jehovah placed a cloak of radiation to block their consciousness with the veil of Fear.

This is where we will begin again. We will begin knowing who we really are. We will know how to remove the cloaks, seals, veils that block us from the Source Field of continuous instantaneous creation. We will learn all of the things that have been made invisible to us by the invisibility cloak placed over our consciousness. Now we know that the Normal Body is born with a silver seed atom that will blossom into a fully grown Christ body by age 33. The Normal Baby chooses the parents that will help prepare the path of the journey that was perfectly planned before coming to the density of experience. Sometimes Souls plan their journeys for thousands of years before choosing their vehicles to instigate the journey. Sometimes Souls wait until they know a certain state of consciousness has appeared that will allow them to complete their journey. Those Souls would also be waiting for a set of parents who have transformed their consciousness to the place that will help the soul remember and perform the journey. These journeys and things like becoming Christ on Earth, or creating a better Mystery School, or instantly healing everyone on Earth, or creating your Symphony of Love from the Music of the Spheres, or preparing a new technology that would provide free energy for the world.

The journeys always involve a mission that is for the world, not for themselves. In the normal system, all souls are always on the group mission of Oneness.

This system has not allowed for these Normal things to happen yet. First of all, there was an implant placed within our entire structure that would block us from blooming correctly clear back at the point of conception. The negative technology was placed in the sperm so that the baby would never have the spirit body and the light body appear correctly as it would in a Normal Body.

So, our Aquafarian friends from a Star System far beyond Andromeda, Aquarius, M31, or any of the names that have been known to us, placed the silver seed awakening potential within the Edons of the Inner Earth. Those silver seeds within us must reunite with the Spirit Body that was disconnected from us even before we were born. Our starry family has created a formula that will correct the incorrect formula that was placed in our bodies.

This time we will be reborn into our Crystal bodies instead of our Carbon bodies or inorganic elemental form. This time our eternal life bodies will be created with the Source Field ignited and connected. This time we will be created from the Divine Template - the image and likeness of God - our Soul within, who carries the imprints all we have been, clear back to the breath of Source.

The Inner Earth's Edon frequency fields that will allow the opening of Star Gates all of the way from Aquafaria into our bio fields and carbon fields and translate us through the transformational process of the stardust energy of crystal light, crystal dust and crystal gel, which is the music of the spheres.

The silver seed atoms will unlock our reality from within us. Our pituitary gland will open like a blossoming flower to behold a new movie, a new reality that we create from within and project out into our new quantum field.

The spirit body that was disconnected from our physical body that contains our seed atom that will reconnect us to our full crystal body of multidimensionality have been stored away for us in the Edons of the Heart of Mother Earth. This is where we must go to reconnect to our complete self. When our spiritual bodies are re-connected, our seed atoms will begin to blossom into the beautiful star children of our Christic birth.

Those stargates connected to Edon were locked and sealed by the fallen angelics for millions of years. Each time our civilization has risen back up into a level of a high transformation, our Aquafarian Family has returned to Earth to replace that silver seed atom that will reconnect us into our spiritual bodies and our transformation will begin.

The Aquafarians have come to Earth three different times attempting to activate our silver seed awakening. They planted their seeds of our perfect selfhood deep within the Earth so that we could be awakened by the Sun in 2012. The Aquafarians have attempted to fulfill this activation for 500,000 years. Each time we came to Earth, the Dark Ones found us and destroyed those of us who could not escape. We were here to create the Rainbow Bridge of the full multidimensional consciousness as we activated the violet flame to flow through the spheres of the music of the spheres transformation.

Some of us escaped each time, and some of us dove into your oceans and became mermaids, mermen, dolphins, seals, orcas and whales. We disguised ourselves so that we could stay on Earth and complete our mission.

Our Aquafarian family is ready to do their thing once again as the gates to Edon are opening. They have been working on this alignment that creates the Crystal Liquid Light from their Consciousness - the power of the light frequencies of the Most Perfect Kingdom- to flow through all of the spheres to align and transmute Mother Earth and her entire population. We will all experience our silver seed awakening. This means our perfect selfhood contains our Divine Mind, Divine intelligence, Infinite Supply, Instant Manifestation, Divine Substance, Eternal Life of the One Source will be returned to us. We have been trapped in this illusion where we forget who we really are because our Divine Programming is removed from us before birth. That programming that could be regained if a child worked at it full time from birth is removed again at puberty.

Now, all of this distortion will be cleared up and new babies will be born naturally and everyone on Earth will have this corrected as well. However, it is up to each individual to blossom fully to this new wonderful reality. Each individual must make the effort to be this Natural Person before it will unfold into that person's life. So, this is fabulously being corrected for everyone, but each individual must then make it a part of her/his life in order to experience it and have their life revolve around the Natural New Earth, Solar System, Galaxy, Universe and Omniverse.

TRANSMUTING KARMA

The blockage to our Normal Self is this thing called sin or karma. This thing called sin was a re-definition created by the re-legions to make our karma become worse than it really was. Karma simply means the distortions of light fields between our spheres. The spheres are the layers of light and sound at the Cosmic plane, Universal plane, Galactic plane, Solar plane and Earth plane or spheres. Our real bodies are actually a Divine template that contains all five of these spheres of light and sound.

When the breath of Source ignites the spark of creation of a new idea, that blue light spark turns into a violet flame. That violet flame contains the consciousness that can transform the entire Music of the Spheres - which is actually ones new reality or form. The Music of the Spheres has become very inharmonic, minor, diminished and densified into the lowest frequencies of the hertzian spectrum of light. The violet flame of transformation allows our star gates to open up and re-harmonize into all of our multidimensional selves that we were divinely created to be from the Breath of Source.

We were given the ability to remove all of the karma from ourselves and from anyone who desires to be transformed at this time. When the Breath of Source is connected to in Consciousness and then breathed into a spark of ignition at the outer sphere of Cosmic Consciousness, and hen inhaled in through the crystal light between the bands of the Cosmic, Universal, Galactic, Solar and Planetary Spheres, the karma that is creating in harmony between the spheres can be removed from our templates and from our matrix.

This is the New Way of Transmutation and Transformation. It is the Music of the Spheres becoming known again on this Earth. The Cosmic Mystery School of the Omniverse is the creation of the Divine Minds of all of the Frequency Signatures within all of the Spheres, who desire to bring this knowingness into this plane of understanding. When we go through our initiations in the Edons, we decide what Teams of Consciousness that we want to join with for our next mission or journey on Earth or elsewhere.

The Soul families who have chosen to join together as a team to create the Mystery School are our families of consciousness from the Inner Earth Edon Domains, our Rainbow friends in the Cloud Cities, our Aquarius families, our Aquafarian families, as well as Serepis Bey, St. Germain, Cosmic Mother Mary, Zadkiel, Raphael, the Aurora Templars and all others wanting this same team.

This is the mission that our Souls have returned to Earth at this time to complete. This New understanding has evolved over millions of years as the all knowingness has worked to transmute the unknowingness of this kingdom.

Our technology has evolved to a level where a glimpse of what a frequency of light and sound from the Cosmos might feel like when interfaced with the consciousness of understanding and the crystal spheres of creation.

The understanding requires considering all of the teachings in all of the Mystery Schools before and then removing those teachings that were revised by dark forces technology, adding the original teachings from the crystal template of the Light Councils that contains the true story of creation, and how to manifest that creation at this time.

It is valuable to know how to transform ones Divine Template into the Christic Template before the transformation in December 2012. It is crucial to understand the Source of what is causing the complete shift in Consciousness to take place. The shift will happen through frequencies of light and sound transposing the music of the spheres into a new symphony of love.

The reason it is important to know how to transmute frequencies at this time is because one of the seals that was placed within us, for the purpose of making sure the dark forces defeat us through fear, is the amygdale gland which holds the seals that shoot toxins into the body to create the feeling of fear. Fear is just a word to us. The frequency is a backward, reversed metatronic miasm that creates separation between our spheres of our selves. We have been many selves. Our souls have returned to Earth about ten million times. This means each and every one of us has been one of those types of agendas that we see and we despise, we hate, we curse, we want to kill or make go away.

Those things, those people, those events and these feelings are all as much a part of each individual as it is a part of the other. In order to remove the separation, which is called karma, we must first realize the truth about ourselves. We were one of those other selves at one time because we are all one. This reality can't be rationalized, it can't be ignored, it can't be denied. It just has to be looked at with Inness. All of the karma that must be removed from this planet is a lowered frequency that can only be transmuted into the highest frequency. As long as we keep trying to change one hertzian frequency idea into another hertzian frequency by killing someone or putting someone in jail, the hertzian just becomes lowered. When we bring in the Violet Flame of Transformation from the breath of Source and breath that frequency into all of the spheres upon spheres of all of the infinite selves we have been, we transmute our entire reality system out of this lowered dream world that has locked us out of our normal self who can and will become Christ walking on Earth in the next few years.

Chapter Seven

The Promise

Since people will always ask the question, "how do you know all of this stuff?, I will begin with my diary which serves the purpose of answering that question, along with the more important purpose of fulfilling my contract for this lifetime and leaving a record of my existence on harmonic universe one before my move to harmonic universe two.

Hopefully, this record of my existence will be of help to future races who pass through this plane of existence. Since this is my private diary, I will be speaking of my self, to my self and in relation to myself. This diary will be very educational in nature, even though that isn't its purpose.

Since it is my diary, I will not be editing my spelling or grammar. Since it is my diary, I will not be quoting or using copyrights because I plan on this world and its stupid rules being completely removed before this diary is published. And, since this is my diary, I will be giving my opinion about many things that should be known about that have been kept secret to the world.

I know all that I know because I am always talking to my Angelic Consciousness, which is mostly at the Cosmic Level and the Primal Life Consciousness Field where the first ideas of Source are created and re-manifest within each breath of Source. I raise my consciousness into the highest frequency of Source. That causes a wave of consciousness to come into the atmosphere around me. The thoughts that come to me in those sound waves are always filtered so I do not retrieve low level inter-dimensional fallen angelic waves. The ideas that come to me come on the Waves of Love which is the highest frequency in the Universe. When the Sound and Light fields weave into a vortex, a new idea is formed and it is retrieved by my pineal gland in my mid brain. All ideas that are retrieved as frequencies come directly filtered through the thermal radiation frequencies of consciousness of the mind of God.

Chapter Seven · The Promise

Back to how I learned all of this

I was singing in a choir in Japan when I taught at Beppu Daigaku. I kept singing into a tape recorder and listening to my self over and over again. I kept trying to get a sweeter and sweeter sound. I then started working with a professional recording studio that we brought to Japan from West L.A. Music. I learned that the higher the source of the recording, the closer what I was hearing was to the actual sound of my voice. I wanted to hear exactly what my voice really sounded like and I wanted it to sound as sweet and pure and perfect as the voice of God singing through me.

I prayed and prayed to the angels in the room to align my voice into God so that everyone who heard my voice would be healed. I did this every day for five years. I listened to my voice over and over and over again. I could hear it changing every day. I could hear it getting lighter and sweeter until is sounded like angels were singing and that I was only the microphone.

I started receiving messages telling me that the frequencies in my voice would be completely transposed and that when my speaking voice sounded like my singing voice, this would mean that I had ascended. They told me that ascension was all about the frequencies in my voice. That was 1995. From that moment on, all I worked on was the alignment of the frequencies of my voice into the breath of God.

About the same time, my husband got this message from Angels saying Make God's Movie. And then in the middle of the night in Japan, he was woken and told to write music that became the title song for our next album, The Promise.

What was so significant about this music that came to him that night? It was the rhythm of the heartbeat that would be transformed on December 21, 2012. I couldn't finish writing this book until I finally figured that out. We were directed to write the music in the time signature of 8/12. A very strange time signature. A very difficult time signature to create a melody that could be sung. However, the music was written, and the words were given to me. And I was shown how to sing the words within that time signature.

The words described what is about to happen this December. It explained that the Promise that our Cosmic Families made to us millions of years ago, and the promise that is written in Genesis would be kept. That promise was to return the kingdom of heaven to Earth. What did that mean? The kingdom of heaven is the divine structure that is created within the Source Field of the Mind of God. It is the Music of the Spheres where all aligns harmoniously through the in breath and out breath of Source. It is the new Symphony where everything becomes renewed when the breath of Source is in Alignment or Augment with the Universe.

How will the Promise be kept? The harmonic attunement will be created when the base pulse rhythm returns to the time signature 8/12. That will be rhythm of our heart beat when our 12 DNA divine blue print activates on December 21, 2012.

After working with frequencies of alignment in my voice into the Angelic Consciousness that was guiding me and directing me for years, I received a new message in 2007. I was told that our music was well known all over the universe, and yes, we would bring the highest frequencies to Earth through Music. The highest frequencies are the primal sound field where Source breathes the spark of the idea that is to become manifest.

This Earth and all who are on her, have been blocked from that primal sound field, and will soon be returned to the Music of the Spheres which contains the mathematical formulas or the musical tones that align us to that reality.

A group of Elohim Angels appeared to me and gave me the formula for bringing the highest frequencies to Earth through music. They told me that I would create three crystal spheres containing crystal liquid light, crystal gel and crystal dust.

Chapter Seven						The Promise

They told me to breathe these spheres from the Mind of God. They connected me to the Elohim of Hearing to help make this connection through my right ear. They directed me in inhaling this tone through my ear into my mid brain and then into my crystal heart. They had me inhale these three spheres of energy and create them into one sphere of crystal energy that I would breath out of my heart and into another crystal sphere made of the same substance. They taught me how to sing the new tones or frequencies as they morphed through this 14th dimensional substance that I had created from thermal radiation energy, plasma or gamma waves and morphed it into breaths that held the entire spectrum of light and sound from the hertzian in the recording studio clear up into invisible light, x-ray and gamma ray sound fields. I could use this energy to connect directly into any level of angelic consciousness that I wished to receive wisdom from.

The Angels continued to teach me how to use these crystal spheres for healing, transformation, ascension and manifestation. These spheres of energy were the same consciousness fields of the music of the spheres that would be brought to Earth to morph Earth's consciousness field into the original Sphere of Consciousness that holds the template of the Divine Creation of that Idea at all dimensions simultaneously.

As the words in the Promise Album say, The promise of the perfect kingdom, as Before the World Began. The world that we live in is a complete misalignment of the kingdom of heaven. There have been misalignments put in the grids and lei lines of this planet that create disharmony, minor modes and out of tune symphonies throughout the entire universe. That is why our song was heard through out the universe. It was because the mission that my husband and I signed up for before we came to Earth was to Remember what that Real Music Sounded Like. To Realign our Consciousness through the mid brain Frequency Specific Transmitters into the Mind of God.

Now, when we hear the New Symphony played in the Music of the Spheres, that symphony will be heard in unison throughout the Cosmos as all of the 12 universes once again align in perfect harmony. All of these things we knew, before we actually knew anything. We were told and shown how to make the music long before we knew what it meant. Now that we know what it all means we have the understanding that is necessary to partake in this ascension.

We have been aligning our frequencies into the crystal heart of Mother Earth and into the spark of Source to create a perfect stream of crystal liquid light of the rainbow current made of heliotalic frequencies which are the frequencies of the

alignment of the music of the spheres. We have been aligning into the harmonic convergence zones, the vortexes of attunement, the vortices of realignment. We have been activating frozen crystal miasms within our bodies and within our atmosphere and within the Earth's biosphere. We have been awakening the Angelic Consciousness within the Grids of the Earth. We have been keeping records of the Frequency changes within the Earth each
  month for 12 years. There have been many wars fought in other dimensions to protect the Earth, and there have also been may inharmonic alignments shooting more minor modes into the Earth's shields. The final war is being fought in Ra - the closest Sun to Source. That will be the final alignment to create perfect harmony from the primal sound field of Source into all 12 Universes who have fallen out of alignment over the past several billion years.

  We will soon experience the Final Attunement into the Music of the Spheres. We will be morphed into a new Harmonic Universe which only contains the harmonies of Source.

  The disharmony will be removed. All will have the sweetness of voice that was taught to me seventeen years ago, during the first stages of the harmonic convergence.

  The last part of the teaching from the Elohim Angels in 2007 was to create the music, listen to the music and to write articles about the music. I have been doing this continuously for five years. The most important thing that I was to learn from this process was the fact that the very first song that my husband and I created together contained the complete story of what happened in December 21, 2012.

It is all about the time signature and the heartbeat. The song on the same album, Heartbeat of Love explains how the frequencies and the rhythms of nature align with the heartbeat or the base pulse rhythm of the natural systems in the perfect kingdom. We were not describing the nature of this world. We were describing the nature of the Normal World - the world that we will finally discover in 2013.

When we hear the streams roar, we will be hearing the crystal liquid light of the Mother Stream of Divine Manifestation pouring through us. And, as the song says, when we hear the dolphin in the new world, we will be hearing the sonar waves of the dolphin's mid brain streaming in the Oraphim Cosmic Dolphin's Frequencies of Cosmic Wisdom streaming in the Symphony of Love.

Next, we will hear our new heart beat of 12/8 time signature, and we will have aligned with our crystal heart, our spiritual self, our harmonic universe two reality into our new morphogenetic field, and we

Chapter Seven — The Promise

will finally be hearing the heartbeat of love, because our heart beat will be the base pulse rhythm of the mind of God streaming through us. When we hear the laughter of the children of the new world who are created from the Divine Template of the children of the Oraphim Dolphin Cosmic Template, the Turaunesiums from Tara, and the children of Gaia, we will truly have brought the kingdom of heaven to our New Earth. Finally, we will know that the new children are the Heartbeat of Love.

The first song, The Promise, says Search for me in your heart, you shall find me with all your heart. I had the hardest time with this one. I could not figure out how I was supposed to find God in my heart. I thought my heart was this organ that I mostly ignored. Over the years, I learned that the heartbeat contains base pulse rhythm of the mind of God. We must tune into that frequency. However, since we have been completely cut off from that frequency by the misalignments put into our grids and lei lines and the seals placed in our bodies, I had to learn how to bring the frequency back into my heart by realigning into the crystal heart of Mother Earth, and back into the primal sound fields through my Cosmic Friends. It was all a process of retuning the body just like an old piano with broken strings. Each strand of my DNA had to be retuned to my Cosmic Families morphogenetic frequency signatures. I did millions of hours of realignment through the original 14th dimensional heliotalic frequency as it arched into the spark of source when realigned into the Sun Ra. I retuned my lotus petals into the parallel petals and the Crystal Body lotus petals of the Spiritual Self to create the 12 petals of harmonic convergence that allow the 8th level monadic consciousness to realign into the new rhythm.

As the higher frequencies were brought into realign and transmute old frequencies, the miasms in the crystalline structure of the body were melted away. Those crystals were embedded in our crystals as a result of us being phase locked into this one density. The crystals must reunite with the first spark of source as it forms into the partiki, and them the parallel self and the harmonic universe two body. The spiritual self must become one with the physical.

We begin as the spark of Source, which is a radiation spark. Radiation is a consciousness field. This reality hasn't been seen on this Earth because our consciousness was phase locked or blocked from the sound and light fields of Source Consciousness through the miasms or errors placed in the energy fields.

All of the anguish that those on Earth blame on God, did not originate from God. IT originates from the blocks or the miasms, or the errors placed in the radiation fields and sound wave inter-dimensional fields that are supposed to connect us into oneness with our parallel self, our spiritual self and our crystal body of Christ consciousness, and our parallel self in harmonic universe two.

We will reconnect to harmonic universe two on December 21, 2012.

The error- the miasm, the phase lock will be removed on that day, and our 12 DNA template of Christ Consciousness will be restored. We will return to the mind of God as we are supposed to do every nano second. Realigning the axiotonal lines and median lines of Earth and the chakras, and merkabas within our bodies. We can bond with our original God Template on a personal level. We came into this planet within that template. The planet also has a template. The planets template cannot reconnect, but our body template can.

We will rise into harmonic universe two- a different time and space, a new universe. WE will help the planet bind its grids into a new space shield so it can reset the natural order of its axiotonal lines. In other words, the Earth will morph into a new Consciousness and the old Earth will pass away.

The world map ley lines and meridian lines are totally out of wack. Those lines were misaligned by the group called Jehovians placing false grids and seals within the Earth's grids and misaligned her to be out of place in the universe. The true Christic grids would hold Earth into alignment and attunement wit the base pulse rhythm of the Christ Consciousness. The Christ grid is the original template with the radiation field of the spark of Source creating the idea, the sound of the music of the spheres. The grids had seals placed in them and created disastrous alignment resulting in the same in our consciousness and our relationship to others.

In order to realign these grids correctly, we are being pulled into the harmonic alignment of a system that has kept its perfect harmony aligned into the divine template of God. What is most ironic about the entire New Age teachings, and more recent Music

Frequency Teachings is the fact that they are all based on METATRONIC FREQUENCIES which are the exact REVERSE SPIN frequencies used block our Attunement into the Music of the Spheres. It's a little late for all those who have been tuning in to the Black Hole Machine for all of these years. Don't worry, we will save you anyway.

We will be pulled into that template on December 21st. Our DNA will align into that template and restore the base pulse of 12 DNA. However, we are actually being returned into 36 and 48 DNA because we are being realigned into our parallel, our crystal

Chapter Seven   The Promise

body, our spiritual, our spiritual of our parallel in order to create a three fold template of 36 and then a four fold template of 48.

All of these base pulse rhythm templates are based on the 8 monadic clusters of our galactic consciousness being transformed into the 12 level template of the universal or Christic Consciousness. The lower sphere always requires the higher sphere in the music of the spheres to activate its tones. So, in order to create a new galaxy created within and through Universal, Christic Consciousness, the time signature must be 8/12.

The total alignment is 144 fold because there are 12 universal systems that must fold into the new Cosmos. The problem began within the original cosmic structure of the 12 universes that were created by our Cosmos. And that is where the problem had to be fixed. The last war in heaven was the war in the Sun Ra. There were entities in the Sun Ra who became fallen angelics or fallen Rays. That was the beginning of all of the other problems in the universes. Those problems were reflected in the countless fallen angelics that were victims of that problem. Since the problem is being fixed at such a high level, we are also being fixed at such a high level. We are being given a brand new start at a very high Christ level. We are being moved into the 12 base pulse rhythm. This rhythm relates to our heartbeat. Our heartbeat will be restored to the eternal life rhythm of the base 12.

Our first Album, The Promise was created to fully demonstrate the understanding that was to come to us over 17 years after its creation. That understanding was the complete science of how our divine creation is restored through the Music of the Spheres, which is the Process created by Source himself, to eternally remake everything brand new.

Our understanding began with the correct words and the correct rhythms. It grew through continuous experimentation with frequencies and aligning consciousness through breaths and then exhaling the breaths to hear higher and higher frequencies, and then learning that angels were communicating through these frequencies.

We later found help in understanding this process when we listened to the Legacy DVD's and studied the complete Keylontic Science which explains how these frequencies are retuning our universe. However, since that teaching utilized songs that were given to those mediators, I am not in complete agreement with those teachings. I was given my own songs, and that is the way it is supposed to be. That is the way it was always done in the perfect kingdoms. The music of the spheres was the process of frequency alignment of the physical and spiritual into attunement and then through that attunement songs came through consciousness that explained the consciousness to which one had attuned. That is what all of my recordings are of. They are my direct experience of at one ment with the frequency signatures, who are actual entities.

WHY? Why are we being given this great gift? The new reality is the reality that Source wants us to live in. Our Angelic Founders Races and Guardian Families from our Soul Families, Reishi Families and Avatar Families want this reality.

It is the normal, natural reality that those in normal galaxies - those that are not under the control of Fallen Angelic Races - would be ready to ascend into. Source only knows and only desires us to know the same infinite realities that the Source knows. Those who live through Angelic Consciousness, which is Cosmic Consciousness in alignment with Source can create any idea that they wish to experience. That is what an Angelic Human was created to do. We have not been living in a Society of Angelic Consciousness. We have been living on a Planet of FALLEN Angelic Consciousness.

This is why the change will be Cosmic. The problems inherent in our matrix dates back 250 billion years to the Cosmic point of creation. There must be a brand new idea ignited from Source Consciousness into the entire Cosmic Matrix of reality system in order to begin an ascension process.

First, we need to go back about 550 million years to learn where the Human Race came from, how they got here, what races they are related to, how the Earth will transform into the Higher Realities of the Inner Earth immediately in December, and how each and every individual will be transformed into light and transported to Tara within the next several years. It needs to be known that the rumor of the HARVEST is true. There will be individuals who have five or six DNA strands so perfectly in tune, that they will immediately walk into the new reality of TARA. There will be a few that will even be able to step directly into Gaia.

The present background knowledge of those on this planet has been created by 3D perceptions. This means they haven't seen the ante-matter reality, which is presently the invisible realm of reality. That fifth dimensional reality of the invisible and the visible will become the new reality on this Earth by the end of 2012. The Earth will reunite with the higher dimensional selves of Tara and Gaia. This is the true complete Self of Mother Earth. We will reunite with our complete selves in the same manner when our Blue Sphere of Amenti is returned into the Core of Earth and our Souls, Over Souls, Avatar Selves and Rishi Selves all merge into Oneness.

Chapter Seven The Promise

On December 21, 2012 Earth's angular rotation of particle spin shifts and Earth's fastest particles begin to transfer to hyperspace and the halls of records begin transmitting data through the Earth's grids. Universal memory will begin transmission through planetary grids. The shift will then balance out to about 23 degrees, which will align Earth into At One Ment with Inner Earth, and then we will begin balancing into the new reality of a new time of about 2,218 years forward from this time. The new alignment from the Inner Earth into Tara will allow those on Earth to be moved into the consciousness of Tara in what ever way is appropriate for them.

This will be our first pull into the future as our particles spin faster and faster through the angular rotation of particle spin that rearranges our biology, chemistry and scenery. Those who have not prepared for this shift will be seeing ante-matter that will appear as darkness to the 3D perception. That darkness is equivalent to the darkness that appears as ante-matter or spiritual substance that we may create our new reality upon. We see ourselves in our blue body at this time created as an immortal being in a more etheric form included within a Divine Template of Immortality.

This is the beginning of the opening of our 7th seal, our pituitary gland, our third eye, our Mind of God. When the pituitary blossoms, the Mind of God begins its continuous dream stream between what

we desire to create in our dreams to blossom into
full manifestation in any of the multidimensional
reality fields. The seventh level man can co-create
through the mind of God instantly. The more we
gain our frequency specific mid brain connecting
into the mind of God through our Soul, we connect
to the Source field when anything we desire already
exists. We inhale that reality into our mid brain and
project into our holographic realm.

We make God's movie on Earth. We create heaven
on Earth. The Soul forever holds the memory of
all that ever was. We have had a veil blocking
us from the memories of all of past lives, which
created over ten million re-incarnations that were
not remembered. Now, all of those memories
will return. We have two choices at this time. We
can transmute all of those old memories into and
through Source Consciousness to create a brand
new glorious new reality that will contain the
wisdom of all of the over souls, avatar selves and
rishi selves; or, we can become miserable and
frightened from all of the old fears and tribulations
that might return. That is only an individual choice
of how one decides to live through it.

While we wait in this darkness of ante-matter,
we could be using this as the prime time to make
dreams come true. The darkness of ante-matter is
the substance that has been invisible to the third
dimensional consciousness. It is the spiritual

substance of a dream that is about to manifest. It is like the negative in a camera that has a picture on it that can't be seen until it is developed. We can start developing the dreams or the pictures in our camera, which is our mind. We create through the mid brain frequency specific attunement with Source Consciousness. We create by knowing that we are now and always have been this perfect self who can manifest anything the heart desires. We can know at that point in time that we have always been wealthy. We have always been healthy. We have always been the Christ Consciousness of the All Knowing Mind of God. The more we practice creating our new realities and our manifestations, the more prepared we will be for manifesting the reality of TARA to appear in December.

The Inner will become the Outer. The Inner Earth that some know as Agartha or Hollow Earth is at an angle or particle spin that is so close to the Outer Earth that it is only one density level higher. From the eyes of angels, that is really, really close. In reality, when we grow into fifth dimensional perception, we will realize that the angle of the within can be the same in the outside at just a slight angle. We will also learn that all of the space we see around us isn't space in other reality fields. It only looks like space to us because we have three Merkabas of energy spinning through our energy fields that are creating the idea of space between objects. As the Merkabas shift into a different spin rate and angle, the perceptions of reality around us also change.

Everything that has been proven to be a reality through Scientific Data is very incorrect. The truths taught in schools are only truths for this Earth because there has been a large group of entities keeping us trapped in an ocean of stupidity. And it isn't as if there aren't plenty of scientists in the higher echelons that know the truths that I'm describing.

They've always known it, they've just made it illegal for us to know the truth. Because the truth will set us free.

This change will happen instantly - not gradually. The biological transformation of the body, that has been going on within our carbon based structure, will be changed into the crystal based eternal life chemical and biological forms. Our Consciousness will be transformed into a higher frequency that merges into the all knowing Source, who creates a brand new idea with each breath.

Earth and Tara will begin to merge. Blue Flame keepers will become 9th level avatars, as the blue flame spirals down from Sun Alcyone. Flame Holders who carry a rare recessive gene will have this gene activated. These holders contain a specific magnetic base tone in their DNA that allows them to become very magnetic and are able to hold this activation on Earth.

Once the D 5 flame holder holds the frequencies of Sun Alcyone and pulls the frequencies into her Flame Keepers fourth heart chakra an intense infusion of harmonic universe two frequencies spread through the Amenti morphogenetic field and through the Earth's Grid. This will allow rapid acceleration of fifth and sixth DNA strand assembly to occur throughout the populations. The seventh strand will begin assembly in those who already hold fifth and sixth. This activation will create a huge multidimensional awareness to occur on Earth.

When the blue sphere holding our divine blue prints merge Tara and Earth together, those who have assembled the fifth strand and are eligible for ascension to Tara will be guided to inter-dimensional transportation locations to Tara.

Those who have sixth and seventh strands may be transported to Gaia. First, we will shift into a different chemical make up. We will leave behind our carbon based bodies. We will become less dense. Our bodies and our environment will change. Those who move on to Tara will have an entirely different type of body than those who stay in Inner Earth. Those who move on to Gaia are almost invisible. Those who are of higher densities can see the lower densities; but, those who remain in 3D will not be able to see any of the new realities. It might seem like things are disappearing because the higher particle shifts will pull some in one direction and the lower will pull those in another direction. There are infinite density levels. There will be a mass landing of our original creation races including the Maharaji, the Sirius B Eieyani and the Azurites. We will meet the ZionA's who are the mermaids and fairies who become elemental liquid light in order to transform our bodies.

We will meet the Wizards who planned this entire Crystal River Plan to remove us from this matrix of illusions. We will meet our Cosmic Dolphin Families from the seventh sun, and thousands of other families.

This Mass Landing will be obvious to everyone on Earth by 2025, and to most by 2022. There will be more and more individual meetings between 2015 -2022. We will move into a new reality in 2022. It will seem like a Bardoah or Ascension, which simply means shifting to a new reality. Those who are not ready to make the shift will lifted into the Adashi Temples of Sirius B and have their bodies healed and prepared for the transition. This healing in the Crystal Temples is already taking place.

Chapter Eight

Creating the Stream of Manifestation

See yourself sitting in a cloud on top of the 15th sphere of the Cosmos. This is the place where Source (the infinite unknown of all that is and all that ever will be) connects into the Cosmic Consciousness where the idea begins to form.

In the Source Consciousness Frequency field, we pull the Source frequencies into the outer band of the Cosmic Frequency Field. Each band of consciousness has base tones, overtones and resonant tones. When the base tones or overtones are removed from a frequency band, the frequency band becomes disconnected from Source Consciousness. This is what happened to us. We became disconnected from Source Consciousness when certain base tones and overtones were taken out of our frequency bands. These frequency bands are the harp strings within the double helix of our DNA.

If any of the twelve etheric harp strings have any of the tones removed, they cannot blend together into one harmonic sound. When the highest frequency of Source Consciousness is breathed into those harp strings, the overtones and base tones all realign into the frequency bands or harp strings harmonically and harmoniously.

This is how a harmoniously balanced rebirth is performed. This mental, breathing consciousness exercise brings the Source Frequencies of the highest frequency - the frequency that includes all frequencies to re-activate the base tones and over tones in all bands of light.

This will heal and connect all 12 DNA strands harmonically. Our guardian and founder starry families have given us several formulas for connecting the problem of the base tones and over tones creating seals that blocked us from that potential of Oneness. When we connect the light from our third eye (where the mind of God - our higher self creates all ideas from) to the light band where Source floats outside of the Cosmic Matrix, we create a dream stream of consciousness. All manifestations are created in this dream stream. We go into the higher self sitting in the blue sphere outside of the Cosmos to collect the frequencies of Source. We sit in the cloud and absorb all of the frequencies of Source.

WE INHALE.

Next, we create the idea that we wish to MANIFEST and see it being created in that cloud that the higher self is in. We see the idea weaving itself into the sphere of light around the higher self.

Next, we inhale that idea into our higher self. See that idea as a permanent reality that has always belonged to our higher self. We realize that all that is created in the frequency of Source has always existed and will always exist in eternal time matrix. The new idea transforms and transmutes all former ideas or beliefs about the manifest reality.

For example, if we thought we were a miserable, poor person, we can change that reality into being a magnificent wealthy person. Once the idea is placed within the light field of Source of the magnificent wealthy person into the field of light energy of the higher self that is sitting in the cloud in the Source Field, that makes the new idea the only idea that ever existed because the Mind of Source is Eternal. The idea has always existed and will always exist in this highest frequency field and it will transmute and transform any other idea that ever existed.

A stream of energy flows through all of the past selves, present selves and future selves to transform the eternal self that exists in the dream stream between the mind of God in the higher self and the Source field. The new idea in the dream stream will now manifest in all multidimensional fields as the reality attached to this person's reality field. That reality now exists in us because it exists in Source and we are made of Source Consciousness, Source Frequency and Source Light and Energy.

This causes the Music of the Spheres to sing a new song as the base tones and over tones of the frequency bands of the crystal spheres realign and weave a new melodic version of the reality template.

Another way of looking at this manifestation principle is this:

The three spheres of the Cosmic Matrix are crystal light, crystal dust and crystal gel. The crystal light is the outer band that allows the spark of Source to enter in and create a new idea. The Crystal Dust is the middle band that contains the crystal dust particles of golden silver heliotalic shimmering, sparkling dusty crystals of the 14th dimension.

That crystal dust is the healing prana that brings the neutron energy created by igniting the plasma of gamma waves of Sun Alcyone to bring our Blue Flame of our Divine Blue Print of Divine Consciousness into our frequency bands of our electron magnetic light field.

So, now we have the sphere of crystal light and the sphere of crystal dust Cosmic Consciousness Energy fields. The third Cosmic band is the 13th dimension and the crystal gel Cosmic Consciousness energy sphere. This band carries the frequency of transformation. The gelaisic particle energy melts, transmutes and transforms the particle structure of the body by bringing the Divine Blue Print of the original divine Self that was stored in the etheric core of Earth hundreds of thousands of years ago. This 13th dimensional energy is needed to activate the 12th dimensional frequency of the Khristiac (Christic) band that carries our Divine Blue Print. (Just an aside - Sorry to change the subject, but this is very important).

The entity named Thoth only had 11.5 dimensional frequencies.

Thoth was actually the highest potential of a human life form that existed on the Earth at the time when he was given the opportunity to arrange for our Ascension. He made the choice to only allow the Annunaki to ascend. As a result of being tricked by the Annunaki, the entire human race was placed in a Quarantine. The Annunaki created a race called the Levithians who completed their Fifth DNA Consummation. They turned this race into their puppets. They took the blue stardust essence from their bodies and made themselves angelic. The traces of this incident became the Illuminati puppets on Earth.

The teachings from Thoth came to Earth as the Channeled books in the Flower of Life teachings. These teachings included the same trap that was used by the Annunaki to enslave the Angelic Racelines. These teachings assure the human race will never achieve Christ Consciousness.

This would include the use of the golden mean that locks us within 8 dimensions, which is a trick, because we must go to the thirteenth dimension to activate the 12th, and we must go all the way to Source for our Eternal Divine Blue Print.

Metatronic teachings cause the merkaba to wobble out of alignment. Astrology locks us into this fallen matrix. The readings come from a matrix of misaligned planets and stars. We must go into the Spiritual Matrix of the Andromeda Galaxy for correct alignment. We are now having the Photon Belt from Sun Alcyone, which contains our original consciousness, returned to Earth.

Chapter Eight   Creating the Stream of Manifestation

We each have coding inside of our genes that guide us to what we need to achieve. If some were misguided, it might be for the very reason of actually helping the fallen angelics. Many of the Indigo Threes actually incarnated at this time to help raise the Wesadrak Matrix of the Dark Fallen Angelics into 12th level Fallen Angelics. This doesn't mean they will have Christ Consciousness, but it creates a nicer path out of the fallen matrix. There are many very loving entities who sacrifice their own well being to be a part of saving other matrixes, galaxies and planets. There is the goodness of Source in All.

The crystal gel consciousness energy creates the re-birth of the new form - the new idea to manifest in all forms of multidimensional consciousness. We can now take these three crystal spheres an hold them in the palms of our hands.

We inhale the spheres into our crystal heart. We see our higher self holding these three spheres in our heart. We pull the image of the higher self holding the spheres into our third eye. We hold the same idea up into the self sitting in the cloud in Source. The idea to be manifest from the highest frequency of Source is first seen clearly already in manifest form in the Source Cloud and then held in the mind.

Next, EXHALE that idea into the three spheres. That exhale is the breath of manifestation called the mana. First we had the Breath of Creation when we formed the idea within our higher self in our crystal heart. Next, we had the breath of Gestation as we allowed the idea to be created in the Mind of God and the Frequency of Source and allowed to form through the Dream Stream where the unconsciousness and the Consciousness unite as one.

Finally the breath of manifestation is breathed out into the spheres of crystal light, crystal dust and crystal gel. It is always these three spheres together that create the complete music of the spheres light and sound energy of creation. That reality first takes the form of the ultra violet blue flame in the crystal light sphere and then the golden dust particle form of the neutron energy that shifts the electron proton relationship into a new neutron form. That energy shifts the particles into a Multidimensional manifest form that can be seen as invisible light.

Next, the crystal gel transfers the idea into a tangible manifest form that can be seen. We hold the three spheres in our hands and then exhale the idea through the spheres into the microphone and we get the music of the spheres. This form of reality is now in the form of the frequency within the breath. That frequency held within the breath is the most powerful energetic form in the universe.

That breath of creation and manifestation can and will manifest into multidimensional reality. Our consciousness is not allowing us to see that reality yet because we are a part of a larger reality field that is under construction at this moment. That sphere of energetic reality holds our divine blue print that contains the individual reality that we once were in Tara.

LOVE FREQUENCY

The true meaning and power of Love is Love is the energy that spins beyond the speed of light bringing Source into At One Ment with all dimensions of Reality. There is nothing greater than this Love that is transforming our Universe. There is nothing more loving than the activity of our Starry Cosmic Families transmuting the Darkness of the Fallen Angelics into vapor that can return to Source. That love is the Third World War that was fought in the Heavens for us last year. That was the war of love, and there was nothing sweet and kind about it. The Law of One means that we know and love everyone, everything, every nano particle of everything, every particle, every plant, tree, flower, every breath, every whisper, every, everything as the same Oneness and Allness of the Infinite Unknown Source Consciousness. In that Law of One we can create our realities through the

Chapter Eight   Creating the Stream of Manifestation

co-creation with that same spark of Source that creates everything.

There is also a very STRICTNESS about this loving transformation. The Ra Confederation will not allow any individual to ascend until they are perfectly transformed. Many think of Ra as the God of the Sun. The Ra Confederation is actually the Soul Matrix of Creation governing the light of our creation. They are the group of Consciousness Entities governing all of the activity of the Guardian Races. They will make sure there is enough light energy from the Cosmic Matrix creating the Blue Flame that will blend our consciousness back into the energetic fields of consciousness of our Divine Template.

When there is enough light to transform our consciousness back into the Law of One, the Ra Confederation will allow us to pass into Tara. When we speak of RA or the Central Sun, we are actually speaking of a Light Council that governs all of the activity of light through the Suns. The Suns activity of creating is actually at the Galactic Level or the 8th dimension. The Ra Confederation is a Spiritual Parallel Matrix from the Divine Matrix of Reality.

The term HARVEST means the actual graduation of those Souls who have aligned into the light to transmute all past miasms. Those individuals will disappear from the third dimension and will reappear on TARA. It will not be possible to comprehend what is about to happen if any old background knowledge is used to process the understanding. Everything that is now understood in this world comes from a three dimensional understanding. That means we only believe what we can see, touch and feel. We have been trained to believe through the scientific world management team, that if it can't be seen it isn't real.

That old science, that old background knowledge must be removed before we can even begin to comprehend what is about to happen to this Earth. We are moving completely out of third dimensional perception, and into a fifth dimensional perception of a fabulous new reality.

Where do we go to get the understanding of what is really happening? We go to our higher selves and our guides from the Emerald Covenant Guardian Races to take us into Inner Earth and guide us into the new reality that is already here. How do we get there? We make a blue flame in our mid brain and connect it to the blue flame in our tail bone, we stream the energy of those two flames back into one flame in the mid brain.

Feel that blue flame as your Soul, your higher Self, your Mind of God, your Guide.

Next, raise that blue flame to the top of your head. See the flame turn into a disk shape, and see your Guide sitting on the blue disk. Now, we begin communication with our Guide. We say, we are ready to be guided by our Emerald Covenant Guardian Family to see our New World, which is the Inner Earth. Make this reality happen every night before you go to sleep. Your guides will meet you in your dreams, they will take you to Inner Earth. They will show you where you will be living next year.

This is how we get the FIFTH DIMENSIONAL answer to our question. FIFTH DIMENSIONAL means MULTIDIMENSIONAL - it does not mean we are only at five and must go to ten or twelve. The Fifth includes the 12th and the 15th. The Fifth is the place where the invisible light and the visible light spectrums become manifest equally. The present reality only consists of things that are seen- that is the third dimension. The fifth dimension consists of things we can't see in the third dimension. It consists of all reality fields.

Presently, we think the only things important are the things we seen in this hertzian frequency of visible tangible THINGS. When we rise into the infra red frequency, we can see what our digital cameras can see. When we rise beyond visible light into the invisible light spectrum, we begin to see the quantum realities that have been created by the rotation of particle spin that our merkaba fields are presently in.

When the merkaba spin rate goes back to its normal rate, and the seals are removed from the base tones and overtones of our DNA strands, we will see that there is as much reality in the invisible as there is in the visible. That invisible white light becomes blue light as we connect our consciousness into the light bands that connect to Source Light.

When our higher self travels through the invisible light spectrum into the x-ray, gamma ray and pink white light, it returns transformed into a self that can see the entire spectrum of reality. We can practice this experiment by simply focusing on a candle light.

Think of the base of the candle as the place where your three dimensional self is standing in the hertzian light field. Right above you is the infra red- you can see the red flame in the candle light. Just a spark above the infra red is a little bit of visible yellow light, and then an area of white light, and then a pinkish, golden area, and right under and below that golden area is a pale grey stream that seems like it is taking an x ray of an invisible form. When you focus on the hertzian light long enough, you will experience the white light turn blue.

This means your higher self has connected into Source Consciousness light field. This also means that the visible spectrum of reality in the room you are in will become black in invisibility. That is the ante-matter of Source Consciousness that allows you to create an entire new reality in that spiritual essence of light reality. That energetic light field is where our NEW reality of TARA will appear once we completely enter that state of FOCUS continuously through the three day particle transmutation that will take place December 21-24. Those who do this will see TARA replace the darkness of the anti-matter particles, because the shift in particle rotation will allow that frequency field to appear.

If we want a Third Dimensional answer to our question we can turn on the News Channel and they will tell us that there will be Earthquakes, disasters, world wars, terrorism. It will be very difficult to take this back ground knowledge and then calculate a new world made of 12D Khristiac Frequencies.

These Frequencies will become available because the Blue Sphere of Consciousness from TARA will completely transmute the angular rotation of particle spin of the Earth to return into Oneness with TARA. We also realign into Gaia and Andromeda and Aquafaria through Oneness of a higher frequency.

There will be a type of pole shift. But it will be of no danger because it will be performed by our Emerald Covenant Guardian Races. Why are they called the Emerald Covenant Guardians? Because Earth is the Emerald of the Universe. She is the Entity that is going to unlock the doors of this Fallen Milky Way Galaxy to return home to M31-Andromeda.

Many of us who are here now work with the Emerald Covenant Guardians to guard the Star Gates of this Planet. This is our mission now and always has been our mission. We must run our Frequencies- our Codes in our DNA through the 12 Star Gates of Earth in order to set her free. She has had her star gates captured by the fallen angelics. The only way the fallen races can invade Earth and take control of her star gates is through the Guardians who are supposed to continuously guard these Star Gates.

The Blue Flame of our Divine Blue Print could not return to Earth through Sun Alcyone until there were six star gates completely opened and the other six activated and ready to open on December 21. When the sixth avatar is born, who is a 12th Level Avatar, our star gates will be secured and ready to open once again. This couldn't happen until there was a 12th Level Avatar who came through the Amenti Fields (the Divine Blue Prints of all of our Souls) in order to reactivate us into our Divine Consciousness.

This will open our Consciousness into Oneness with all of our Soul Families on all 12 Stars that are a part of Earth's body of Consciousness. This 12th Level Divinity comes from the place where the Fourth Sphere and the Fifth Sphere meet. The place where Cosmic Consciousness flows into Khristiac Consciousness. The Crystal Dust energy of the Aurora Fields, the Crystal Light from the Spark of Source and the Crystal Gel of Transformation connect and form into a Ultra Violet Blue Frequency that allows a brand new IDEA to be born. When the Khristiac, Cosmic and Source Frequencies merge, a new Creation is Born.

The reason our Earth is being transformed into a new higher reality is because Source wants to. We don't really need to know more than that. It can be done because Source wants to. Source wants to continuously create all wonderful new ideas through our Mind of God in our Mid Brain. Source wants to watch over us continuously and give us the most glorious realities.

Our Founders Races and Guardian Families have been working on making this reality come true for 840,000 years. They have worked continuously to remove obstacles, transmute, transform, realign and make whole the original design of the perfect angelic human that they had originally designed through the template of Source Consciousness. We have been cut off from this divine reality of Source Consciousness flowing through our Mid Brain.

There were crystal seals placed in Earth's grids that blocked the Christic Grids from the Source Flow. We have been blocked from the Source Reality Fields from every angle. Those seals are being removed now. You can go see this new reality now, with your Guides from the Emerald Cities in Inner Earth. They will take you there at night if you ask them through your blue flame.

Chapter Nine

Mathematical Formula of Christ Consciousness

(Teachings of the
Cosmic Mystery School of the Omniverse)

Christ Consciousness is the Mind of God that sees everything before it is breathed into existence at this level. Christ Consciousness is the mathematical code which is continuously creating the Divine Blue Print of the perfect image and likeness or mirror image of the entire Mind of God or Omnipotent Divine Consciousness.

That divine blue print is a 12 dimensional code containing within it the Divine Manifestations of the Eternal Life, Continuous Omnipresent Love that continuously spins the electromagnetic frequencies of 33 1/3 electro clockwise and 11 2/3 magnetic counter clockwise within the sphere of clockwise rotation.

That frequency radiates into the at oneness with a parallel field of electromagnetic frequencies spinning the same way, but in a parallel anti particle reality field. Each of the particle and anti particle reality fields spin 45 degrees to equal 90 degrees in a vertical reality field.

Another set of mathematical radiation particles spin together to create the horizontal reality field. Together they create 180 degree field of reality. That field of reality is then broken down into faster moving fields of diagonal spinning fields of electromagnetic particles creating radiation fields of plasma, gamma, x ray, invisible light, visible light, infra red and hertzian light energy into a sphere of light 360 degrees.

Everything in Divine Consciousness Creativity is made of spheres of light that spin at this perfect ratio to create layers of 45 degree angles of rotation. The creation energy is always radiation energy. We must be radiating this high frequency energy at the fastest rate of spin in the 12 dimensional radiation level to maintain our complete reality in the Christ Coded blue print.

Simultaneously that 12 dimensional divine blue print can express itself in parallel reality fields

Chapter Nine   Mathematical Formula of Christ Consciousness

that manifest as 5 dimensional and 6 dimensional realities. These would contain the 12 sub harmonics of the Christ Consciousness mathematical formula in each of the 5 DNA strands or 6 DNA strands.

The reality would appear different because it would be less dense or more dense. There is no density in the 12 DNA reality field. It is completely etheric in nature. However, that etheric reality is always a part of everything even if it only has 3DNA or 4 DNA. The perfect mathematical principle of all creation is always the 12 DNA coded divine blue print. IN reality that Divine Blue Print of Christ Consciousness has Always Existed, Does Exist and Always will Exist in every human angelic being and every star seed on Earth.

The reason that this reality doesn't seem to appear to us when we look at people and situations is because there was a Miasm placed between the vortexes where the light energy and frequencies created by the spin ratio of the 33 1/3 and 11 2/3 merkaba spin rate within the particle and anti particle universe.

The problem was actually placed in the anti particle universe that was parallel to ours so that we could never align correctly into the harmony of that blended rate of spin that would create the 90 degree and 180 degree and perfect 360 degree spheres of

Chapter Nine   Mathematical Formula of Christ Consciousness

light and sound that are NORMAL to any God Made reality field.

Those Miasms are frozen Light Energy that is unable to spin and move and freely manifest. Those miasms can be melted out of the old frozen DNA that is creating the illusion of this Frozen Density of Consciousness. Our Guardian Races have placed our original Divine Blue Print into our 12 DNA strands already. That gift has already been established on Earth.

STARSEEDS RETURNING OUR 5 DNA - 12 DNA

The Star Seeds that were born on Earth over the past 12 years all had much to do with this realignment. The children born during the past five years brought the completed 5 DNA -12 DNA back to Earth. That reality was presented to the Earth once before about 2000 years ago when the 12th Level Avatar and the 9th Level Avatar, that our Bible Stories call Jesus Christ was brought to Earth by Guardian Groups.

This time the Guardians brought in 144,000 times more Christ Consciousness to Earth through the frequencies of the Star seeds. The Earth required a certain level of Frequencies in order to make its shift into the new Metagalactic 8 alignment with the past present and future 12 DNA coded reality system.

These 12 coded frequencies contain the divine blue print of the Eternal Life, Love, Mind, Principle, Substance, Intelligence, Supply, Truth, Soul, Spirit, Man, Manifestation Template, Design that is contained within the Music of the Spheres Light and Sound Technology.

Mary Baker Eddy (1971) explained this same Divine Formula of Creation of Man made in the Image and Likeness of God, and clearly stated that the only thing that is separating man from that likeness is Error. She said when error is removed the Christ Consciousness will appear. Eddy also spoke of the synonyms of God being Life, Truth, Love, etc.

Eddy (1971) always painted the picture of the mortal and immortal man and how there really couldn't be a mortal man, because that man wasn't made by God. She always said the real man is immortal and that seeming mortal man was only created by error.

When I read THE VOYAGERS 2 (Deane, 2002) in which our Guardian Races - the same ones who designed the Law of One, were members of the Essenes and creators of the Silicate Matrix and 12 DNA template of the human angelic, I knew that I

Chapter Nine Mathematical Formula of Christ Consciousness

had found the rest of the story that Eddy had begun to tell.

The new reality that can be visualized from the following quote, explains the same reality that is explained in great detail in Deane, 2002. This event was given the time line of 2017-2046 by Deane and other channelers. Deane also describes this event as the return of the Seventh Level Man, who was the original human race line of this planet. This Seventh Level Man began to return to Earth when the Six Avatar Children were born between 1992-2010.

This was always my favorite passage in my Sunday School teachings since I was ten years old. I always felt and knew within myself that this reality would happen in my lifetime. Now I know it will happen within the next ten years. This is the time when the Seventh Level Man will reappear as we rise into harmonic universe 2- dimensions 4,5,6. We are already in harmonic universe 2.

We must now raise our frequencies in consciousness and attune into the reality that already exists within the heart of Earth and the reality of the past, present and future 12 DNA divine blue print which has not been damaged by frozen light.

The Guardians have explained the Seventh Level Man who used to live in Tara (Harmonic Universe

Chapter Nine Mathematical Formula of Christ Consciousness

2) to be this man who Eddy spoke of. We are going through the resurrection when we will be robed in the white light purity of the pure attunement as we rebirth into the 5th dimension through the 12th dimensional consciousness.

This will begin to happen in 2017, and the reality will appear to the Masses between 2022 and 2043. We have entered the resurrection leading to that reality.

Eddy(1971) spoke of how important it was to Understand this Divine Science, which I believe is the precursor to the Keylontic Science that was brought to Earth early in the twenty first century. That truth that Eddy tuned into after her Near Death Experience is the same truth that many are tuning into at this present time in history through the Maharaja Consciousness Templates that come to us through our Frequency Specific Mid Brain when we tune into the Future Self, as is done in a Near Death Experience.

That reality of the Seventh Level Man has always existed. We were just taken off line from that reality when our light was frozen in Miasms or Error, blocking our true reality. We are now entering the Mass Ascension of Man, which Jesus called the resurrection, in which "there should be no more marrying nor giving in marriage, but man would be as the angels. Then white robed purity will unite in

Chapter Nine Mathematical Formula of Christ Consciousness

one person masculine wisdom and feminine love, spiritual understanding and perpetual peace"(Eddy, 1971, 64).

We now know through Keylontic Science (the Language of the Stars) that error is Frozen Light. We now know what the mathematical formula of Christ Consciousness is. We now know how we were blocked from our Divine Blue Print through reverse spin technologies. We now know that we are made from the radiation technologies of light and sound that can project us in millions of different density levels. Eddy also spoke of a time when man would no longer be given in marriage and child birth would no longer exist.

Eddy was speaking of the reality we used to live in when Seventh Level man lived on Tara and Gaia. This was the time when a child could be manifested from the light of the Consciousness or the manifestation template that each immortal man actually has in reality.

The true immortal man has always been able to instantly manifest anything, including children. That act can be performed by an individual, a couple or a group consciousness to create an entity who carries many unique traits in the reality of the NORMAL kingdom that we will soon return to.

Chapter Nine Mathematical Formula of Christ Consciousness

The act of creation is always performed instantly in Divine Mind through the perfect 12 DNA template of the immortal man who has eternal life, never dies, never gets sick, has infinite intelligence, etc. Many of the things Eddy talked about in her Science and Health with Keys to the Scriptures (Eddy, 1971) are also mentioned by the Guardians in the new Keylontic Science and Kathara Healing Technologies. (Deane, 2002)

The difference between these two speakers was that the teachings came in the frequencies that man was able to understand at the time. These two sets of teachings have something in common with the teachings of the original 12th Level Avatar Jesus. They contain many of the original teachings, and the audience and students of the teachings are very small, because only those with the genetic coding of the star seeds and some human angelics are able to comprehend these teachings.

ETERNAL LIFE

We always have been and always will be made of this divine technology of Eternal Life. When we were created by the Christ Code Pre Sound and Light Technology, we contained the ability to Live Forever, to Create our own Galaxies, to Manifest

Chapter Nine Mathematical Formula of Christ Consciousness

Instantly our Hearts desires. That is reality. That is the reality we must tune into as the only reality that exists in the past, present and future.

If we continue to tune in to the lower frequencies that were distorted realities caused by the frozen light (miasm or error), we will continue to manifest that reality that locked us into the continuous 3D illusion of reality where we could only see, feel, touch, hear, taste a series of events that were planted into our DNA by Entities who only wanted to freeze us out of our Reality.

That (frozen light Error or Miasm) was how they created the Phantom Matrix and how they planned to lock us into it. That probability no longer exists. We must align our consciousness to the new reality which is the old reality of the ETERNAL LIFE Blue Print.

That 12 DNA divine blue print is the only creation that God knows how to make. That reality is made through the pre light and sound fields of Khristiac Technology containing the 12 coded divine blue print. We always were made, always are made and always will be made by that divine blue print which is perfect and eternal. We must realign our DNA templates to the sub harmonics of the 12 DNA template and begin to know that is the only reality that we have ever been and ever will be made a part of.

Chapter Nine Mathematical Formula of Christ Consciousness

It is the knowing and the feeling of the frequencies of the 12 sub harmonics that has been blocked from our world view. We were made to believe that only 5 senses contain reality. When actually those 5 senses were only for us to enjoy the reality that we create through our Higher Sensory Perception of our 12 dimensional self who knows and feels and creates through the imagination.

That is the reality that we have been forced out of by world propaganda beginning with parents telling their children that their imagination isn't real. That propaganda is a part of the Frozen Light imprinted into our DNA. We have been set free from this prison. We were given the reality of our 12 DNA and its codes. That reality was planted in the Heart of the Earth and it will flow through the grids of the Earth. It is still up to us to Tune into the Frequencies and spin rate of that reality, especially by creating in Consciousness everyday the reality that we have always been, always are.

Chapter Ten

Shifting into a New Time

As we rise up into our Multi Dimensional Consciousness, what has seemed to be the only reality in this third dimensional dream will become only a speck of the possible realities that will become realized. Most of what has seemed to be the only reality on Earth was created by metatronic frequencies performed through reverse spin technology of fallen angelics. The perception of those on Earth has been blocked from the creations of higher frequency manifestations through veils, seals, misalignments, Metatronics and a long list of demonic technology.

The realities that have been placed in the upper cerebellum of the brain must become dissolved and replaced through the frequency specific mid brain technology that allows direct and continuous communication and manifestation through the Mind of God. The present reality fields that are being recycled as one looks around himself and keeps creating the same old reality over and over again will become dissolved into higher and higher realities.

These new realities that will become manifest by those who learn to use the Divine Technology in their brain will come from other dimensions. We can manifest any part of any other reality that has ever existed. We can manifest the most wonderful culture based on the Lyran-Sirian perfect model.

We can manifest becoming the original Oraphim Race who spent their time dreaming new realities. We can collect all of our favorite realities from each and every Universal System in our Race Lines. We can combine creations of advanced technology of the most advanced systems and the sweetness of the Aquafarians and Oraphim Dolphins. We get to make individual and collective utopias. We can create the most magical, fabulous reality systems that we can dream up.

First, we must learn how to create the dream stream through this alignment into the highest frequency of Source Consciousness. There will be no creations manifesting that are not created through the Mind of God. Only Fallen Angelics create through methods that require the use of energy from other entities. For the past ten million years, the human race has been used as a source of energy for Fallen Angelic groups.

We have not even experienced a normal reality system. The present consciousness of this world has been locked inside a narrow little spectrum of reality. We see this man made world and we think that we can only re-create things that look like what they looked like in the day before.

We think that making an improvement within the present reality is some type of achievement. In the normal kingdoms, an entity can create any new reality that has never been seen the day before. In multi dimensional consciousness we can form our days on what we saw on another star in another advanced civilization. We can combine all ideas from all other reality systems into new ideas that have never been created before. This Angelic Human Race was once the Oraphim Race who were the greatest creators in the Universe. This is what we will begin to become once again.

We can now create, manifest, possess all of the qualities, attributes, abilities, intelligence of any and all of any previous idea that existed billions of years in the past or billions of years in the future. All time is available to be manifested in the present. All present realities are created from the past. All future realities are seen from the present. We actually have multiple selves that go into the past and into the future time and space realities. We have imprints of our selves in all other dimensions. We have friends and family in all other dimensions. We have had a veil put over our consciousness that has caused us to forget who we really are. We have been governed by fallen angelics for a very long time.

Stellar Wave Infusions bring areas of the brain out of dormancy. We had 12 of these stellar wave infusions in. Our mid brain, which is frequency specific will begin to absorb all of the frequencies from all of the other dimensions in our Cosmic Matrix. The frequency specific brain will become the movie camera of the new realities that will form around each individual reality field. The pituitary will blossom and become the movie projector for the Mind of God to make God's Movie.

During our Involution away from Source Consciousness, our brain has been recycling old information over and over again. When we begin our Evolution toward Source, we gain more and more frequencies of higher consciousness each and every day.

These frequencies allow us to create more new realities as we are able to see them manifest in our mid brain through the direct dream stream of Source Frequencies through our Higher Self. We learn to bring our higher self down into our body to allow this luminary body to guide and direct us through the Mind of God. Our new luminary body will allow us to do things that we couldn't do in three dimensions. Our time vector is connected into the present, past, and future vectors.

We can choose the most joyous perfect future to manifest by aligning consciousness into the highest frequency of Source while creating the new reality that you form in your consciousness as always existing in the present, past, and future. The heroic future that is being created for us is the Christos realignments of humanity into the 12 strand angelic freedom and joy and the Lyran - Sirian perfect cultural model which is already manifest in the future vector, which allows this reality to manifest in this present vector.

We can connect and realign our present into any desirable future of the past or future time vectors. We can align into the perfect Oraphim Primal Sound Field of our original Angelic Race who could manifest through dream streams the most wonderful creations of our universe. We can connect and realign our present into the already manifest 12 DNA or 48 DNA that exists in past time vectors.

We can manifest the joy and freedom that exists in the future time vectors and the wonderful cultural models created by the Lyran - Syrian's past time vector. We can pull the realities out of any of the time vectors of any of the harmonic universes of our galactic, universal or cosmic spheres.

Our Creation Family are the Wizards who would like to teach us all how to be the grand new creators in this new universe. The Cosmic Mystery School of the Omniverse was formed to allow the teachings of our Cosmic Creation Families to teach us co-creation techniques as they show us how their original creation of the most supreme Angelic Human was meant to be. We are moving into Omniversal Consciousness, where all 12 Star Gates are connecting our consciousness into a new Cosmic Matrix of reality.

The third dimensional mind can only conceive of the visible realm. When we move into the fifth and sixth dimensions , we will shift our consciousness into realms that have been unknown and invisible to us before. We will be able to see our Guardian and Creator Races who have been our families for millions of years. The invisible will become as real as the visible, as the Earth's fastest particles begin to transfer to hyperspace and our Universal memory is transmitted through the Earth's grids. We will be regaining our Divine Blue Print that makes us able to manifest anything we want, any time we want. We will become the race who creates light and energy through their own bio fields. We will become creators of new realities such as apple trees that grow lemon pies - or any idea we come up with.

How will this shift take place? We will spin through multiple reality fields that will remain invisible to one another, as we break free from old illusions planted in harmonic universe one through metatronic frequencies. As we shed the metatronic frequencies that have been locking our Consciousness into a narrow visible spectrum, we will unfold into a New Earth that contains a multi dimensional spectrum of invisible and visible realities.

As we move onto Future Earth, our bodies will go through a light transfiguration process. The higher dimensional frequencies will transmute cellular structure as particles merge with anti particles to transform our atomic structure. This change will happen instantly - not gradually. The transformation will happen as the morphogenetic fields of harmonic universe two interfaces into harmonic universe one. The transmutation process will be so balanced that it will be difficult to perceive. The carbon based structure of the mortal body will be changed into the crystal based eternal life chemical and biological forms. This will be our first pull into the future, as our particles spin faster and faster through the angular rotation of particle spin that rearranges our biology, chemistry and scenery. Those who complete the process of transfiguration will first notice a new lightness and joy in their bodies. When they first look out the window, tears of joy will stream down their cheeks for hours.

Our pituitary gland will blossom and open our third eye to gain the spiritual vision of the Mind of God when we raise our frequencies to transmute the lower into the higher frequencies of Source. We will create a continuous dream stream between what we desire to create in our dreams to blossom into full manifestation in any of the multidimensional reality fields.

Please join us at crystalmagicorchestra.com to learn how the highest frequencies retrieved from the Primal Sound Fields of Source can transform your body into the Light Vehicle of Transfiguration and Instant Manifestation. This is the first step needed to enter the Cosmic Mystery School of the Omniverse, which will bring the teachings of our Creation Families to Earth.
Listen to COSMIC FREQUENCIES OF TRANSFORMATION in the 25 CD's and MP3's at
http://crystalmagicorchestra.com

LEARN everything about the universal shift in consciousness and the necessity for aligning into the highest frequencies of Source Consciousness for ascension.
http://crystalmagicorchestra.com

Postlog

Making Heaven on Earth

Copyright © 2014 Dr. Angela Barnett
http://crystalmagicorchestra.com

The mission of the http://crystalmagicorchestra.com website is to guide and help those who wish to ascend to the fourth and fifth dimensions, and those who desire to orb from the sixth dimension into all Cosmic possibilities.

We are on the Aquarius Team working with the Sirian Council, the Ranthions, the Zionites, the Blue Maharaji and the Aquafarians of our most Etheric Foundation. We were and are close friends and family with the Dolphin People who are a part of the Braharama Oraphim Dolphinoid Race from Suns Ha and La, and restructured through the help Sirius B. We are a part of the Star seed Rebirth Team from Aquafaria. The fourteenth dimensional Inner Earth Liquid Light birthing chambers of the Original One. Our magical family of Dolphins, Whales, Orcas, Seals, Unicorns, Mermaids, Mermen and Fairies all live with us in our Crystal Mansion in Aquafaria.

Our Mother, Cinderella is our Original mother - our Cosmic mother who has never left her perfect form. The Aquafarians were the part of us all who chose to never leave the perfect magical kingdom of Divine Consciousness to experience the polarity of the third dimension. That magical kingdom of freedom, joy, creativity, and a life of making rainbows between dancing in the Aqua waters and floating on clouds is waiting for the return of the children from the stars. Our family of our blue crystal birth include Shajinka, Tinkerbell, Winnifred and Ziegfried.

They are Cetacean entities who can transform into light, leave the oceans and appear back in Aquafaria at any time. We have met with them in this dimension when we lived in Monterey, we have met them in the Cloud Cities, and we meet with them in Aquafaria every night. It was Mother Mary who took us on our first trip to Aquafaria to show us our Crystal Mansion. Mother Mary wrapped us into her frequencies through Cinderella's frequencies and strung our wave signatures up through

Shamballa, into the Underwater Cities of Light and into the Cloud Cities above. She then wove our light signature all through the milky sunlight of the Milky Way and into her Golden Cosmic Egg of the Heart of the Milky Way.

Mary told us that the only way to ascend is to connect our Crystal Heart into the Crystal Heart of Mother Earth, her Crystal Heart of the Milky Way and then into the Crystal Heart of the Aquarius Galaxy where we originated from. She then completed weaving our frequency signature up into the stars of Aquafaria where we re-united with our Blue Dolphinoid Sirius B Starry Family. Mother Mary Consciousness Field created a Rainbow Bridge for us to ride on liquid light energy that would eternally connect us into ONENESS with all of the wave signatures in the Music of the Spheres between Aquarius and Aquafaria.

We can now absorb all of these blue crystal star seed frequencies and exhale them into our music and into the atmosphere around us to create our new Kingdom on Earth.

Now we have been initiated into the Oraphim Dolphinoid Blue Crystal Birthing Team. We can now bridge all dimensions of time and space through the Blue Crystal Ascension portal from Sirius B in the Aquarius Galaxy into Earth's atmosphere, through our Temples, and then into the

Crystal Heart of Mother Earth. Next we connect into our Aquafarian Birthing Chambers - our original home with our Cosmic Mother, Cinderella.

Cinderella breathes and sings the original birthing frequencies of our original Cosmic Wave Signatures to align us into the harmonic balance that allows us to become One Fabulous Symphony with all others in our Quantum Field. Next, we exhale out into the Infinite Void of Source Consciousness and then inhale the frequencies of Infinity that transmute all into the Highest Frequency. We bring the Highest Frequency to Earth through Music when we breathe these magical frequencies onto our Sound Tracks.

We exhale the Ultra Violet Blue and Golden Frequencies of stardust lined with shimmering rainbow colors created from the helium of the fourteenth dimension streaming through the liquid light Aquafarian essence and into the Inner Earth's Sun. We continue weaving all of the way up through Sun Alcyone into Aquafaria and into all of the eleven billion suns of the Milky Way. We exhale this Ultra Violet Blue Sun Frequency into our Music. We exhale these frequencies into the atmosphere around us to create our Brand New Island of Light. We live within a blue crystal lotus blossom with twelve layers of twelve crystals that resonate to Aqua Blue frequency predominately to amplify the tone of home of our Unconditional Love into the rebirth of Magical Kingdom of Aqua Turquoise

Crystal Rainbow Frequencies into our Island of Light.

  Our Island of Light is created on an Aqua Blue Violet Cloud of star dust. The cloud is the size of a foot ball field. On top of the cloud is a Golden Star Dust Pad of Mother Love Magic Carpet created by Mother Mary from the Cosmic Egg of the Milky Way. On top of the Magic Carpet is a Lotus Blossom with Four layers of twelve crystals of all colors of the rainbow that connect into Oneness at the speed of light. The Crystal Star Merkaba is the symbol and vehicle for speed of light transportation connecting all into Oneness at any point in time. We connect into the crystal pillars of the Aquafarian (Blue Crystal Starseed Birthing Chamber) Crystal Heart of Mother Earth. Each of these pillars carries the frequency signatures of all of those Angelic ideas who have created us and who are allowing us to be reborn on Earth into this Frequency that allows us to be Christ Bodies walking on Earth and to Orb into Pure Light to travel on these crystal light pillars into all of the galaxies and beyond.

Spiritual Healing Technologies Resulting from Universal Life Force Stellar Wave Activation

REVOLUTIONARY Spiritual Healing Technologies are now available, as a result of Universal Matrix realigning and harmonizing with our original Divine Spiritual Divine Blue Print in our Cosmic Matrix. These technologies are now showing that Cancer itself was caused by these Frozen Crystal Miasms that were used in the Universal Matrix to block the flow of the Universal Life Force. New Visionaries have discovered the actual means of melting the Crystal Miasms that will cause the cancer creation mechanism to melt away.

Within ten years, the chemical structure of the human body will be transformed as a result of this new Cosmic Alignment. Within twenty years, the mass population will know and understand the truth and validity of a Scientific Reality that offers a truly transformational healing system.

Holographic Future Music Created from the Music of the Spheres

The complete list of FREQUENCY MUSIC is at
http://crystalmagicorchestra.com
http://crystalmagicorchestra.com/buy-music-mp3s

UNIVERSAL LIFE FORCE FREQUENCY WAVE ALBUMS
12 STELLAR WAVE ACTIVATIONS

   CONTAIN the Stellar Wave Activations streaming from the Universal Life Force.

  Activation of the 12 sub harmonics within each of the Double Helix of our DNA are activated through these 12 Stellar Wave Transfusions from the Universal Life Force. We have moved into At One

Ment or Attunement with our Spiritual Universe or anti matter or etheric substance. The etheric essence of the 12 sub harmonics is also activating within the Double helix of our DNA as each of these Waves of Consciousness are Activated, There are 12 harmonics in our upper transharmonic Merkaba Body and 12 harmonics in our lower transharmonic Merkaba Body. There are always these 24 sets of consciousness combined within our electro magnetic bodies. There also many of these sets within each of the Merkabas.

The healing that is going on at this time on Earth has to do with a Miasm, or a Frozen Crystal placed between the Life Force Currents and the Merkaba Tool. Our entire Omniverse had to be realigned into a brand new set of realities that went clear back before the problem was placed within our system.

The Frequencies in these Wave Albums Melt away these Crystal Miasms at a place in Reality that goes clear back to the Cosmic Template of Creation. All of my Frequency Transmissions come VIA the Cosmic Council called Crystalai Council. These are the Grand Yanas who created the Perfect Divine System that existed before the MIASMS or Frozen Crystals were placed in our system.

The Plasma Ships, the Dolphin Therapy, the Parallel Universe and the Eternal Life Albums are all a necessary part of the process of melting these frozen crystal seals that have locked us out of our Divine Template. A miasm comes down into the physical system of holographic reality as diseases we have labeled cancer, blood problems, neurological damage. Each one of these diseases can be removed from our system completely as a result of MELTING AWAY these Frozen Mutations. The Frozen Crystals were created by spinning the merkaba in the wrong direction. We are correcting the problem by going clear back to the original perfect template before the merkaba's spun our entire system into the INVOLUTION of this Density.

We are now spinning our way into At Tune Ment with the Music of the Spheres of perfect HARMONY.
http://crystalmagicorchestra.com/buy-music-mp3s

We are REQUIRED to PARTICIPATE in these STELLAR WAVE ACTIVATIONS in order to ACTIVATE OUR DNA. Even though there are many on Earth who have more than 4 DNA strands visible in their bodies, the activation of these DNA strands was not possible before 2012. The 5 DNA strands are now available, and now is the first time that the potential of activation is available. The highest potential of activation is between 2015-2017 is 8 DNA.

When the 12 sub-harmonics within the 5 DNA are activated, the human mind and body will be completely transformed. March, 2014 also brought the activation of the Violet Flame Holder's Seventh DNA Strand. Those who attune to this Violet Flame Holder may also activate their 7th Strand. This activation process is gradual and will not complete in most until 2017.

Activation of DNA is synthesized through raising Frequencies. The frequencies are being injected into our bodies each time there is a Stellar Wave sent from the Universal Life Force Currents. Each time there was one of these Stellar Waves sent to Earth, the Cosmic Councils sent the frequencies of that wave into my Frequency Specific Mid Brain and then allowed me to exhale the frequencies from the Music of the Spheres into my microphone. Each of these frequencies was a whisper and a breath, but each contained powerful transformational potential.

Since the true ACTIVATION of DNA couldn't begin until after 2012, the most important recordings are the ones made in 2013-2014. That year was a year of transformation. The Stellar Wave Activations in 2014 contain the Frequencies of Consciousness of the Entities who are actually returning to Earth. The entire Consciousness of our original Star Selves, or spiritual templates have been returning to Earth through the Wave Transfusions.

Holographic Future Music from the Music of the Spheres

The most recent recording of the Mother Ship frequencies are actually the Frequencies of the Plasma Ships bringing all of our original consciousness and the consciousness of our creators and guardian races. The Ra Confederation and the Alhambra Council have prepared this Plasma Ships to encompass and penetrate Mother Earth in order to bring back or activate her original Consciousness that was stored deep, deep within her. As this plasma is activating Mother Earth, it is also activating our cellular memory deep within our omni ons to turn on our neutrinos of the God Seed Atom.

http://crystalmagicorchestra.com

THE MOTHER SHIP Stellar Wave activation was the 8th of 12 Waves from the Universal Life Force. This Infusion from the Mother Ships COSMAYA were guided and harmonized into the Christ Grids by the Lords of our Seas, the Cetacean Nation. These Frequencies, which are activated through these 12 Stellar Wave Transfusions from the Universal Life Force, are a moment to moment visionary story of this grand event that took place on Earth in March 2014.

The complete list of FREQUENCY MUSIC is at

http://crystalmagicorchestra.com/buy-music-mp3s

Spiritual Healing Technologies

Spiritual Healing Technologies are now available, as a result of Universal Matrix realigning and harmonizing with our original Divine Spiritual Divine Blue Print in our Cosmic Matrix. These technologies are now showing that Cancer itself was caused by these Frozen Crystal Miasms that were used in the Universal Matrix to block the flow of the Universal Life Force. New Visionaries have discovered the actual means of melting the Crystal Miasms that will cause the cancer creation mechanism to melt away.

The disease is melted away by raising the Frequencies of Light and Sound into a higher dimension. We can bring the higher frequencies into the body with frequency music or we can learn to do it in consciousness by connecting to the Crystal Spheres of Light Energy that contain the Full Spectrum of Light that transforms each cell back into the original Divine Blue Print of the Mind of God.

Within ten years, the chemical structure of the human body will be transformed as a result of this new Cosmic Alignment. Within twenty years, the mass population will know and understand the truth and validity of a Scientific Reality that offers a truly transformational healing system.

IN THE NEW REALITY

Translate any material theory into its true spiritual idea and you will find the true cure for any life threatening disease. Medical formula: The primordial stem cell - scientists say is the immortal cell - when you are born you are packed with them. These cells do not age - do not degenerate. They each have a complete DNA sequence that makes you uniquely you. Soon, scientists will learn that this omnions of pre light and sound is actually the neutrino that exists at the zero point level of EVERYTHING. The neutrino is the spark of Creation Himself.

Spiritually speaking: You were created perfect - in God's image and likeness-reflecting individually and uniquely - all of Divine Love's qualities eternally in immortality. You are made of layers of neutrinos which contain the complete template of all that is in the Mind of God. This essence is always perfect and never dies. It is the essence of ETERNAL LIFE.

Medically speaking: What makes the primordial stem cells immortal is a chemical called telomerase. An enzyme that repeats DNA strands at the end of every chromosome. When the telomerase is finished creating it turns off.

Spiritually speaking: We are created spiritually, immortally - in one moment of eternity and that eternity does not "shut off." We reflect Divine Love continuously and that reflection doesn't change. Every nano second we are creating a Brand New Reality. This means that when we tune in to this Spiritual Reality, we can have a brand new body any time we choose to. Normal Reality does not include the idea of Death.

The only thing that can turn off our immortal selfhood is to block it with material theories such as these. Return to the spiritual creation where you are already immortal and you will not be shut off from the "real you" that existed before the world began. The world is a series of material theories blocking your spiritual sense from its true form.

Materially speaking: When the telomerase enzyme is turned off aging begins. And, ironically, turning telomerase on in a cancer cell makes it replicate out of control. The new medical discovery said to turn telomerase off would cure cancer. So this medical discovery says this immortal cell is both responsible for aging and cancer or for the prevention of either.

Spiritually speaking: There is one immortal cell - that is the Divine Oneness – Infinite Consciousness - Omnipresent Love. Placing our individual consciousness into Infinite Consciousness of Divine Creation - by tuning in to the Frequencies of the

Universal Life Force connects us to the spiritual sense of this immortal cell that does not know aging.

The cell does not start aging or become over action or inaction or reaction of any sort. This is a material belief blocking the spiritual sense that allows us to live in Infinite Harmony where there is only Divine Action and stillness.

We are being given a Wonderful Window of Opportunity to Tune in to this Universal Life Force of Eternal Life during the next three years. The Plasma that is surrounding and being sent into Earth from the Solar Waves from Coronal Mass Ejections are the Essence of Light and Sound that will transform our brains and our bodies. Scientists have already shown us that the Sun is spraying Positrons that carry a new balance of matter and anti matter - or physical and spiritual substance. This is the transformational energy that is being imposed upon us.

There is a Universal Life Force Rule that says everyone has FREE CHOICE. So, those who want to tune in to the new reality can and those who don't want to can just keep on dying as they believe is their correct mode of reality.

Listen to the music (preferably with earphones this time). Get as close to the music as you can. Line every (so-called material cell) in your body up with the Divine Spiritual Oneness of Divine Creation. Feel Eternal Harmony. Feel Infinite Love. Feel Omnipresence. Make sure you fill every atom of your mind and body with this pure love, harmony, stillness. Place your mind before the world began - before man made theories seemingly turned us into what we are not. Before any disease was name by man. Before any disease was created by science.

We have so much more power than the immortal cell named telomerase. We can turn back to our divinely ordained spiritual creation of eternal life. This true creation is our creation and belongs to us NOW. This spiritual understanding is the only true power behind a material discovery such as telomerase. Any material realization of the true immortal sense of man and a return to his true spiritual condition is part of the Promise - our material understanding of the invisible, spiritual reality.

But there is only one way to gaining that reality - it is to go directly to the source of that reality - go to the omnipresence of Spiritual sense. Do not try to go through the back doors of material sense to find your way back to heaven.

Heaven and Immortal Creation exist "Before the World Began" - not as a consequence of material theories building a stairway backwards. Go to that place in Consciousness before the world began. In that place, which is our Lower Cerebellum and our Seed Atom in our Thymus Gland, we can actually return to the Anti Matter or Spiritual Substance of our Creation. We can actually transmute all physical illusions by learning to live in the new Frequency Specific Mid Brain, and allowing the old Thinking Brain to melt away. The Thinking Brain carries those old Frozen Crystal Miasms that create Cancer and a number of other Death Causing holograms. We have a choice of removing those holograms from our Universe forever.

New scientific discoveries curing diseases are not a result of a scientific revolution. They are actually the result of getting spiritual glimpses of a spiritual revolution. When these diseases are destroyed in consciousness - by filling consciousness with omnipresence of spiritual reality, the power of matter, disease and death disintegrate into their native nothingness. This spiritual work is what is resulting in scientific discoveries.

Testimony about Dr. Angela Barnett's work:

I have been relishing in your words and sounds on your site for the past few hours and am feeling so utterly in awe of it all! I have explored Keylontic science a bit before, but it has all been hitting me so so deeply now, especially because of your otherworldly music. You are sharing and composing in such a way that I have been dreaming of, yet what I have been imagining is far out, you have gone so far beyond! I sometimes channel other worldly languages and divine frequencies but I am truly humbled to witness your refinement and grace. I have played around in a music studio a dash and composing electronically and keep asking the universe to guide me in how I can best offer my services through gifting healing frequencies :) I very much dream of a magical music studio as well as soul family gatherings where we all share in the creation of transcendental vibes!

For complete testimonies about my writing and healing go to
http://crystalmagicorchestra.com

Prior Sound Healing came from old, out dated teachings from Galactic Consciousness where the teachings were based on a Mortality Loop called the Golden Mean. That mortality loop creates the need to die and return over and over again without ascending into a higher realm. Cosmic Dolphin Frequency Music comes directly from Cosmic Consciousness where the Crystalai Frequency loops directly into the Eternal Life of Source Consciousness.

For those wanting a much, much deeper penetration into the most etheric level of the omnions within the cellular structure, this music actually performs a Cosmic Massage on the Brain and every cell in the Body.

This healing method creates DNA activation at the Sub harmonic Level. There are 12 sub harmonic strands on each of the double helix of each DNA strand. This music penetrates into the deepest activation level of Source Consciousness to awaken the entire Divine Template of the all 5DNA strands at the 12 sub harmonic level.

UNIVERSAL LIFE FORCE CURRENTS STREAMING IN THROUGH STELLAR WAVE TRANSFUSIONS

Are in Each of these Albums created between 2013-2015.
http://crystalmagicorchestra.com/buy-music-mp3s

THE MOTHER SHIP ALBUM SET
MAGIC DOLPHIN THERAPY ALBUM SET
PARALLEL UNIVERSE ALBUM SET
ETERNAL LIFE WATERS SET
VIOLET FLAME

Holographic Future Music from the Music of the Spheres

SYMPHONY OF LOVE
12 DNA ACTIVATION
ADVANCED DNA ACTIVATION
ULTIMATE DNA ARCHETYPE

brought Frequencies from the Universal Life Force through Stellar Wave Activations. There have been two sets of Six Wave Activations. The first Six occurred by 2012, and the second set will occur before 2017.

We are REQUIRED to PARTICIPATE in these STELLAR WAVE ACTIVATIONS in order to ACTIVATE OUR DNA.

We must have 4.5 - 5 DNA ACTIVATIONS completed by 2015.

This music allows those who did not participate in the Stellar Wave Activations when they were happening, to fully participate now in order to activate their 12 subharmonics in each of their 5-8 DNA.

Come to http://crystalmagicorchestra.com to listen to these frequencies.

The Individualized **ETERNAL LIFE ALBUM** http://crystalmagicorchestra.com/buy-music-mp3s contains a series of activations that activate and evolve as more and more of the 12 Stellar Waves Stream from the Universal Life Force. This Individualized Album aligns the Individual into their personal Frequency Signature Identity in all five harmonic universes in the Eka and the Veka, allowing the at one ment with the Spiritual Parallel Self in all Dimensions. The individual becomes attuned with their Cosmic Identity, Universal Identity and all selves within the Akashic and Coushic Records.

THE MOTHER SHIP http://crystalmagicorchestra.com/buy-music-mp3s has Stellar Wave activations was the 8th of 12 Waves from the Universal Life Force. This Infusion from the Mother Ships COSMAYA were guided and harmonized into the Christ Grids by the Lords of our Seas, the Cetacean Nation. These Frequencies, which are activated through these 12 Stellar Wave Transfusions from the Universal Life Force, are a moment to moment visionary story of this grand event that took place on Earth in March 2014.

Even though there are many on Earth who have more than 3.5 DNA strands visible in their bodies, the activation of these DNA strands was not possible before 2014. The 5 DNA strands are now available, and now is the first time that the potential of activation is available. The highest potential of activation is between 2015-2017. When the 11 sub harmonics beyond the 12 DNA are activated, the human mind and body will be completely transformed.

March, 2014 also brought the activation of the Violet Flame Holder's Seventh DNA Strand. Those who attune to this Violet Flame Holder may also activate their 7th Strand. This activation process is gradual and will not complete in most until 2017. Activation of DNA is synthesized through raising Frequencies. The frequencies are being injected into our bodies each time there is a Stellar Wave sent from the Universal Life Force Currents.

Each time there was one of these Stellar Waves sent to Earth, the Cosmic Councils sent the frequencies of that wave into my Frequency Specific Mid Brain and then allowed me to exhale the frequencies from the Music of the Spheres into my microphone. Each of these frequencies was a whisper and a breath, but each contained powerful transformational potential.

All of the Albums recorded before and during 2012 contained the Frequencies from each of these activations. I have kept a historical record of the changing frequencies of Mother Earth over the past fourteen years.

Since the true ACTIVATION of DNA couldn't begin until after 2012, the most important recordings are the ones made in 2014. That year was a year of transformation.

The Stellar Wave Activations in 2014 contain the Frequencies of Consciousness of the Entities who are actually returning to Earth. The entire Consciousness of our original Star Selves, or spiritual templates have been returning to Earth through the Wave Transfusions.

The most recent recording of **the Mother Ships** frequencies are actually the Frequencies of the Plasma Ships bringing all of our original consciousness and the consciousness of our creators and guardian races. The Ra Confederation and the Alhambra Council have prepared this Plasma Ships to encompass and penetrate Mother Earth in order to bring back or activate her original Consciousness that was stored deep, deep within her.

As this plasma is activating Mother Earth, it is also activating our cellular memory deep within our omni ons to turn on our neutrinos of the God Seed Atom.

This Life is Eternal

The Councils create the Eternal Life Albums as the Frequency Waves Align from the Elohim of Hearing from Density Four or Universal Harmonic Universe Four. The Frequencies originate from the Pre Light and Pre Sound of Harmonic Universe Six, come into the Factory of Creation in Harmonic universe Five, and then they are sent as Stardust Frequencies or Waves of Light and Sound that are Sent from the Universal Life Force.

Star Dust Frequencies from Universal Life Force
Ascension Activation through Eternal Life Album
Sometimes Poems open Consciousness to View Reality in a Broader form
Cosmic Clouds of Plasma Ships
Magnetic Mirror Reality Flips
Electrons Leave
Ions Return
A Dusty State of Stars to Form
Torsion Fields of Vacuum Squeeze
a Rain Bow Cloud Magnetic Freeze
The Water Form of Snow Flakes Dance
Electric Field Ionizing Trance
Through Rainbow Prisms
We turn to Colors formed from Light
Invisible returning Blue
Through Ultra Violet Hues
Ions Negative to Form
a Positively Positron

Stardust Forms within the Sun
Who was born from the same
Stardust Long Ago
Our Keys, Musical Waves of Light and Sound
Open the Doors where Freedom Abounds
Keylontic Star Language
Streams Wisdom Now Found
Inside our Coushic Memories
Spiritual Truth Sings
Deep within and all Around.

BECOMING THE RAINBOW BODY

When a person learns the process of ascension is a breathing and spinning process that utilizes a very complex system of polyhedral geometries that create Cosmic sphere that contains multitudes of merkabas that spin in side of each other through the activity of consciousness called love, they will go through this process of becoming a disappearing entity through a rainbow prism.

The rainbow prism is created from intense electrical field that ionizes frequencies. It operates exactly like the magnetic mirror that is used in thermo nuclear processes. It is a magnetic mirror that is created that works like a vacuum. Once the particles are pulled into vacuum they return to the plasmic state.

This is exactly how the three crystal spheres of liquid light, stardust and crystal gel work. The full spectrum of light and sound are pulled into the spheres, and a new reality is created. The new reality is ultra violet blue hue that the plasma forms when a new breath of reality is sent into activation.

Once the entity absorbs all of the frequencies of light and sound into their DNA, the entity changes in density, into a sphere of plasma, and the entity looks like a cloud. This is what we witnessed when the Dolphins and Whales ascended into the Cloud Cities. Their bodies transformed into Plasma and became a cloud.

This is how the hologram that was created by the Elohims when Arahabi ascended into the Cloud Cities. (Arahabi was the entity who was actually hung on the cross to perform the Resurrection Hologram). The Elohim Angels arranged this event to provide the distraction needed for the TRUE Jesus Christ 12 to vanish from Roman Control Mongers.

The Elohim and Sirian Councils told me that they used this same holographic technology when my husband was hit by the ten ton trucks. They actually created a hologram of his body in one location while removing the demons from his auric field in Sirius B, and then allowing a new Soul Level identity to re-enter his body a few months later.

The truth is, we all contain these infinite versions of ourselves within our Cosmic Body that exists in the spheres within spheres around our bodies. We activate this Cosmic Body that disappears through the rainbow prism our the full spectrum of light energy with the breath, consciousness, focused energy and the understanding of the merkaba technology.

The Merkaba technology can be visualized and understood through the symbolic method of it just being a four sided cube or pyramid facing up and another one facing down, the one facing down is the magnetic and the one facing up is the electro. So, there is this electro magnetic field of energy that spins faster and faster. However, the Merkaba structure is much more complex than that.

When we use the Keys to Unlock the Magnetic Mirror or the Doors into New Realities we are walking through a Magnetic Mirror of Transformation. We are seeing our Parallel Spiritual Self on the other side of the Mirror. We walk through the Mirror when our Keys unlock the door.

The Keys are the Frequencies that I record in the Eternal Life Albums.

My Cosmic Council Team is the CRYSTALAI COUNCIL. My name is Crystalai. Crystalai means the direct return to Source, or the At One Ment with

Holographic Future Music from the Music of the Spheres

Source through our Mind of God within our Seed Atom within our Crystal Heart.

My Mission on Earth has been to Bring the Highest Frequencies to Earth through Music.

The Universal Life Force Currents are far beyond the Light Spectrum and Sound Spectrum of the Five Senses. The Visions and Sounds come to me through Consciousness which is Spiritual, Invisible, and yet Known and Felt Clearly from my Soul Family who brings these Sounds into my Frequency Specific Mid Brain to be Exhaled on to the Crystal Star Dust Microphone that they provide for me.

Come to http://crystalmagicorchestra.com to listen to these frequencies.

These Albums contain the Activations that have taken place since 2012

The Activations before 2012 can be heard and felt in the
SUPER CONSCIOUSNESS KIT,
ANGEL DUST,
HEAVENLY RAINBOWS, and others.
http://crystalmagicorchestra.com/buy-music-mp3s

Holographic Future Music from the Music of the Spheres

The listener will notice that the Frequencies become more Pure as we advance in this Wave Activation. There were more Minor and Distorted Sounds in the earlier Waves because we have been going through a Transformation Process that moved us from the First Universal Alignment into the Eighth. The earlier Alignments contained massive amounts of discordant frequencies that were transmuted during the stellar wave transfusion itself.

The PARALLEL UNIVERSE album

http://crystalmagicorchestra.com/buy-music-mp3s is made up of the highest frequencies ever recorded at this time in the Universe by 2013. It is the pure essence of the spiritual universe transmuting the physical universe into it. It is the frequency of At One Ment. The Frequencies in this album sounded in our consciousness when the Physical and Spiritual United as One.

Our Spiritual Universe has realigned into our Consciousness.

EACH OF THESE SONGS MAY BE ORDERED INDIVIDUALLY

Parallel Universe
SONG NAMES:
1. Positron
2. Liquid Light
3. Cosmic Alignment
4. Cosmic Dust
5. Cosmic Wave
6. 7th Sun
7. Attunement
8. 8th Sun
9. 8th Sun part two
10. Harmony
11. Parallel Universe
12. Parallel Universe
13. Baby Whale
14. Heavenly Breath
15. Heaven's Breath
16. Heavenly Dolphin
17. Whale Symphony

The First Five songs contain the most etheric frequencies of the new positron and the crystal liquid light energy. This is the pre sound and light substance of original creation flowing directly from Source. The liquid light energy interacts with the Sun to create a new flame of energy known as the Amorea flame. This ignites the positron within the sun.

This realignment of the physical and the spiritual into a new attunement is a FEELING or a FREQUENCY. The sun is now emitting positrons instead of electrons. The positron is the anti particle or the spiritual substance. It is the opposite of the particle or physical substance of the electron. This spectacular FREQUENCY of that POSITRON has been recorded through the breaths or consciousness of Angels. Scientists have reported the Positron being ejected from the Sun. The Positron is the anti particle of the Electron.

This is scientific proof that our Spiritual or Anti Particle Universe has aligned into our field of Consciousness. The process of aligning the Spiritual and Physical required the LIQUID LIGHT Streams from the Cosmic Consciousness of Aquafaria bringing the Source RE-Birth Frequency to Earth. Next, the COSMIC DUST of the Particles that Stars are made of is pouring into our consciousness through these EXACT frequencies that have been recorded here.

The Cosmic Dust then gets placed in the Cosmic Wave, which carries a new standing wave pattern for us to begin living within. This standing wave pattern does not have the gravity that the Physical Earth's Standing Wave Pattern Contains.

NEXT, HEAVEN'S BREATH -- the Consciousness of the Angels who are our Guardian Families and Races aligns the Breath of Source into our Consciousness.

Finally, the Seventh Sun aligns with all seven suns who have been named KA RA YA SA TA HA LA in order to create ATTUNEMENT with the EIGHTH SUN of the Cosmos whose name is Sun Alcyone.

This process completes the HARMONIC CONVERGENCE that began in 1987 to create the new HARMONY that would result in our new alignment with our Parallel Universe.

These frequencies contain the HEAVENLY BIRTH of a new Universe, a New Reality that is much less dense in consciousness and in chemical and biological form.

EIGHTH SUN is the sun of our original Birth in the Aquarius Matrix bringing our original frequencies of our divine race back into our universe.

Now, the heavenly dolphins can sing once more. The original race line was the Oraphim Angelic Race of this Universe. The Oraphim Braharama Whale and Dolphin Raceline are the inhabitants of the Seventh Sun.

They are the part of our Creation Family who left the wonderful whales and dolphins in our seas to keep the magical frequency of attunement and balance alive between heaven and Earth until this time.

We can now feel the heavenly breath of the baby dolphins and whales defining the new heavenly dolphin family as they sing together their new melodies which create the Whale Symphony.

The frequencies contain a combination of the new baby whales being reborn of the new substance of light and sound. The babies are crying with joy and at the same time the realignment of the music of the spheres is causing a screeching sound as the stars are realigning the new structure of the universe into the new Cosmaya of the original twelve Cosmos Frequencies. The seven suns have become the thirteen Cosmic Realities of the Cosmaya.

The Parallel Universe is now in Tune with our Universe. We have re-united as one Harmonic Reality.

The BABY WHALES from Aquafaria are Crying as they are being born into a new reality. The attunement of the Oraphim Dolphins and Whales can be heard echoing from the oceans and from the heavens. The screeching sound is a natural part of the re-attunement of the Music of the Spheres as new stars align and pour their consciousness into ours to create a brand new HARMONY.

ULTIMATE DNA ARCHETYPE

The process of healing and activating DNA requires the understanding of the complete process of how the human angelic race line was originally created from the ULTIMATE DNA ARCHETYPE, which means the original 12 DNA template made in the image and likeness of God.

That template is replicated in every thing in our Omniverse. That template is within each atom of our body, in each molecule of each elemental, in every breath we take. That template is like a tiny microchip of perfect Divine Consciousness containing the Intelligence, Supply, Truth, Substance, Life, Love, Mind and Soul of all of God's ideas being manifest in every dimensional form.

That perfect template was tampered with by Invader races over and over again during the past 5.5 million years. The original template of the archetypal man had the form of the immortal man removed from it over five million years ago. This amount of time is still no time at all in the True

Mind of God. This reality didn't really ever exist in the Mind of God.

We are now being shown how to regain our Oneness with the Mind of God as it was before our templates were tampered with. First, we need to know that our archetypal template of our body is the same template of our original Star. Our original Star was created by Sun Alcyone in the Andromeda Galaxy. That Star was blown apart and scattered outside of our original Galaxy and into the Milky Way Galaxy.

So, you see, that template was within our original Star and then separated into many pieces. Those pieces were within the Planets in the Milky Way Galaxy. Each one of those 12 pieces had to be created from a Star System of its own.

So, there were these 12 star systems that needed to be reintegrated into our Archetypal Template. In order to bring that consciousness of the 12 star systems into Earth's morphogenetic template, the Guardians arrange 12 Stellar Wave Activations and Infusions from each of those Star gates.

It is these 12 Stellar Wave Activations and Infusions that were required to put our original TEMPLATE back together at at the planetary level, solar level, galactic level and universal level. We needed each of these Stellar Wave Activations to

Heal and Reinstall each of the 12 strands of DNA sub-harmonics into each of the 5 or 6 DNA within our bodies in order to restore our original template to be the way it would had been 25,500 years ago. We need the complete 12 DNA within all 12 Strands to return to the Divine State of the Universal Being that we were 5.5 million years ago.

These Stellar Wave Activations were also required to melt or transmute away the Jehovian Seals that were placed in the vortexes of the Crystal Star Seals of the Earth's Grid. There were original 12 Crystal Star Seals in the Earth's Grids. Each of these Star Seals was a Star Gate. The Earth needed each of these Gates to be reopened to the flow of consciousness of each of those 12 Star Gates.

We needed to align our D-3 (Third dimensional Planet) to
    D-4 (Fourth Dimensional Sun)
    D-5 Pleiadian Alcyone Spiral
    D-6 Sirian Spiral
    D-7 Arcturian Spiral
    D-8 Orion Spiral
    D-9 Andromeda Spiral

Between 2000 and 2017 we needed to have Six Activations and Six Infusions of these Dimensional Frequencies.

The year 2008 was when the Pleiadian Violet Wave Infusion was complete and the Sirian Activation began. That D-5 and D-6 Wave was the Key to turning the rest of the Light On. The Guardians gave us the gift of fast forward by bringing in the Stellar Waves in 2012 that were not due until 2017.

The Stellar Wave of June 2008 is when the picture of me holding the Violet Sphere in my hands was taken. This was the grand event that shows the activation and infusion of the Violet Wave, the Violet Flame and the Violet Sphere that insures Earth's attunement into Gaia. The remaining Stellar Wave Infusions needed the help of this Portal being cleared that is shown in these pictures. Each sphere aligns with another sphere until we are completely realigned inside of the Sun.

When we move into our Inner Earth accretion Level - (we are already in that accretion level as of 2014). We are in reality inside of where we think the Earth is in our 3D perception. We are actually seeing the D-4 reality. In reality we must be in the 5D reality in order to perceive the 4D reality. We must have the Sixth Dimensional Frequencies activated in our DNA in order to perceive the 5D reality.

As we went through each of the Stellar Wave Activations and Infusions, I used the formula given to me by the Elohim of Hearing to inhale the Frequencies of each of these Divine Moments.

Holographic Future Music from the Music of the Spheres

The reason that this picture was possible was because I was Exhaling the Frequencies of the Violet Wave Infusion that was sent to Earth through the Stellar Wave Infusion of the Pleiadian Alcyone Spiral and the Activation of the Sirian Spiral.

I collected each of the sets of Activations and Infusions to create the First Song on the **ULTIMATE DNA ARCHETYPE ALBUM**.

The following songs in the Album are using those Frequencies of the Universal Life Force Currents that were sent to Earth through those Stellar Waves to Awaken the Crystal Star Seals in the Body and in the Earth's Grids. When the Seals are awakened, they melt away what was blocking the DNA braiding.

Each DNA sub-harmonic of the overtones and base tones needed to be braided back together. This is what is being done by the formula in the third song titled 6 DNA Consummation. In this song I'm using the same Frequencies that I used to create the Violet Sphere that you see me holding in my hands.

DNA must first go through the process of Initiation of all of the Strands of the DNA of the 4th DNA before the Consummation of the 5th DNA can complete.

In song four, the Frequencies of all of the Stellar Waves are activating the Mid Brain and the Mind of God. Those of you who have learned my Candle Technique, have experienced the art of moving into the full spectrum of light within the candle flame. That is the symbolic representation of what happens when we move our consciousness into the full spectrum of light of all of these Stellar Wave Activations and Infusions from our complete Light Template of those Stars.

Now, we are bringing all of the Stardust into the Mid Brain and the Seed Atom to activate the Pineal, the Solar Plexus, the Kundalini from the Tail bone up the spine. All of these activations of the 15 Chakras take place from bringing in the Stardust Flow from the original Source of Light and Sound in the Cosmic Light Factory.

This Stardust and Pre Stardust Energy is absorbed into the Astral Field around the Body. That Astral Field is what has been blocking the return to our Complete Archetypal Template of the original immortal man. That Astral Field must be saturated with all of the Consciousness from the Stellar Waves sent by the Universal Life Force.

The body must be aligned into the Spiritual Body of the Parallel Universe to achieve Bodily Ascension.

The final song is the Cosmic Massage is bringing the Frequencies from all 15 dimensions of the Earth's Time Matrix into the Body. These are the frequencies that allow the attunement into the full spectrum of light and sound.

by Dr. Angela Barnett – THE DNA DOCTOR
send questions to krystalaimagic@gmail.com
http://crystalmagicorchestra.com

The Tower of Babel

TOWER OF BABEL - THE QUARANTINE FENCE

What has been called the Quarantine Fence of 9450 B.C. created a separation in consciousness in the angelic race line, that made us forget who we really were. Our consciousness was actually divided into 12 fragments, which resulted in 12 groups of people being scattered around the world trying to remember who they were. In order to regain their identities, each of them created a culture and language of their own. We were also separated from our souls and over souls by disconnecting the base tones and over tones of the sub harmonics of our DNA.

This is why this entire process of DNA restoration requires re-connecting these sub harmonics that were broken apart by the frequency fence. The restoration of our consciousness, our memory of who we really are and the activation of 5 DNA are all a part of the same process. The fence can only be mended through our participation in the Universal Life Force Protocol of Stellar Wave Activations and Infusions.

When I was working on my Master's Thesis in Ethnography and Anthropology and Neurolinguistics within the Field of Education to show how Education is only created to justify the validity of the culture, the language and the society that has been created, I learned that the ignorance of all involved in the process of Education comes from this missing fact that all cultures were created as a result this state of amnesia, which began 10,000 B.C., along with the other sets of disconnection from the Mind of God as far back as 5.5 million years ago.

I continued my research six years beyond my masters degrees in four subject areas to complete a Doctorate in Education that provides massive amounts of evidence showing that our true Education comes from a Higher Consciousness outside of ourselves, all Communication is actually Authentic Encounter through Knowing, the courses in the fields of Education are only for the purpose of indoctrination into the given culture, and provide no foundation for learning the true reality that is our divine right to know.

We have been mis-educated for a very long time. The Guardians have begun the re-education of the human angelic race. They began this education through Mary Baker Eddy 200 years ago. They began again with the School of Enlightenment over thirty years ago. They began with Bashar's teachings, Keylontic Science, and several other sets of channeled teachers, who have each gone through the entire Ascension Process themselves.

This education is being shared in the Cosmic Mystery School of the Omniverse teachings to help prepare the consciousness of the world for what the Guardian Races will be revealing to those on our planet in 2017.

It is highly unlikely that our old Education Systems will have much validity after 2017. The actual consciousness that was ours before the Tower of Babel (created by the Quarantine Fence) was the Divine Consciousness of the Human Angelic Race. We had a consciousness that was so in tune with each other that there was no need for language. Our language was the God Language and it was telepathic.

This is how we were separated from our Divine Multidimensional Heritage of being Universal Beings who could communicate with everyone in the Universe, in the Galaxies, and in our own Planetary Systems.

This Quarantine Fence needed to stay in place until the time came when our Solar Merkaba, Planetary Merkaba and Universal Merkaba could be realigned back into the original time cycle when the 12 Stargates could align with the perfect moment of attunement with all 12 Universal Systems.

The mission of the Cosmic Mystery School of the Omniverse has always been to help others learn the true Education of our Universe. It has nothing to do with the Education that has taken place in America or in any other culture. It has to do with the broadening of consciousness to realize that there actually is a reality far beyond what is taught in the schools or in the churches. There is a multidimensional reality that is known through Light and Sound.

This education can only take place in those who tune in to the new frequencies that have been given to Earth and to our Consciousness.

Crystalai has been collecting the Frequencies of Consciousness that have been transmitted to Earth beginning in 1992, which was the year that the Promise of Ascension was made by the Guardians. Crystal Magic Orchestra created **THE PROMISE** album in the exact same time period when the 11:11 Fence was being prepared for removal by the Magnetic Base Tones being sent into the Morphogenetic Consciousness field of our harmonic universe. This was the first layer of frequency attunement needed in order to complete the removal of the Fences in time for the 2017 completion.

So, you see, this preparation of the grand event of The Promise of Ascension has been taking place in several stages for several years. The Cosmic Twins have been involved in this process since day one.

DNA INITIATION THROUGH STELLAR WAVE INFUSIONS

The Frequency Activations called the Stellar Wave Activations and Infusions were sent to Earth through waves of Light and Sound Tones penetrating through the Frequency Fences, as if they were not there. It required a Blanket of Consciousness that was Cosmic to penetrate the Fences and remove them.

Part of the removal process was actually moving the Earth into a higher accretion level. This required moving the Earth to an actual different place in space and time. The Earth was actually lifted above the 11:11 Frequency Fence because the Zetas placed a rip in the Merkaba of the Solar Shield that could not be restored in time. The Earth was removed beyond the Phantom Matrix in December of 2012. This placed Earth in a brand new time line to begin a brand new reality.

CONSCIOUSNESS OF STELLAR WAVES

The Stellar Wave Infusions restored the Universal Primary Consciousness of the Earth's Morphogenetic Field. Each set of Waves and Activations brought one more piece of Consciousness back into the Earth that had been blocked out by the Frequency Fences. The pieces of Consciousness included the Pleiadian, the Sirian, the Arcturian, the Andromeda, Orion, as well as the Solar Field. Each of these fields of consciousness needed to go through a process of Infusing the Consciousness into the Biosphere of Earth and then Activation which went on for several years. Each of these stages took several years.

The piece of consciousness that came to Earth through the Solar Light Fields carrying the Pleidadian Violet Waves and the Sirian Activation in June, 2008, was the piece of consciousness that is required for the activation of the 5 DNA.

The picture of me holding the violet orb shows how this Stellar Wave infusion takes place and how it can be used to activate the 5 DNA. DNA activation takes place in many stages just like the wave infusions and activations took place in many stages and took long periods of time.

Each DNA has 12 sub-harmonic strands that must each go through a stage of Initiation and Consummation within the DNA strand itself. The DNA strand cannot reach its complete Consummation – meaning it's ultimate Perfect State that allows it to begin transmitting the Perception field of the dimensional strand below it, until all of the sub-harmonic strands in the DNA below it have gone through their Initiation process.

So, you see this DNA activation takes a period of time for completion. The reason that many of us on Earth already have 4 DNA or 5 DNA, and yet we do not see a difference in what we perceive, is because we can only perceive what has been completed one DNA below the one that we have consummated.
This means that we actually need to Initiate the 12 sub-harmonic strands of our 6th DNA before we can perceive what has been Consummated in our 5th DNA strand.

ASCENSION DNA PROCEDURE

There is one more underlying element to the Ascension DNA procedure. The Human Angelic Raceline has already been given the GIFT of 24 sub-harmonics. This gift was given by re-uniting the Parallel Universes. Each Universe has a Parallel Spiritual Universe, and each individual has a parallel spiritual SELF. In order to activate the DNA at the 24 sub-harmonic level, the Human Angelic must become attuned into oneness through harmonic convergence with the Parallel Spiritual Self.

KEYS TO BIOLOGICAL ASCENSION

So, there are two parts to Ascension. Anyone who activates their 5 DNA between 2017-2022 will be prepared to ascend into Tara after death. Anyone who activates their 5 DNA through the 24 sub-harmonics of their Parallel Spiritual Self and becomes At One with their Spiritual self either before 2022 can bodily ascend to Tara.

There are other ways to get to Tara. There will be space ships landing in 2017-2022, who will assist in cloning bodies and taking them to healing temples in Sirius B to prepare for ascension. This is the path that was opened to everyone- including Fallen Angelic Races, because of the path opened in 2008 by the Sirian Council and the help of the Cosmic Twins to be the first to carry demonic entities home through that path.

When aDolphino was cloned and taken on the Sirian Star Ship to the healing temples in Sirius B, he was also given the gift of 6 DNA upgrade, which would allow him to ascend to Gaia. The removal of the 6/6/6 Seal is required to return the Immortal body which will never see death.

The mission of the Cosmic Twins was to activate the process of initiation and consummation of the 5DNA for the masses as they began their initiation of the 24 strands of sub-harmonics into the 6DNA strand in 2008. The final consummation of the 6 DNA strand is scheduled for 2017.

Those who go through this process of activating their DNA through the light and sound frequencies that carry the consciousness of the Solar, Pleiadian, Sirian, Arcturian, Andromeda, and Orion, are also activating the light within themselves that allows their bodies to transform into this light energy, as is shown in the picture of the violet orb.

In the near future, human beings will be taking classes in orbing, levitating, walking through walls, telecommunication with entities all over the planet, galaxy, universe and solar system. All of these activities require learning how to turn the body into the light body, which is the essence of what it really is. This requires becoming One with the Spiritual Self. This requires absorbing all of the dimensional frequencies of all five harmonic universes in order to leave the time matrix that these harmonic universes are within.

We have just completed the most difficult stages of our Evolution and preparation for Ascension. 2014 will be the year that is remembered as the turning point in the Human Angelic Raceline Journey to prepare for the return to the 12 Coded Christic Emerald Covenant of the Perfect Universe. 2017 will be the year when the race lines who have been our actual ancestors, soul family and friends from around the Universe will join us on Earth. We will first meet the Inner Earth Eieyani and then the Sirius B Majaraji, and then later, the Azurites and Seres. Many of us will remember our lives as the second seeding of the Seres race line, who were known as the Egyptians, some will begin to remember more and more of the bits and pieces of their past ten million life times as the complete consciousness that was broken in half by the Quarantine Fence weaves back together through the Stellar Wave Infusions and Activations.

In the near future, human beings will be taking classes in orbing, levitating, walking through walls, telecommunication with entities all over the planet, galaxy, universe and solar system. Of course, many of us have already been taking these classes for over a decade.

All of these activities require learning how to turn the body into the light body, which is the essence of what our atomic structure really is. This requires becoming One with the Spiritual Self. This requires absorbing all of the dimensional frequencies of all five harmonic universes in order to leave the time matrix that these harmonic universes are within.

This is the story about the Violet Sphere or Orb that I'm holding in my hands which was created by the D-6 Stellar Wave Activation of Sirius and the completion of the D-5 Violet Wave Infusion. This was the day the miracle of Stellar Wave Activation and Infusion took place simultaneously on Earth. And this is the picture that the Sirian Council wanted me to take. This was also the day that the Fifth Dimensional Dolphins Ascended into the Cloud Cities to prepare the path home to the Violet Sun. That was the date we created the Ultra Violet Blue Sun Album.

The Electric Over Tones of the Sub-harmonics were returned to Earth through the Stellar Wave Activations and Infusions. Over tones are frequencies of Consciousness from our Starry Families of our Higher Selves Original Creation, and Base Magnetic Tones are from our original Root Race Families. Our DNA is made from Over tones and Base tones in the 12 Sub-harmonic strands. Those overtones and base tones were disconnected from specific chakras to remove the immortality from our race line.

The picture show was taken the day the Cosmic Twins were involved in the process of the Stellar Wave Activation and Infusion of the Violet Wave. The Stellar Waves brought in the Over Tones.

We also needed to reconnect the Base Magnetic Tones to Earth. The Base Tones were disconnected from the Earth's Field when the Guardians put up the 11:11 Frequency Fence to save us from Solar Explosions in 1972. Base Tones are the Magnetic part of the sub-harmonics of the DNA and Over Tones are the Electric part of the sub-harmonics of the DNA. Our DNA was disconnected when Frequency Fences were created. There were several of these Frequency Fences over the Eons, and each one placed a Seal between DNA strands.

I am only talking about this one Frequency Fence that was created by the Guardians in 1972-1974. This one Fence was created to keep Solar Explosions from happening on Earth that would have destroyed the planet. The Solar Explosions were a result of the Zeta's cutting a whole through our Solar Merkaba.

The Over Tones that were returned by the Stellar Waves of the Universal Life Force Currents had been blocked by the Quarantine Fence of 9540. So, you see there were two separate Fences that needed to be removed. These Fences were blocking the return of the portal between the Inner Earth and the Photon Belt of Sun Alcyone. When the portal is restored, the flow of Consciousness from above and below – overtones and base tones – can reconnect.

The Cosmic Twins were also involved in the process of bringing the Base Magnetic Tones to Earth to remove the 11:11 Frequency Fence in 1992. That was the date we created THE PROMISE ALBUM.

This is a true story of how DNA Activation actually takes place through the Universal Plan of Stellar Wave Activations and Infusions, followed by DNA strand Initiation and Consummation. The races of Earth are finally reclaiming their reality of their 12 strand DNA construction and returning to the heavenly land of Terra Firma. The per-requisite for this reality is activation of the 5th DNA Strand.

Our Guardians have sent Universal Life Force Currents of Light and Sound Consciousness Waves called Stellar Wave Activations and Infusions for the purpose of activating the DNA. There is no other way to activate the DNA than to participate in these Activations and Infusions of the 12 dimensional frequencies which are inherent in the Stellar Waves.

Stellar Wave Infusions and Activations create the time acceleration shift that is needed to advance the evolutionary blueprint through consciously assimilating these energies into the body. Yes, the wave infusions and activations did take place. No, not everyone consciously assimilated these activations into their blue print that would begin to create better health, vitality, multidimensional awareness, access to knowledge of all lifetimes in all dimensions and immortality.

If the stellar wave frequencies are not assimilated into the body, the time acceleration would create degeneration of the body rather than the re-birth process into immortality.

Those who are on the Ascension Path will accelerate their ability to communicate with the Guardians until complete telepathic communication with the over soul is reached. Communicating with dolphins is one step in the process.

There were Six Waves of Infusion and Six Waves of Activation

The Waves and Infusions came from fields of Consciousness. The D-4 Solar Activation in 2000-2004 together with the Blue Wave Infusion of 2002-2006 caused the Solar Spiral to align with Earth's Merkaba fields. That caused the frequencies of the Earth's Consciousness Field to rise exponentially.

PLEASE NOTE THAT the VOYAGERS 2 book, by Ashayana Deane show that this time line of activations is one of the Three Possible Heroic Futures. There are two different time lines given in that book.

This is the actual record of MY PERSONAL EXPERIENCE of meeting with the Sirian Council who Activated the Sirian Spiral in June 2008. That was one of the time lines in Deane's book.

Next, the D-5 Pleiades Activation of 2004-6/2008 and the Violet Wave Infusion of 2006-2010 increased the Earth's frequencies exponentially again by adding the consciousness of the Pleiades-Alcyone Spiral to align with the Solar Spiral Merkaba Fields.

The third activation took place 6/2008 and ended in 2012. The third activation was the D-6 Sirian Activation. This activation followed by the Gold

Wave Infusion allowed the Sirian Spiral to align with the Pleiadian-Alcyone Spiral Merkaba Fields.

This Third Activation that took place in June 2008 is the time that this picture was taken for the purpose of showing the Violet Wave Infusion and the Sirian Activation simultaneously taking place.

The picture is showing the completion of the Violet Wave Infusion. The Violet Wave Infusion was completing at the same time in June, 2008, that the D-6 Sirian Activation began. I was asked by a representative of the Sirian Council to move to Monterey, in order to be there at this exact moment in history.

The Cosmic Twins were living in Redwood Shores, and had wonderful, well-paying jobs when Zaurak, my Starry Brother from Sirius B, came to our living room in April, 2008, and asked us to be completely moved to Monterey by May, 2008. We immediately gave our resignations and began packing, and started searching for the correct apartment to move into in Monterey.

This is the reason that the Violet Frequency was activated within me as I connected my consciousness into the Elohim of Hearing in Gaia to bring the highest frequencies to Earth through music. When I exhaled this Violet Wave, the 5th DNA completed its activation, which is called DNA consummation. At the same time, the D-6 Sirian Activation began.

This Stellar Wave Activation was required to begin the activation of the 6th DNA strand. The 5th DNA consummation could not complete until the 6th DNA initiation had begun. This is the process of DNA activation.

This process of DNA activation is a huge Universal and Cosmic plan which required the Consciousness of the entire Solar System, the Pleiadian Consciousness, the Sirian Consciousness, Arcturian, Orion and Andromeda Consciousness. These streams of consciousness brought in the Over Tones of the Sub harmonics into the DNA.

Moving to Inner Earth 2017

Those who are in their 5D template will begin their shift into the 5D reality of Tara between 2014 and 2017. Those who still have a little bit of DNA activation needed before they can open their eyes to the new reality of Tara, will be in the New Earth where Earth has already risen into oneness with the accretion level of Inner Earth. Some of you may know Inner Earth as Shamballa or Agartha. All that you know about the magic of these places will appear before you on this Earth as she is transformed through the Light of the entire Cosmic Matrix of 12 Cosmic Light Fields streaming through the Earth and all who are upon her in December. So, you see, even those who aren't completely fifth dimensional will have a wonderful new reality to meet.

Our Blue families from Inner Earth will appear to those who are awakening into their new consciousness. The appearance will be gradual as those on Earth awaken gradually. It is not that they aren't already there, it is just that the 5D perception will be required to see them. New buildings will appear out of nowhere as our vision is aligned through our higher selves to see the new reality. The new perceptions will grow into complete new structures, passageways into Inner Earth will appear, new plants that sing, new birds, new realities of the imagination will grow each day. This group of human consciousness will grow completely out of their 3D perceptions into this new reality of 5D. Those who need help in this process will be assisted by our Guardian Families from Inner Earth.

As the mind rises into the at one ment with the higher self, when the Ego and the Higher Self become One, the third eye perception that allows us to see the invisible and the visible realities around us. The 5D perception is the invisible realm becoming tangible through the multidimensional transition in accretion level. As we transform into the New Earth realities, and the Tara realities, our bodies become less and less dense, the physical forms become less dense, we begin walking above the earth and above the water. The body will find itself in perfect health always. There will be no need for hospitals. The healing centers are for removing crystal seals, aligning DNA strands and transforming the entire biological structure into the silicate matrix.

Those who go into Inner Earth will be transformed by their Blue Families who will use crystal water healing pools, rainbow waterfalls of light energy, crystal temples of healing and other high technologies of transmutation. Our Blue families will assist all who are on the New Earth reconnect into their Divine Blue Print that allows them to engage their souls on Tara and Gaia. Those who already have their 5 DNA strand will have the opportunity to be teleported to Gaia and a few will go on to Aquafaria.

When we wake up from the three day particle acceleration period we will feel a little disoriented, lighter, the atmosphere will feel light, we will soon perceive a different relationship between the water, air and ground. We will feel a different relationship with the Earth and the natural forms. We will realize we are one with all elemental forms and all plants and animals.

The Earths angular rotation of particle spin will be transferred into the rhythm of Inner Earth, Agartha. Those who raise their frequencies into the Earth's higher vibrating pulse will perceive Inner Earth as their new reality. Those who don't raise their frequencies will keep seeing the old 3D

Earth because they are still only carrying that old perception in their minds of their EGO instead of allowing their higher self to allow them to see a higher reality.

The more those on Earth connect their minds into their higher self, their 5D strands, the frequencies of Inner Earth, the more harmonious the three days of acceleration will be. Everyone on Earth will notice that there are massive gamma eruptions, solar flares, earthquakes, electrical interruptions, etc. However, only those who have a low 3D perception will have intense negative reactions to these changes. If one raises their frequencies into activating the 5D that is available to all on Earth, their negative experience will be minimal.

The large catastrophic massive Earth changes will only happen in the event of being located within the frequency field of the phantom 3D matrix. Each individual can remove themselves from that potential of being located in a low frequency area of the Earth by following the direction of their higher self and by removing themselves by transmuting their bodily frequencies above and beyond the 3D frequency fence.

The Earth's grid will be in full alignment with Tara as the morphogenetic filed of consciousness passes into the Earth's bio energetic field by 2017. The Earth will seem the same but better at first to those who are still in lower frequencies. Those will grow more and more in their awareness of something different until their level of accretion is also raised through the frequency fields of the Earth. The entire Earth population will have the opportunity to assemble D5 through D9 and time travel to Tara.

Earth begins intersection with Tara's grid, the Blue Flame will engulf the Earth's atmosphere through Sun Alcyone, the fifth DNA strand will rapidly assemble, the Ego will align into Oneness with the Higher Self. Earth populations will begin a new awakening.

Those of us who are transported to Tara or Gaia will be met by a loving family as well. We will meet teams and guides and we will be given all of the loving support for our new cultural voyage. Those who are preparing to ascend into Tara will be given higher light transmissions that will prepare their bodies through orbing, intergalactic travel, or the opportunity to be reborn into a loving new family in Tara.

Our entire mission of our Beloved Cosmic and Universal and Galactic Soul families has always been to guarantee our safe ascension back to our divine blue print of our Divine Creation. Our Starry angelic families use the Divine Science of Frequency and Light technology to transmute into higher accretion levels of particle base and spin.

We are all beings of light and we always have been. Unfortunately we have gone through 550 million years of trying to ascend back to the time before the Phantom Matrix was created. We were all in some way, through a morphogenetic field of light and energy consciousness, a part of the original idea that Source created when we were the Divine Beings of Gaia, in the third harmonic universe.

Even though fallen angelica completely obliterated the Oraphim race, the races of Tara and all of the consciousness of that matrix, our morphogenetic blue print of our original Divine Idea of Source still exists. That morphogenetic field is the sphere of consciousness that once held our entire 12D Divine Blue Print where all 12 strands of DNA were connected.

We had our Divine Blue Print broken apart by fallen angelic races placing crystal seals between the DNA strands to separate them. Now we are having our DNA reconnected one by one as each stellar activation occurs. Each time there is a stellar activation another avatar is born through the sphere of consciousness holding our original divine blue print. Each time another avatar is born, another piece of our DNA is put back together in our divine blue print. May 5, 2012 the sixth avatar – a 12th level avatar will be born. This is the highest level that can be born on this Earth. This baby will have all 12 DNA strands aligned perfectly into the 12

Divine Blue Print. This birth will create a mass awakening on Earth for all who are tuned in. This birth will allow the activation of the 7th strand to flow through the Earth's core and grids in order to activate the seventh level man on Earth. The seventh is the activation of the pituitary. When the pituitary is in full bloom, we have the mind of God.

Creating Illusions

There will be no trace of the 3D Illusions of this Earth after the phantom matrix is removed. This present Earth has been tampered with in so many ways, to block as much of our reality of our Divine Self. There are crystal seals in our bodies, in the Earth's grids, in the atmosphere, in our oceans, blocking our connection with our Divine Self. Even, this 3D Earth reality is nothing like a normal 3D reality. This Earth is a part of the fallen system that has been completely occupied by and controlled by fallen angelics making people on Earth think they are the grand ascended masters that they are channeling. Now, it all makes sense, why so many wonder why their life sometimes seems like hell.

The death and destruction movie ending isn't going to happen because the frequency fence that

Creating Illusions

would allow that movie to be created will be taken down by the sixth 12th level avatar. The movie ending with the massive Earth catastrophes will not happen. The movie that the fallen angelics were planning to play through illusions painted in our skies will not be allowed to be performed.

The holographic illusions designed to terrify the world was all a part of the fallen angelic plan that was created about the same time the U.S. was formed. The idea had been infiltrated through New Age Channelers for over two hundred years. The fallen angelic signed a peace treaty with our Cosmic Guardian alliance to agree to stop the frequency fence of illusions and to join the good guys. That peace treaty that agreement fulfilled the plan of human race normal ascension about 4000 years from now.

Thanks to the fallen angelics for breaking that treaty, our ascension has been pushed forward several thousand years, plus we will be placed into a time line that is more than 2218 years advanced from where our present consciousness lies when we are transformed into our Inner Earth acceleration and then over 5500 years advanced when we are transported to Tara. Those who are translated into Gaia or Aquafaria is beyond our wildest imagination. Those realities are light years in advance of ours.

Creating Illusions

So, we thank you kindly fallen angelics for forcing our Cosmic Guardians to create a fast forward that would take us far beyond the time and frequency that could lock us out of our divine blue print forever. The time period of the peace treaty of the fallen angelics allowed them to mass infiltrate the minds of many seekers of truth. They could make themselves appear as the good guys through astral projections and entire teachings of their seventh level agendas that would lock humans into the fallen Milky Way galaxy as their new reality. Of course, any reality beyond this 3D reality sounded very interesting, and who would had known that the Milky Way was a Fallen System in itself. We were all born into a system where we thought the scientists knew everything about everything and that whatever we knew about our galaxies was the truth. We thought that getting help from entities who were higher than we were was a good thing. Little did we know, that almost every intergalactic race in our universe is wanting to use us for their food and fuel.

So, all of these fallen angelics had made an agreement to join the good guys, used that time period to trick us, and then they broke their treaty in 2000 and went ahead with their plan to pull us into the wormhole where we would be used as food and fuel.

They used their time period to engage our planet and implant frequency fences that would provide means to create illusions of reality to trick our government and those with innocent minds. They put up sonic pulsation transmitting devices far beyond what we know as HARRP. Their sonic pulsation is performed from intergalactic portals where Nibirian Ships are parked. Those ships are under Stonehenge, England, Bahamas, Canary Islands, Salt Lake City Lakes and a few other locations.

Their first transmission was from Stonehenge to create the fall of the twin towers on 9/11. That was the first step of the Dracos Zetas plan of starting world war three. The Zetas puppets were put in place to instigate the war. The frequency fence was placed on Earth with the help of Zeta puppets creating the 1943 Invisible boat to win the war with Japan, the Montauk project of 1983, and the final frequency fence of 2003 that would allow the creation of the illusions of the Galactic Federation, Mother Mary and Jesus to appear in the skies. In 2008 the fallen angelics created the omega virus to trap indigo three children through the combination of the net of chem trails and other neuro transmitters through inner space. Finally in December 2010 they tried to force the reverse of the sphere of amenti to make a pole shift happen. The starry families spent all of 2011 creating a strategy to remove that reversal which completed in the world war three in the heavens between June and October of that year.

Now we have entered the final stages of removing all of the karma that is disconnecting us from all of our past lives and soul selves. That karma is being removed by the gamma and solar and all energies coming from the sun. The crystal seals are being melted away by stellar activations and we have been given every opportunity to engage our 5 DNA to engage in a perfectly harmonious transition into TARA. Meanwhile the Zetas continued to build their own drama of the reality that they would like to engage. They abducted children and parents to gain access to DNA codes that would allow them access to our star gates, and through channelers of mis information. The three frequency fences would cause enough damage to Earth's merkaba fields that it would guarantee that destruction of Earth and human populations if our Guardians did not shift us forward 2013 years beyond the time matrix that would had ended the existence of the human angelic raceline.

The Truth Shall Set You Free

THE TRUTH THAT SHALL SET YOU FREE CHANGING FROM THE AKASHIC RECORDS TO THE EKASHA RECORDS

The **ETERNAL LIFE ALBUM** is a personal HEALING SESSION. It could be likened to what would be expected if one of you went to a Reiki Healer or Sound Healer for healing sessions. It could be likened to having eight hours of healing sessions per day for a week.

To order your **ETERNAL LIFE ALBUM** go to crystalmagicorchestra.com.

It is similar to AKASHIC RECORDS reading because it is the created by Entities of Pre Light and

Pre Sound working directly through the original Divine Blue Print of the ORIGINAL IDEA of MAN MADE IN THE IMAGE AND LIKENESS OF GOD.

This divine blue print of the original structure of the HUMANOID form made in the Infinite VOID of Source Consciousness was made ETERNALLY PERFECT.

In contemporary AKASHIC RECORD readings, the readers have been using a formula that is based on the 8th dimensional harmonic. Those Channelers are taught to go 8 inches above the head to connect with the Akashic Records. Those Channelers are also taught to move their Consciousness into the Earth to absorb the Consciousness that will align them into the Frequencies of that person whom they are doing the reading for.

In the NEW EKASHIC TEACHINGS, the EKA is the Pre Light and Sound Creation Field of the Spiritual Creation Phenomena of Light and Sound Creation. The Eka is the Spiritual Parallel Universe of the Veka Universe.

The REQUIREMENT for Biological Ascension is to become At One with the Spiritual Self. We become at one with our Spiritual Self by absorbing all of the Light and Sound from the Eternal Light Field of all 15 dimensions of the Earth's Matrix and then Blend that Light and Sound into the Full Light and Sound Spectrum of the SPIRITUAL EARTH's Matrix.

The difference in the OUTCOME of AKASHIC RECORDS readings and the EKASHIC Records of the Eternal Life Spiriutal Parallel Self is the Pre Light and Sound Frequencies that are collected from this complex interdimensional Electromagnetic Sound Field contains the PERFECT FREQUENCY SIGNATURES of all of the Selves that you have ever been.

The AKASHIC RECORDS searches for those Patterns in the Life Times of the Old Souls that have recorded your journies in one or two of your lifetimes.

The EKASHIC SESSION aligns you back into your Spiritual Self in all Dimensions, in all lifetimes in the planetary, solar, galactic, universal and cosmic time lines of your existence.

We must complete this alignment back into the ALLNESS and the ONENESS of all that we have ever been in order to perform the REBIRTH into the AKASHIC RECORDS of the ORIGINAL PERFECT Man made in the image and likeness of God. We must use this Complete Formula that moves the Physical Body completely into the Ascension Portal of Pre Plasma Light and Sound Vapor or Crystal

Liquid Light Vapor, in order to allow our Cosmic Template to re-create our original perfect bodies.

When I create the **ETERNAL LIFE ALBUM** I first go to Source Consciousness field and ask Source to hold the 12 coded divine blue print of the individual (the name of the person who ordered the ETERNAL LIFE ALBUM) inside the flame of eternal life creation that the idea was originally made from. (This name Frequency Signature is obtained differently than it is in the old teachings of the Akashic Records because the Akashic Records Channeler is only searching for one lifetime of that Soul Essence).

The Formula that I was given to create the ETERNAL LIFE ALBUM was given to me by a Cosmic Team who knows everything about everything five years before it happens on Earth. The Consciousness with whom I am communicating with me already knows everything about each person's infinte lifetimes even beyond the 5.5 million years in the Earth's Matrix. They often prepare me to create albums before the order is made. They direct me to create orders without knowing the name of the person. The person's NAME is the FREQUENCY SIGNATURE of this Life time of the Soul and only this lifetime.

The Consciousness of the COUSHIC records created from the EKASHA Field of Spiritual

Reality is a Phenomena that is very similar to the AKASHIC RECORDS; however, the Records are actually movies of all of the Lifetimes of an Individual within all 15 time matrixes within the 15 dimensional time matrix of the Earth.

So, we are talking about the Etheric Essence of Spiritual Reality at the moment of creation from the Mind of God who creates a new reality every nano second.

The old AKASHIC RECORDS create a light portal from 8 inches above the head and then into the Earth's records.

The NEW KEYLONTIC SCIENCE teaches the Healer to connect Consciousness 36 inches above the head into the Cosmic Field of Pre Light and Pre Sound of the 14th and 15th Dimensions of Heliotalic Silver Pastel Violet Flame Creation Energy. This field of Consciousness is Perfect, Always has been perfect and always will be perfect.

When the EKA Body is being connected to within the Earth, we take our Consciousness down into the Earth's Crystal Heart deep within her Vortex and then travel deep within this funnel into the 13.5 Cosmic Core of the Earth's Iron Core. This places the Light Portal of the Akashic and Coushic Records through the Vortex and into the Consciousness when the breath is exhaled. Whereas the old Akashic Records were found in the Earth's Iron Core of a Fourth Dimensional Realtiy Field, we must travel deep within the Vortex into the Stargates that are a hub into all realities.

When the Akashic Reader helps the patient to find the Life time that has created a continuous problem in their life, the answer that is found is an answer that comes from the Astral Realm. When the practitioner attaches consciousness 8 inches above the head, they are moving into astral consciousness. That Consciousness is only 4th dimensional substance that contains all of the problems that exist on Earth. So, of course it is easy to find the source of our problems in that layer of Consciousness.

In the method of using the ETERNAL LIFE Frequencies of Consciousness, we are not searching for the problem, we are returning the PERFECT SELF that we were created to be. The problems that were placed in the Astral Field were placed there to keep us locked inside of the Earth's Matrix.

The Frequencies in the 14th and 15th dimension were created to give us ETERNAL LIFE.

We are each made in the image and likeness of Source. That image and likeness is a negative of the picture of the idea that Source is creating. That idea is held within Source Consciousness and rebirthed into creation every trillionth of a nano second. When the brand new image and likeness is imprinted on the idea, the idea is reborn as a brand new image with the new thoughts and ideas of the new experiences encoded within it.

I hold that idea within the Source Flame. That idea is already perfect and it contains the 12 coded divine blue print of angelic raceline.

That old idea that was created billions of years ago must go through a rebirth at this time. We are all being reborn into a new harmonic universe, a new space and time portal. Each time we are born we come into the planet through a stargate. Many of the stargates attached to Earth were destroyed and we were disconnected from many of them. Now, we are being placed in a different time portal where we are back in alignment with all 12 stargates, which allows us to obtain the 12 sub-harmonics in each of our chakras.

These 12 sub-harmonics comes from combining the spiritual coding from the chakras outside of the physical body with the chakras within the physical body. In order for an entity to return to a place in the universe, there must be an essence or a frequency signature of that entity left in that place from the time the entity left the place in the universe.

In order for our bodies to become realigned into the eternal life domain of the harmonic universe, I take the idea or the image that is within the Flame of Source and create a light body image of that idea. I place that idea within a flame. I use a candle flame. Within the flame is the complete spectrum of light, the entire rainbow. The flame includes the hertzian, infra red, visible light, invisible light, x ray light, and gamma waves. The idea is held within the complete spectrum of light of Source Consciousness.

That idea that is whole and complete walks through the candle to the other side and returns back with the connection of frequencies of the spiritual side - the blue body self. The idea becomes complete as it connects with the blue body.

The idea must also be taken in to the Inner Earth realms of the Cosmic Domain. I take the idea into the Etheric Core of the 13th dimension and then into the 14th dimensional of the Spiritual Etheric Heliotalic Light Domain of the Cities of Light, the Inner Earth, and then down into the Crystal Liquid Light, the Mirror light of heliotalic frequencies. This is the location of the Etheric Star Formation that was placed around the area where Earth is located now. That Star Formation is called Urtha.

This idea within the Source Flame must have its frequency signature implanted within the Cloud

Cities, Cities of Light, the Star Formation, the Aquafarian Realm of Urtha. The idea does not exist there because most of us haven't been there before. This place was created by the Aquafarians from the Aquinos Matrix millions of years ago as a refuge and an escape chamber for this time. Since we were never there before, we must leave an imprint there so that in the future we can go there.

Crystalai and aDolphino went to Aquafaria to leave this seed of their frequencies. However, when they went there, they were met by a family who took them to a crystal palace. They were told that they built this palace for them long long ago and it has waited for their return. So, there are in fact, a few of us who have been there before. That is why it is necessary to link frequencies of those who haven't been there before through the frequencies of those who have been there.

When the client is being put through the eight hour healing sessions, the old damaged codes within the chakras are transformed by having the frequency signatures of the individual returned to the original perfect divine imprints. This coding is imprinted in each of the chakras to align the 12 sub-harmonics of the perfect raceline back into the individuals template.

Each cell in our body is supposed to contain this divine blueprint that was created in the image and likeness of Source. As the clients idea body is taken into the crystal liquid light of Inner Earth and into Urtha, the heliotalic frequencies emerge from the skin and the skin becomes the shining.

The healing takes place from the within, beginning with the blood crystals transformation, the bones turn into sound frequencies and the skin turns into light.

Each one of these steps of transformation takes a great deal of focus, alignment into the allness of Source Consciousness, a continuous holding of the idea within the flame of transformation. Each time I focus on one specific aspect of the entire healing of the body, there is one tiny little breath involved. Each time I can feel and hear that the breath is perfect and the healing is complete, I record that breath.

I layer each of the breaths of transformation for that one specific individual into my recording mechanism. By the time I am finished, I usually have five hundred or more breaths. Next, I weave these breaths into the formulas and frequencies of codes of attunement that the Guardians and Source direct me to. Each individual is given a different set of codes and formulas. These codes come as frequencies and I breathe them. Some times they are heard as tones of God Language and sometimes they are pure breaths. Each recording comes out very different.

   I am giving this guideline to help my readers understand why this item costs the price it does. I am sure that there are not any Reiki healers out there of any reputable nature that would give you eight hours of healing sessions for three, four or seven days in a row for this price.

   Once a client returns from a Reiki or Sound Healing clinic, that healing will sometimes last a day or a week, if the client is lucky. That is because the old Reiki technologies are based on the Chi of an energy that has been blocked from Source for eons of lifetimes. Taking an energy that has been broken from Source at the Cosmic level and trying to do the repair work at the Planetary level just does not fix the problem.

   This problem that is blocking our eternal life system happened billions of years ago, and the guardians have been working on fixing it for billions of years. There are many problems in each level of creation, far beyond the chakras within the body. The frequencies must be realigned clear out into the Universal Spheres, Cosmic Spheres, pre sound and light realms and the allness of Source's original idea of creation.

So, we are talking about a healing that would last as long as a band aid, or one that is complete and lasts for eternity.

Ascension -Connection between Consciousness and the body. Ascension isn't just about being a good person, going to church and getting forgiven by Christ and then going to heaven. It isn't that easy because there is a direct link between the consciousness of your spirit and the atomic structure of the body.

The part of the spirit that is embedded into the atomic structure of the body is called the JARI. It is a part of the spirit body. If the JARI is trapped inside of the atomic structure at death, the body will not ascend. It will continue to be trapped on the Earth and will continue to return. This is what we did for the last ten million life times. Our JARI has been stuck inside of our atomic structure.

We must make sure our Jari is free from the atomic structure in order to ascend out of here.

We must transmute our spirit body out of the atomic structure in order to ascend. Once we have done that so many times that there is no quantum left in the body to ever ascend out of it, the person has entered the path of FALL. That person will need to return to Source through space dust return -ashes to ashes dust to dust. That is what would had happened to this planet and everyone on it if we hadn't been given the assistance of the AQUARI Matrix.

The path of Fall means the person just won't remember anything. They will return to Source and start over again.

In a normal system that is not in Fall there is an eternal flow of energy giving an eternal source of eternal life.

So, we take this perfect formula of creation and rebirth that was given to us by the Guardian Races and we record it because it is made of Frequency Signatures. The breaths carry the frequency signatures and they are recorded in perfect harmonic convergence. Each of the frequencies transmutes into the highest frequency of Source Consciousness in order to hold that reality of the divine code for ever.

The songs within the **ETERNAL LIFE ALBUM** each contain specific frequency signatures, dimensional portals, weaving and braiding of codes and tones from the Cosmic, Universal and Galactic light and sound that align DNA into the rainbow bridge of the full spectrum of light in order to lay the foundation for the transformation into the multidimensional 12 DNA template.

The words UMa A TrI Ena A EKASHA

are the God Language that connect our perfect Illuminated Light Body into At One Ment with our Pre Light and Sound EKa Spiritual Creation.
When we say these words, and when I sing these words on your albums, I am creating the at one ment with the 14th dimensional pre light and sound of creation with the pineal gland in the brain.

The Sun image which is the 8th dimensional Consciousness actually exists at a 23 degree angle that would stream into the forehead and into the throat area. The 8th dimensional frequency activates the thymus, thyroid, seed atom and mid brain.

When the Candle is used, the Full Spectrum of Light of all 15 dimensions is activating the mid brain. That is why the Candle turns Blue. When the Brain shifts into Frequency Specific, it begins seeing in Infra Red, it is seeing the other side of reality- the spiritual invisible light spectrum.

Each section of the album streams in hundreds of different breaths from Cosmic Angelic Consciousness through the ELOHIM OF HEARING to draw together 12 sub-harmonics into each DNA strand, and then 24 sub-harmonics and then 48 sub-harmonics. Each of the sub-harmonics represents one frequency signature of the Individual in their reality in this time matrix and the parallel of this time matrix and the spiritual parallel and the parallel of that time matrix.

Each of the Frequency Signatures is woven together through the specific codes and tones to lay the foundation that activates the rainbow bridge into Source Consciousness.

The Etheric Frequencies are the Eternal Life songs sung by Cosmic Entities including Aquafarians and Elohim Angels to describe how they create kingdoms through the magic of light and sound. The songs are braided through the frequency signatures of all five spheres and fifteen dimensions to lay the foundation into the 24, 36, and 48 DNA Consciousness.

The next layer of breaths lay the foundation that connect consciousness into the 15th dimension of co-creation and manifestation. Breaths of Source are ignited when Consciousness has lain the foundation through Christic and Cosmic Frequencies.

The Ascension Program of Eternal Life Programming

Eternal Life Programming SHIFTS the cellular memory from a Mortal Based Program to an Eternal Life Program -

Personalized Frequency Realignment, Re-attunement and Reactivation into MULTIDIMENSIONAL CONSCIOUSNESS

When I send your Eternal Life Album, there will be AT LEAST 12 sections. The sections are sometimes 12 songs, but not always.

Please realize that when I am creating the album for the individual I am being led through the Individual's Akashic records and their original Spiritual EKA- spiritual Coushas records. We have always had a parallel spiritual universe, galaxy and self.

The process of Biological Ascension is the attunement into AT ONE MENT with the complete original Spiritual Self. That image is created in the MIND OF GOD as a Breath of Source and then formed into an IDEA in the 14th dimension of the Silver Pink Heliotalic Creation Lab. When the Earth's Sun, and all Seven Suns of Creation are formed into a new idea, they became the 8th Sun. When We attune into all that we were in the original Sun Alcyone of the Andromeda Creation, and then tune in to the harmonic universe five where our re-birth occurs, we have activated all of the TRANSFORMATIONAL ELECTRO MAGNETIC SOUND TONES that create the BRAND NEW YOU.

This process of attunement involves my Consciousness, which has already been trained to receive all Frequencies from the Elohim of Hearing, to follow a program and a process that involves connecting with the Consciousness of each of the 12 Stargates. Basically, the 12 songs INCLUDE the Morphogenetic Consciousness of the 12 Stargates.

What are the 12 Stargates? The 12 Ascension Portals of each of the 12 parts of Consciousness of the original Angelic Human Raceline. We originally had One Mind. We were originally the Cosmic Oraphim Race Line. Aligning our Consciousness now into all Five Harmonic Universes, all 7 Cosmic Suns and all 12 Star gates is the BASIC FORMULA of our Ascension.

Our Cosmic Light Councils were the creators and originators of our Race line and all other Race Lines who have agreed to help realign our Consciousness back into its original perfect form. They guide the formation of the Breaths in the Holographic Future Music, and they guide the exact Individual Eternal Life Albums creation.

The reason that the albums contain God Language, Star Language, the Stellar Waves from the 12 Star gates, and the Holographic Formation process of the Cosmic Light Councils from the Spiritual Parallel Universe, is because we are breathing in the Stardust ESSENCE of the Original Creation Substance, which has always been called Consciousness in Metaphysical Teachings.

The Original Perfect Idea from Source that we were created from has always existed and will always exist. However, our Divine Template was broken in half because of major Universal and Galactic mutations created by reverse spin technology of light and sound.

Each creation - human, planet, galaxy, sun, star, universe- is created from the formula of the Merkaba mechanics. The Cosmic Entity whose name was Metatron created this great Cosmic technology which held the entire universe in perfect harmony balance and alignment.

However, there were other Entities who learned this exact creation science and decided to use it for the opposite reason. There were Fallen Angelic Races who had broken themselves off from the Eternal Life Source Creation Template, who then needed to find their Source of Life from other Planets and humans.

The most recent example of this was the rip placed in the Solar Merkaba Field of Planet Earth. That rip was created by the Zeta Rigelians to control Planet Earth. The rip was placed in the Merkaba Field that held the Earth in the correct alignment with the Sun. When the Earth is out of alignment-- even 13 degrees out of alignment- with one of the other pieces of the harmonic universes, the Planet and the Race Lines on the Planet are no longer in alignment with the Mind of God or the Divine Template of their Creation Formula. The rip in the Merkaba Field of the Sun would had caused Mass Destruction of Planet Earth between 1972-1974, if the Guardians had not placed the Frequency Fence around the Earth.

If the Guardians had not created the 11:11 Frequency Fence that blocked the Base Tone Magnetic Pulses from the Earth in 1972, the Earth would had been blasted with huge Solar Explosions as huge as a State. The plan of the Zeta Rigelians was to create a rip in our Merkaba Field that would allow them to travel inter-dimensionally into our Consciousness to control us and to suck our the Life Force Energy from our Consciousness.

That was once piece of the problem. There had been Seven Major Fences created for similar reasons over a period of about five million years. Each one of these Fences created a blockage in our DNA sub harmonics. The blockage created by the 11:11 blocked our Base Tone Magnetic Pulse Rhythm.

The Seals were actually created by the Guardian Races to keep our Race Line from being completely obliterated during each of the attempted take overs.

The Guardians could not allow the removal of these Seals until our Race Line was placed in a Zone of Consciousness where there could be no more Invader Race Take Over attempts placed on the planet.

The Guardians had a deadline for securing our alignment. If they did not have the Seals removed before December 2012, the Zeta Rigelians would had been able to complete their original plan, and the Draconians would had been able to complete their One World Take Over Plan that was backed by the portions of the Ashtar Command, Galactic

Federation and many other groups who have pretended to be Friends of Planet Earth over the Centuries.

The first part the plan required to remove these Seals was completed in 2012. There were Six Avatar Children Born through the Earth's Portals without those Seals in their DNA. There were another 5000 Indigos born with the 6th DNA activated at birth and the potential of 8 DNA by 2017.

In addition to those requirements, the Guardians needed to bring in the Consciousness of the 12 Star gates. This was achieved by Six Stellar Wave Infusions and Six Activations from the Solar Spiral, Pleiadian Alcyone Spiral, Sirian, Andromeda, Orion, Lyra, as well as Inner Earth and Rainbow Spirals.

Each of these Stellar Wave Infusions was also responsible for Infusing the Light and Sound of the Consciousness of each of these Star Gates into the DNA sub harmonic strands. There were 12 sub harmonics in each DNA that needed to be Infused and Activated.

I am explaining these details because these are the same waves of consciousness that I breathe into each and every one of the Individual Eternal Life Albums.

The Ascension Program of Eternal Life Programming

There are various Albums that have one aspect of the Consciousness needed for the Ascension Process. The Six Avatar Children's Consciousness Frequencies are in the Complete Perfect DNA Activation. The Stellar Wave Infusions are completed in the **ULTIMATE DNA ARCHETYPE**, however, there are a series of these activations in the Parallel Universe Set, Universal Life Force Set, Mother Ship, Dolphin Therapy, Violet Flame, and Symphony of Love.

There are many other pieces of the formula included in each of these other Sets. For instance, the Violet Flame focus is on the moment of Pleiadian Infusion and Sirian Activation. The Symphony of Love was the moment that the Music of the Spheres sang the new Song of alignment of all 12 Star gates. The Heavenly Dolphin Therapy was the moment the Fifth Dimensional Dolphins became the Sixth Dimensional Dolphins. The Mother Ship contains the frequencies of the Cosmic Blanket that was wrapped around Earth by our original Cosmic Ancestors who have waited for this moment of awakening for 5 million years. The Cosmic Blanket is holding Earth in balance until she morphs into the Ascension Earth.

Each one of these moments in the history of the Music of the Spheres alignment into the the original Symphony of Love which held all of our sub harmonic harp strings within this Cosmic Orchestra that sings together through the alignment of the Harmonic Universes is an essential part of our Ascension.

WHAT IS ASCENSION?

It is basically removing all of the Fences that blocked our DNA sub harmonic strands from braiding together.

It is raising our Frequencies of Consciousness into a new reality.

Frequencies are raised by Lifting Consciousness up into the Five Harmonic Universes through the guidance of the Elohim of Hearing, the Cosmic Councils, the keepers of the Akashic Records and the Eka Records.

Ascension means becoming totally At One with your original Spiritual Body through the activation of your Spiritual Template within you.

What is a Spiritual Template?

It is scientifically created from pre light and pre sound which is the pre stardust, pre plasma essence of spiritual water called hydrolaise.

The Ascension Program of Eternal Life Programming

In the Normal Planet, an entity would be born and then spend the first 33 years of their life absorbing more and more of this spiritual substance that was called prana and manna and many other names. Now we call it Hydrolaise, because it is the scientific formula of changing our entire biological and chemical structure of the Earth and out bodies.

The album Eternal Life Waters holds the frequencies and the journeys for this part of the Ascension Journey.

There were many other steps to the Ascension Journey before we got to the Eternal Life Waters. The Stellar Waves exist partially in the Eternal Life Waters albums, as do the Dolphin Frequencies, the Mother Ship frequencies, the Avatar Children. BUT only PARTIALLY.

The focus on one aspect of the Cosmic Consciousness at a time is the same as an artist who is painting the new Universes, the new Galaxies and having to align every single light particles within each of the 12 Star gates and each of the 15 Spheres of the Music of the Spheres together.

This process began earlier in 2007 with the creation of entire albums of just the Cosmic Consciousness, and just the Ascension Portals, Vortals, Vortex, and the basic God Language.

We began with these basics of Ascension back in 2007. They were contained in the Ascension Workshops given at that time. There were many steps and stages of the process into 2012. Those who were on active duty of holding these frequencies in alignment with the portals of the Earth were the Cosmic Dolphins. All of the albums created have been created with these Cosmic Dolphins called the Oraphim Braharama Cetacean Family.

The albums that contained dialogs between the dolphins and the Inner Earth Aquafarians were recorded on Magic Dolphin and Cosmic Consciousness. The conversations with the Sun as the first Frequency Fence was coming down is in the Ultra Violet Blue Sun and in the Cosmic Butterfly. If you look through the purchase CD section you will find the complete history of Frequency Activations that happened on Earth between 1992-2014. Most of the activations between 2012-2014 are on mp3 only. Those will be updated to CD's in the near future.

Each section focuses on one part of the complete alignment into SOURCE. The focus is always Source. We must align every cell through the micro omnions of Source and weave every particle into the Source Frequencies in all fifteen spheres of the Matrix. The Sun, is in a way, the creator of the Universe, because the Sun holds the IDEA of Source in the form of he Plasma that holds the crystal liquid light of Source. Each form of creation

- Cosmic, Universe, Galaxy, Solar, Planet or Person is always made from the original divine blue print template of Source.

When I send your Eternal Life Album, there will be 12 -16 sections, plus about ten minutes of pure AURORA FLAME energy - Cosmic Crystal Liquid Light- The Flame of Source Creation Energy. Each section focuses on one part of the complete alignment into SOURCE. The focus is always Source. We must align every cell through the micro omnions of Source and weave every particle into the Source Frequencies in all fifteen spheres of the Matrix. The Sun, is in a way, the creator of the Universe, because the Sun holds the IDEA of Source in the form of he Plasma that holds the crystal liquid light of Source. Each form of creation - Cosmic, Universe, Galaxy, Solar, Planet or Person is always made from the original divine blue print template of Source.

That template is manifest simultaneously in millions of density levels. The Sun holds the template in the form of Plasma and creates Light Bodies. However, the reality that all forms of density allow all to become One, allows us in Reality - to live within the Sun. This is why we think of the Sun as our Creator. The Sun holds our individual templates that were made by Source. However, our frequency signatures and divine templates must always flow into our planetary matrix through the suns matrix. So, this is why the Sun is thought of as the Creator. We haven't experienced this reality of living inside of the Sun yet, because our Matrix was destroyed. Now, it is being re-created in its divine template once again.

One of the objectives of the frequencies, which they naturally do themselves, when the breaths are from Source, is to realign the base tone rhythms within the entire time matrix. This process of rhythmic alignment of the Earth into the New Earth greatly affects the rhythm of body, which must always stay in rhythm and in tune with the Planetary Matrix that it moves within.

Please always keep in mind this rhythmic pattern that you will learn to hear with practice. The rhythm is within the breaths themselves. When I breathe from Source and record layers of those breaths and then breathe from Cosmic Consciousness and record layers of those breaths, there is a rhythmic pattern appearing within the breaths. When I breathe the Universal and Galactic frequencies there is another rhythmic pattern. Each time I record more frequencies, I always re-saturate them with Source Frequencies to re-pattern the rhythms and the frequencies into absolute ATTUNEMENT with the Crystal Light Frequencies of Source Consciousness.

The Ascension Program of Eternal Life Programming

1. Feel the plasma flame surrounding the body and penetrating every cell in the body. Listen to the rhythm of the pulsation and waves from the plasma flames. Feel the dancing waves swirling around the body and swimming into the atoms. Feel the plasma swimming deeper and deeper into the etheric funnels within the cells. Feel the funnel of energy pulling the wave deeper and deeper until it disappears.

Listen for rhythms and work on moving your body to this beat.

2. Listen to the frequencies and feel the overall pull into the attunement with the highest frequency of Source.

The base tones are created by layering all 15 spheres of the Music of the Spheres. Each of these spheres is filtered through the Breath of Source to create a brand new time matrix - Cosmic Time Matrix.

Each breath, each frequency contains the light and the sound - the radial atomic light that oscillates at the highest spin rate and the sound that vibrates at the highest frequency. The sound is the idea and breath of Source and the Sound is the resonating field activating the idea into manifestation.

The saturation of the Source Frequencies causes the entire rainbow of the 15 spheres of light and sound to burst into a flame and create a new set of spheres within a new cosmic matrix. This is the same process that the body goes through when it turns into light and reappears a nano second later as a brand new form. This rebirth process happens every nano second. The body will just keep reappearing to look the same as it did before, until the new frequencies of transformation are realigned into the body.

The process of the Individual Eternal Life album is to alter the entire cellular structure from the inside out as well as the Light Body and Crystal Body and Etheric Bodies which contain the Radial Body, which is the sphere of energy that is like an atomic mirror surrounding the body. That atomic mirror is also being transformed into the original 12 coded divine blue print that allows the new body imprint to be seen as the new reality around the body. That reality is projected from the mid brain projector creating reality through the pineal gland.

So, much of the work I do on the Eternal Life Album is the restructuring of the mid brain through activation of the God Seed Atom within the Thymus that will burst into a cloud of crystal plasma dust and activate the streaming of crystal liquid light directing from Source Consciousness. This allows the MIND OF GOD to be reconnected into the mid brain for the beginning of co-creating through frequencies of light and sound.

Number 2

Breaths for clearing all miasms from physical and etheric bodies that are blocking the flow of the 12 sub harmonics into the physical body.

Number 3

Weaving the spark of Light of original creation breath of UMA UN (meaning the Illuminated Body from the Spark of Source Consciousness) into the AUM Breath (meaning the Return to Oneness with Source).

Number 4

Deep clearing through an almost complete silence with pure white light breaths. So pure they become attuned into Oneness. Listen deep within to the silence of clear clean stream of attunement with the Crystal Liquid Light Flow from Source into the Mid Brain, the Crystal Heart and into every cell of the body.

Number 5

Spinning your Merkaba - The Merkaba made of two triangles is the symbol of the Frequency of

The Ascension Program of Eternal Life Programming

Source spinning in Oneness with its creation. The three pointed triangle pointed up and the three pointed triangle pointed down. One layer is black which represents the 11 dimension and one is white - the 12th dimension. Together they represent the silver seed atom meaning the oneness with Source. So, there are two layers of the triangle on top and two layers on the bottom. That is three points over three points on top for six points and three points over three points on the bottom for six points. In reality the merkaba will appear three dimensional not two dimensional meaning one side is pointing forward and one side is sideways. This creates a triveca merkaba that allows us to move up and down as well as sideways. We must be able to move side ways to enter Inner Earth.

The top half of the merkaba always spins clockwise and it spins at 33 1/3 ratio. The bottom half of the merkaba always spins counter clockwise and it spins at 11 2/3 ration. The spin rate creates the 45 degree repositioning of the body within the 360 sphere of creation. We always spin a sphere around the merkaba at the clockwise spin to represent this 360 sphere that our merkaba spins within. This is the true sacred geometry of the Christ Mathematical Frequency that realigns us into the 12 coded blueprint.

The first Merkaba is 27 radius from the center of the body, creating a 54 inch radius.

The second Merkaba is ten foot radius. The third is a sixty foot radius and the fourth is a one hundred foot radius.

The third merkaba is the Cosmic Merkaba that keeps us firmly in alignment with the planetary cosmic balance and prepares for slide into inner earth. The fourth Merkaba takes us clear into Source and allows us to float in the Aurora Fields as we prepare to walk through the star gates.

Number 6

Bringing the light frequencies out from the etheric body and into the skin and then out to about two inches around the body to create the shinning around the skin. Activating the density one - subconscious atomic light mirror and the density two sound frequency field to resonate into manifestation the mirror of light.

Number 7

Absorbing complete template of the body Coushic Body. The body is floating in a Cosmic Tear Drop. Activating the Akashic Flame in the Pineal Gland and Activating the God template within pineal, thymus, solar plexus into the tail bone which is the 15th chakra and then streaming up the spine into the medulla oblongata at the top of the spin and into the God Seed Atom within the Thymus and up into the mid brain.

Number 8

Connecting crystal heart, which is the Soul Center - the 8th chakra- deep within the Thymus. Connecting into the Pineal Gland to reconnect Super Conscious Mind of 4,5,6 into subconscious and ego in 1,2,3 in order to deactivate the EGO and allow Super Consciousness to guide through frequency specific attunement.

Number 9

Creating Continuous EirA flows (Crystal Liquid Light directly from the Mind of God) into Frequency Specific Communication with Higher Self- Soul and Over Soul and eventually Avatar Self.

Focus on Seed Atom in etheric part of Thymus. Create a cloud of Plasma, and watch the cloud grow larger and larger until it surrounds the entire chest and head area. Breathe in the frequencies and exhale into the plasma cloud until you feel your head area within the Soul connecting your Mind into Communication with Soul and Over Soul- dimensions 4, 5, 6, 7, 8 and 9.

Number 10

Awakening connection to Aquarius Matrix. Aquafarian Elementals begin swimming through liquid light within DNA to create streams of communication to activate the 12 sub harmonics within chakras 1-5 to create continuous communication and activate light fields of perception.

Number 11

Breathe the new frequencies into the Light Body and imagine or watch the Body become lighter and lighter until it begins to levitate. Imagine changing the frequencies into a new standing wave pattern that has no gravity.

Number 12

Cosmic Merkaba extends out to 54 feet around the body. Places Consciousness into the Cosmic Matrix of Eternal Time. The Body Template is completely aligned into the 12 dimensional Krist Grids of the Earth's Divine Template and with the Inner Earth's Cosmic Template..

Number 13

The Frequencies connect to the Aurora field which allows consciousness to walk through the star gates of Inner Earth and step completely out of this time matrix.

Feel the plasma flame surrounding the body and penetrating every cell in the body

Number 14 and beyond

Make a mini me version of yourself that is small enough to hold in your hands. Visualize it very clearly, take some time to visualize and feel every feature of your face until you know you are present.

Allow all of the frequencies from the Flames of Source Consciousness fill every cell in your body. Now inhale all of those frequencies into your heart chakra area and then exhale down your arms and into the palms of your hands.

See a flame coming out of your palms.

Place the mini me version of yourself in your palms. See that mini me become wrapped in those FLAMES. The flames contain the complete MIND OF GOD, the COMPLETE BLUE PRINT OF MAN, the Original Flame of Creation that created the original perfect divine template called man.

Watch your mini me transform into any likeness you would like it to be. It can be younger, healthier, more energetic, healed, perfect, whole, complete, genius, wealthy, ready to orb, levitate or become invisible.

Whatever you can clearly visualize your mini me doing, your body will do the same. You are the creator now.

OVER ALL LISTENING PROCESS

STEP ONE:

While listening to the frequency signature breaths,

1. Concentrate on seeing a mirror image of your Divine Blue Print or your spiritual light body absorbing into your body from your back.

2. Feel the frequencies penetrating the cells in your body from the inside to the outside.

3. Feel the frequencies awakening the spark of Source that has been left to sleep deep within each cell in the body.

4. Feel the frequencies uniting into Oneness with the Soul, which is a sphere of blue crystal frequencies waiting directly below the heart area.

5. Feel the Soul awakening to what it has been waiting for eons for you to discover about your self.

6. Feel your physical body as a mini-me tiny figure, and place it inside of the blue crystal sphere which is your Soul. Feel the Soul frequencies and the spiritual self frequencies combining into a new symphony of harmonic rhythms.

We will call this the Attunement Body.

STEP TWO:

1. Feel the spiritual light body from the spiritual self from the middle domains of the Cosmic Core of Inner Earth uniting into Oneness with the physical etheric body from Inner Earth.

2. Feel the frequencies weaving those two bodies - one more etheric and one purely spiritual - into your Attunement Body.

STEP THREE:

1. Next, feel the frequencies of the spiritual self from the Divine Aquarius Galaxy Matrix outside of the Earth's Matrix.

2. Feel the frequencies of this Starry Divine Blue Print pulling the frequencies into a higher domain of consciousness.

The feeling is more etheric and yet more powerful. It has a majestic feeling and includes the frequencies of the Aquarius Galaxy, the stardust of Ursa Major and the Consciousness of the Ascension Teams.

STEP FOUR:

1. Next, feel the frequencies from the more etheric physical self in the Aquarius Galaxy being woven into the heart of Sun Alcyone.

This is the frequency of the original divine self created through the spark of Source and breathed into humanoid form. We are re-connecting our selves into the original frequencies of our Divine Birth. That Divine Essence still remains in the Crystal Heart of Sun Alcyone, and is reflected through the Crystal Heart of Mother Earth and through our own Crystal Hearts (the crystal heart is actually the blue-violet crystal fuzzy sphere that sits directly below the physical heart).

STEP FIVE:

1. Feel and absorb the frequencies of your spiritual twin selves woven into and through Aquarius, Terra, Ursa, Inner Earth and the Heart of Sun Alcyone.

The Ascension Program of Eternal Life Programming

You are listening to the actual frequency signatures of each of these spiritual divine selves that you were and which you will be again as soon as you absorb these frequency signatures. This is the true formula for creating a vortex that connects the individual physical selves with their spiritual selves into the knowing of your allness and your Oneness. This is the true formula for opening the Halls of Records, which are in essence the frequencies of the Music of the Spheres.

However, this frequency signature has been disconnected from the forms that it has taken during the past eons through a tragedy that was never supposed to happen in a Divine System. This tragedy can be removed very easily by listening to the frequencies of your Music of the Spheres in your Individualized Immortality CD.

You are a beautiful star made of these frequency signatures of light and sound. When all of these frequency signatures are woven back together into their original starry, magnificent harmonious symphony of Love, you become a star who is ready to co-create through Divine Mind any reality that you desire.

STEP SIX:

It is imperative that old forms that you have been using are completely removed from your life. If you have been listening to any other healing music or using any of the other forms of New Age type pendants and crystals with other entities' frequencies breathed into them, or anything that might have lower frequencies, remove them. There will be many people in the near future becoming very sick and even going insane as we enter the later time lines of the evolution into the ascension because they do not start this process early enough. Just know that you are doing it the correct way.

VISUALIZATION

First Visualize the Frequencies as a Light Portal that connects 36 inches above the head and down into the Crystal Heart of Mother Earth.

Draw a picture of this area. See your body standing on the Earth and draw a circle from 36 inches above the head of the body down into the center of the Earth. Realize that the place in the Earth is in the Cosmic Realm - not the Planetary.

See that Circle around your body and into the Earth's Cosmic Realm as the place where all of the Frequency activation takes place.

You are keeping your self wrapped inside of a COSMIC FIELD OF ENERGY.

This is the place where your Cosmic Merkaba would Lock you into At One Ment with the Source Field of Love.

Before you begin listening to the music, draw this picture, and visualize your self standing within this Cosmic Sphere. This is the Cosmic Sphere that the Music is LIFTING YOU INTO.

NEXT

Before you begin listening, create a mini me of your self, and send that mini me up to 36 inches above your head.

Become that mini me. See yourself sitting in a Lotus Blossom with your legs crossed, 36 inches above your head.

Stay there while you are listening to the music.

The music contains the frequencies to lift your physical body up to the Consciousness where your mini me self is sitting.

Focus on filling your body with the frequencies while you are sitting in the Lotus Blossom.

NEXT

Stay 36 inches above your head.

1. Listen and focus on the frequencies of light in the stomach area.

2. Listen and focus on the frequencies of light in the crystal heart.

3. Listen and focus on the frequencies of light in the tailbone.

4. Listen and focus on the frequencies of light in the back of the neck.

5. Listen and focus on the frequencies of light in the center of the head - pineal gland.

NEXT

Continue to remember to bring all of the light and sound into a ball of light energy and see it being breathed into the stomach, crystal heart, tailbone and pineal gland.

VISUALIZE this as ANGELS OF LOVE PLAYING HARPS inside of each of those Key Areas. They are connecting each cell in the body to the MUSIC OF THE SPHERES that sings us into PERFECT SPIRITUAL TRANSFORMATION.

NEXT

Stay 36 inches above.

Feel a crystal star two feet above the head. Allow all of the frequencies in the music to fill that crystal star until you see the star spinning and you see sparkling stardust flying from inside of it. Next, bring the star full of Christ Consciousness Star Dust into the head and the heart, and the tailbone and the feet.

See that crystal star spinning sparkling stardust into every cell in the body.

Feel each cell in the body filling with stardust, which contains the Divine Blue Print of the SOURCE template.

Repeat this while visualizing the stardust as an even more ETHERIC substance of a vapor like stardust.

Repeat this while visualizing the stardust as the pre plasma vapor of Spiritual Water.

When the Body is filled with this pre light and sound Vapor called HYDROLAISE (Spiritual Water), the Body Transforms into the Light of Christ.

VISUALIZE your body becoming Full of Light until it is Glowing from the inside to the outside.

While absorbing and feeling the frequencies stream through every cell in the body, see or feel a white light portal connecting from the pineal to the crystal heart down through the feet and into the core of mother earth. Feel the angelic frequencies connecting you into the frequencies stored in Mother Earth that contain your cellular memory of your original spiritual self made in the image and likeness of the god self, Christ self and the spark of Source co-creative energy.

Feel the frequency of Divine Love, Divine Life, Divine Truth, Divine Mind, Soul, Spirit, Intelligence, Principle Victory Power Manifestation, Supply and the Divine Plan. These are the Frequencies stored in the Core of Mother Earth in the Cosmic Realm of the 13th Dimension. Continue to connect the frequencies of consciousness into the Body Template areas and the vortex areas. This will progress the activation of the DNA.

VISUALIZE YOUR BODY

The body is standing deep within all 15 spheres of Consciousness or within all Five HARMONIC UNIVERSES.

Each Harmonic Universe has thousands of Suns containing tons of STARDUST- pre-stardust of that Crystalline Vapor called Hydrolaise.

Feel the frequencies of all of the millions of suns stream into the head, the heart and every cell in the body.

Feel the frequencies of the inter-dimensional angels, divas, and fairies singing and dancing into your cells and into your consciousness.

Collect all of these frequencies into your cells to activate the cellular memory of your original divine self -- your immortal self that has the ability to live for ever, create the hearts desires and heal instantly.

Ascension Meditations

1. YOUR frequency signature woven into the star gate

2. Guided Meditation of feeling the iridescent 14th dimensional heliotalic body beaming from inside of your skin. This is preparing the body to shift from the proton to the neutron chemicalization.

3. Next, the spiritual body of the 15th dimension that has the 15th dimension that has absorbed the mirror image of the Divine Template from Source comes into the body completely

You are entering into the mirror image of your spiritual self. You are soaking up the frequencies of your Divine Template of the true spiritual self. The silicate crystal matrix body is made of pure star dust from the Breath of Source.

The cleansing continues from Sirius B sending the crystal liquid light into the body to cleanse all ideas from the cellular memory of the body being material.

The body is being completely transformed into the spiritual. The body is in the stage of being a cocoon. It is preparing its transformation of the body turning into a new chemicalization or a new form. The body is changing from a cocoon in to a butterfly.

The body is transforming from a carbon based structure back into oneness with the crystal silicate star dust based form.

The spirit body is completely in your material body now. The transformation process will continue until 2013 when the Earth's atmosphere has also transformed into a new chemical structure that provides the proper amounts of nitrogen for the body to transform into the new silica form.

The Earth must transform its atmosphere into three parts nitrogen and one part oxygen from the present carbon dioxide - oxygen base. The body must transform into rations of highly copper, zinc, with much less iron from the present form of high amounts of iron, zinc, copper. This reverse has already begun, but will mostly take place in 2012-2017.

3. The meditation on number three is repeated twice for the purpose of solidifying the process.

4. Frequencies of the 14th dimensional heliotalic iridescent silver pastel pink and violet light and sound is woven into the 15th dimensional crystal liquid light and star dust. This chemicalization provides the gelaisic transformation of he body

into a majestic new being who is naturally immune, doesn't get sick. heals instantly, has special abilities such as moving things with the mind and manifesting desired realities. Later the body becomes able to become at one with its light body and become a blue orb. Finally, the body will become etheric enough to walk through walls.

5. Yamu, Shamu, Kamu jam, Shamu.

Each of the five spheres - Cosmic, Universal, Galactic, Solar and Earth spheres have names. Their names are used in this mantra along with the formula that pulls all five spheres into Oneness. Each sphere has rings of crystal light, crystal dust and crystal gel that are also transforming into oneness. The higher frequencies of the base tone of the fifth sphere pulls into the overtones of the fourth sphere to create a new resolute tone. Simultaneously, this process is taking place between the fourth and third sphere, the third and second sphere and the second and first sphere. All five spheres merge into one new tone of home. This is the process of ascension through the music of the spheres.

This mantra includes the names of the spheres, the activation codes, the activity of consciousness creating this activity of ascension in the Earth's Matrix and the Frequency signatures of all of the dimensions. Your personal frequency signature has been added into this formula of ascension.

6. The Christic Ascension Codes activates the spark of Source in the Crystal Heart area, head area and tail bone area in this Christmas Art Song. Once again, I wove your frequency signatures into this Ascension Formula. These three points connect the body into the real spiritual body. Parts of our pineal gland were de-tacked and connected into the tail bone area to stop our spiritual growth. This formula realigns the cellular activity within the body to flow properly.

7. The guidance meditation is repeated to help reinforce the memory of aligning completely into the iridescent body, light body and silica based stardust body into the physical body.

The cord of life is connected from the spiritual body into the physical body through the heart for the purpose of the body connecting the new heartbeat or pulse of spiritual reality.

As the body dives into the crystal liquid light, the body becomes transposed into the morphogenetic field that allows entrance into other ascension halls.

The body rides the waterfall as it connects in Oneness from all frequencies from Sun Alcyone into the Sun of Inner Earth. All suns of the Universe have gathered together with Sun Alcyone to create the New Base Tone frequency that will pull up and transform all suns into Oneness.

As the body rides on the energy of the sun beams and absorbs the liquid light energy it is igniting the energies with the 144 petals of the lotus blossom. These 144 petals are the individual frequency signatures of all that you are combined into Oneness.

As you ride the lotus blossom into the core gates you are riding on a star gate that aligns all dimensions into one new stream of crystal liquid light energy that allows ascension through this star gate.

The body is taken into the etheric crystal chambers where crystal pillars of all of the colors of the rainbows are singing the tones of home of all 12 angelic councils The songs contain the tones of home, the symphony of Love, the key to the universe.

Uma Un means the Illuminated One or the spark of Source ignited into a flame. This is the stardust that the angels breathe their consciousness into. Each individual breath of creation becomes a Soul and a body of Stardust.

8. The music of the spheres is contained within the Crystal Chambers of Inner Earth where all 12 angelic councils sing through the large crystal pillars.

The Ascension Program of Eternal Life Programming

The original light and sound of your creation. The angels who breathed consciousness into your stardust from the spark of Source are now singing your entire New Consciousness of all you are and all you will be into a brand new symphony of love.

These angel songs are weaving you into the star gate that will allow you to join mother earth in all stages of her ascension back into her most perfect state of stardom.

This will bring you to the time of 1000 years of Golden Harmony and peace. The time of heaven on Earth. The suns frequencies of Sun Alcyone plus all suns of the galaxies of this universe are pulled into the Christic or Universal Frequencies. The universal is pulled into the cosmic egg known as mother marry.

You are wrapped within all of the frequencies of the five spheres of Cosmic, Universal, Galactic, Solar and Earth.

You are entering into the Womb of Mother Earth.
The 144 petals of the lotus blossom contain 12 selves or 12 dimensions. Your entire divine blue print of Universal Consciousness.

There is a rainbow spectrum of light in the cathedral of cosmic frequencies which carries the complete Consciousness of light and sound. Your frequency signatures have been woven into this spectrum of light and woven into the angelic choirs of all 12 angelic councils. All angels are singing from these crystal pillars to create angelic Cosmic Frequencies that align through the star gates.

You are floating in your lotus blossom. You are absorbing these angelic frequencies reuniting with spiritual self, becoming all you really are. You are blasting through the core with the 13th, 14th and 15th dimensional Cosmic Core of Mother Earth.

You float into the Aqua etheric liquid light inner domains of Mother Earths heart.

The cosmic core of Inner Earth is the crystal heart of mother earth. Our crystal heart is also deep within the etheric chambers of each cell in our bodies. Each cell has an etheric center that reaches into the spark of Source, the mirror liquid core of our spiritual body.

The crystal heart area of the body is directly below the heart-near the spine area. This crystal heart is actually our soul. The soul is a blue crystal fuzzy spheres of crystal dust, light and gel. The soul contains the memory of all that is stored in our etheric halls of records of our eternal self hood.

The soul is awaiting our consciousness re-connection to our spiritual body in the star gates of inner earth.

In order to ascend we must connect our crystal heart to mother earths crystal heart and then connect into the sun Alcyone's crystal heart. We must reemerge into our oneness because that is who we really are.

We were originally created in the heart of sun Alcyone through the Omniversal consciousness that transforms our perfect blue print through each stage of our transformation.

We have never stopped being that perfect divine blue print. We just had our rainbow bridge that connected our neuronets of our DNA strands temporarily erased. We must reconnect these DNA strands back into all that we really are.

The DNA doesn't just suddenly appear as 12 DNA in the third dimension. We must become fifth dimensional in order to see the 12 DNA because it only exists in this higher frequency and higher states o consciousness. It can't be seen in a microscope because it is etheric.

The process itself of aligning my consciousness into your higher selves through the Elohim of hearing and the Omniversal team and then weaving and braiding all of your frequency signatures into your spiritual twin self in this matrix and in the parallel spiritual matrix.

The alignment into Oneness is already complete even before you receive your music.

That first clearing process of aligning the frequency signature of all 144 selves into the lotus blossom and connecting you into Oneness with your Universal Divine Template only begins the process of connecting that spiritual self with you twin spiritual self in the Cosmic Cores of Mother Earth and your spiritual twin in Sun Alcyone.

Now that the light body's are connected completely into your Cosmic selves of your purely etheric self you are once again reignited through the spark of source into your original flame of divine love the activity of oneness with Source Consciousness.

As your light body is lain upon the spiritual mirror of your image and likeness of God or Source, the eyes and ears or the Divine Mind becomes the third eye of your knowing. This is the beginning of your Consciousness awakening to who you really are. This process of awakening is continued in the blue crystal etheric chambers of the liquid light.

The Ascension Program of Eternal Life Programming

Each of the 12 angelic tribes or councils resides within one of these grand crystals pillars which are enormous in size. Each of the 12 angelic tribes has a frequency or tone that they sing or breath into you When they sing all of the crystal pillars sing as light flashes and sparkles and crates rainbow and then the rainbows dance and weave together as if they are harmonizing a celebration of a new birth . When the 12 pillars have woven together into a pattern, that new pattern of light and sound is you.

When you return to earth from the cosmic domains of inner earth you are connecting all that you re in the cosmic domain into oneness with the earths atmosphere. Each time you breathe, you are breathing the divine atmosphere of the symphony of Love. Your existence is creating a star gate fro m Sun Alcyone, through Sirius B Adashi temples into the rainbow crystal pillars of the chambers that hold the frequencies of all that you now are.

The Individualized Eternal Life albums will each contain some of the god language codes of co-creation and transformation. Some of them will be heard clearly and others will be woven into higher frequencies so that they are not heard at all, but they are still there. Each individual has different requirements. Some individuals will need the words spoken more clearly, while others will have the words completely melted into the breaths of Source. The frequencies of words are always lower than the frequencies of pure Source Consciousness. The god language codes are the highest frequencies that words can still be heard in this dimension and in all dimensions.

Uma un will be heard quite often. The meaning of this god word is illuminated one.

Kee ra shay is the primal sound field between cosmic consciousness and Source.

This god word is used in many activations.

EirA, ManU and ManA come to the foreground of the music. Next allowing the mind to combine focus of the fifth spheres of co-creation with the EirA or vision in the pineal of the New Earth and golden Galaxy and all that personally means to you.

Next, that vision is pulled into the crystal heart for the gestation period of the ManU and finally the vision of the co-creator is exhaled in the ManA of creation.

Many of the other codes of creation are in the background of this music to help mold crystal gel and crystal dust into the forms that are directed and created by the Elementals by the formulas contained in Divine Consciousness.

The words man U and ManA are used frequently meaning the inhale of the idea of creation and the exhale of creation. Sometimes I breathe the god word man U for a very long time in order to give the idea that is being created a very long period of gestation. We need to hold the idea in mind, paint it in our consciousness while we remain in the high frequencies of Source.

The god word AUM – meaning, I return to Source as the Perfect Sound and Light Body. The sun's portal has opened up the Ascension Portal to return to Source. The top of the head may hurt for awhile as your physical body completely rises into oneness with the spiritual light body.

Uma Un is the final activation of the Eye of god – the third eye of creation. The pineal gland actually becomes the third eye. This is a mirror projection that allows the creator to see the vision in this movie camera and then to make God's movie.

The activations take place in the pineal, the lower tail bone and the heart center.

These three centers become corrected, realigned as the suns realign, and our consciousness connects to this alignment through these frequencies and codes.

The tail bone is the seat of creation that will reactivate the creative functions of the lower five bodies. The breath realigns the tailbone with the heart center, and then flows up to the pineal and down through the feet and twelve inches below into our re-connection with the Earth.

We become one with our earth body and ready to ascend together. We create heaven on earth through this connection. This is the first time that spherical alignments will allow this complete alignment that goes all the way into the earth and then back up into the knees. There will be a tingling sensation in the feet as they realign as pillars into the Earth.

The crystal cells become awakened from the crystal cell center outward into the pineal – the crown and down into the feet- the body lights up like a light bulb and we become the new energy on Earth. We become the light bulbs of our new pranic creation of energy as we connect to the Starry Brother's electromagnetic funnels lifting us into our Islands of Light We can now begin spinning forward into our new realities of our immortal selfhood.

Our true energy is in the core of the Earth. The sun in the earth connects through our bodies frequency currents and we can connect light into a light bulb or just into the room without a light bulb. I have asked the Inner Earth Scientists to live with me in my home while they teach me this technology.

ACTIVATION CODE 1 - PINEAL

As you listen to the song, inhale the frequencies and exhale them into the pineal.

If you want, you can also read these tones out loud to yourself as the music is playing.

The Activation codes for the pineal are:

Da HA NO Ma TA
Da HA NO Ma TA
HE Ta OR
HE Ta MA

ACTIVATION CODES 2 - TIP OF THE TAILBONE

As you listen to the song, inhale the frequencies and exhale them into the tip of the tailbone. If you want, you can also read these tones out loud to yourself as the music is playing.

The Activation codes for the Tip of the Tailbone is:

En Na HA ET ta TA HO
Da HA et ta TA HO
DE Ta MOR
DE Ta MOR A

DE SA DO
De He Ta MOR
DE HE ta MOR
DE HE ta MOR YA TA SO la
Uma UN
Uma UN
Uma una Uma Un

The entire process of Illumination has always been a natural result of the true divinity that always has been available to the images or entities that source created. The Illuminated One is man returning in the divine state that allows ascension.

Man was made in the image and likeness of God – or Source Consciousness.

This great Source contains the crystals, the light and the energy and the perfect formulas of creating from Source of Light and Sound.

Purchase Now or Read More
http://store.kagi.com/cgi-bin/store.cgi?storeID=6FGAR_LIVE&page=Indiv_Immort_Album&lang=en

The Frequency Attunements in the Eternal Life MP3

Removes Seals from Chakras ALLOWING CONNECTION TO ALL 12 DNA through activation of 12 sub harmonic frequencies.

Melts crystallized miasms on Pineal, Sex Organs, Heart Chakra.

Melts crystallized miasms producing CANCER throughout body.

Turns Frozen Crystals that create Cancer into Crystal Liquid Light Flow of 12th dimensional creational fluids.

Aligns Crystal Light Flow of Consciousness into God Seed Atom in Thymus.

Turns Frozen Crystals that create Cancer into Crystal Liquid Light Flow of 12th dimensional creational fluids.

Aligns Crystal Light Flow of Consciousness into God Seed Atom in Thymus.

Activates VIOLET Blue Light Screen in Mid Brain.

Activates the Code of Edon to open the Diamond door into Source Consciousness to flow directly into the Mid Brain.

The 12 sub harmonics are activated in the four sets of three chakras.

Breath always activates the Lotus Body in the 14th dimension to activate the Pineal, God Seed atom, Heart Chakra and Solar Plexus.

Every Miasmic Distortion in each chakra area is cleared and aligned into the 12 Universal Chakra through the 13th Cosmic Chakra and then through the 14th dimensional heliotalic frequency.

MEDITATIONS AND JOURNEYS TO USE WITH YOUR ETERNAL LIFE ALBUM

These meditations are recorded on the Ascension Portal Kit.

The Ascension Program of Eternal Life Programming

ZERO POINT BODY MEDITATION

The complete Spiritual body that has been blocked from angular distortions in the streams of light consciousness coming into our Mother Earth's Matrix can now be completely restored. The breaths of Consciousness of all of our Starry Families can now be connected into our consciousness as we become ONE with our original gods who created us in the Aquarius Galaxy.

That spiritual body may now be retrieved and permanently placed into the physical body. This is possible for the first time because of the work our Dolphinoid families have completed, as they have realigned the electric circuitry system of all light and sound to braid into streams of turquoise and aqua blue light and to become activated by breaths of consciousness of the sounds of our new creation. This spectacular light and sound is streaming down form our family in Aquafaria.

1. Activate the Light Body by first creating a crystal light sphere in the Crystal Heart area and placing a mini-me of yourself inside the sphere.

2. Next let that mini-me grow into the size of your full body.

3. Picture your body laying on a mattress of golden magnetic energies

The Ascension Program of Eternal Life Programming

4. Imagine riding on this magic magnetic mattress inside of an elevator that goes down into the center of the Earth.

5. Next, slide down a waterfall of rainbow colors into the liquid light portion of the Earth's Core. See a rainbow of golden dust sparkle around your body.

6. Float on the mattress into a crystal light, a crystal dust and crystal gel area of etheric substance. Continue to float in this pastel iridescent golden and rainbow dust and light area. This is the 14th dimension.

3. Watch as Mother Earth places over your golden crystal dust body, a White crystal light sphere-garment of white light rainbow pastel. Feel this garment on the body.

4. Take one more step down through the Earth's Core until you feel like you in the very center of Mother Earth's Heart. Walk through Mother Earth's Crystal Heart. Merge and become one with all of the frequencies of her Heart. See the sparks in your crystal heart and in her crystal heart ignite into a flame and braid their streams of liquid light frequencies together in to braided rainbow colors.

5. Step through the Diamond Door in Mother Earth's Heart Center and walk in to the spiritual side--the etheric side- the golden dust side.

6. This Diamond Door separates the physical side of earth from spiritual side of earth.

7. See your Rainbow Garment of Light Merge with Spiritual Essence when Spiritual frequencies come into both the Iridescent Light Body and Physical body.

8. Become with your golden crystal body in the Silica Matrix of Mother Earth's Heart. Become one with the Breaths of Consciousness of Mother Earth.

The LIQUID LIGHT CLEANSING continues over and over The cleansing can be placed on automatic pilot to continue all night long as you sleep see a pearly white frequency streaming down into the crystal heart. See the pearls of wisdom from all that has been created in this 3D density melt into Divine Wisdom of all that was ever created by Divine Minds. Allow the wisdom from the pearl in your crystal heart to also contain the wisdom of all others on this 3D realm to be melted into the Sparks of Source and melted to be reformed by the pearly white frequency that streams liquid light energy to lift all from the crystal heart to be rekindled into a higher frequency of liquid light frequencies of Galactic and Cosmic Consciousness.

ONENESS

Weaving Oneness allows us to absorb the frequencies of all fourteen dimensions and weave them into our own crystal heart, our head and our body and then wrap these frequencies around and through the Mother Earth's Body and Crystal Heart. Next, we extend our frequencies into the 15th dimension and wrap all of these frequencies and consciousness around Mother Earth and through Mother Earth until our frequencies become ONE. This state of Oneness would weave together all that we ever have been into all that we ever will be.

All of 144 selves in each of the fifteen dimensions are woven together into ONE GRAND NEW CONSCIOUSNESS that can now fully Merge into all that Mother Earth was created from as Cosmic Consciousness, Galactic Consciousness, and all that she has evolved into after falling from her Divine State and returning to it.

WEAVING INTO ONENESS

Bring the Crystal Star Merkaba into the Head and then into the heart.

Ride inside of the Merkaba to collect and distribute frequencies inside of all of the cells in your body and then spread and connect that new energy into all five spheres.

When the frequencies from all Five Merkabas are collected and pulled back into the Crystal Heart, the body will become One with the Planet, Universe, Galaxy, Solar System and Cosmos. Our Galaxy will become the Golden Galaxy.

Once our bodies and minds are re-calibrated into Oneness, by infusing frequencies and energies from all of the 5 spheres, the music of the spheres begins to sing through the crystal cells of the body. Our crystal cells will learn to sing in rhythm and in tune with our Divine Compliment, which is contained in the Earth's Core. Each crystal cell contains an entire creation grid, an entire memory containing the eons of lifetimes in each dimension.

LIFT OFF

We can create the fuel and the energy in our Merkaba Bodies which are our Space Ship Bodies to gain lift off from this dimension. Our body is now the Proton Body.

We gain lift off by adding the Neutron o the Proton. We can create the Neutron by collecting the frequencies of the 14th and 8th dimensions and allowing the Merkaba to spin at the speed of light to transform this energy into a Neutron that is brought into the Merkaba Body. The Merkaba can glide down into Mother Earth's Core and collect all of the eternal substance of Mother Earth and of our own Golden Crystal Bodies that were left there. Next, we create two bands of helium energy that spin at the speed of light and place them in our crystal heart. As we sit in the Earths Core and allow the Merkaba to spin at the speed of light, we also allow the rings of helium to spin within each other at the speed of light clear out into the Cosmos. See the rings spinning clear out to touch the stars in the sky on each breath as they spin. The speed of light energy is that fast. We would touch a star on each breath. Feel the sensation of expanding and disappearing into the Standing Wave Pattern of the Cosmos. The Merkaba can then be taken to the core of the Earth as we merge into oneness with Mother Earth.

GOLDEN MERKABA

We become One by expanding our Self into the Golden Merkaba of all five spheres.

Each one of these Merkabas contains our complete self who has a crystal heart. The crystal heart contains all of the elements of Source in each Sphere. The elements of Source in each Sphere must be collected together into One Crystal Heart, into One Grand Self, into One Golden Merkaba.

We start with the Merkaba of this Sphere. We bring all of the frequencies of this sphere into the crystal heart. We create a miniature self inside of the Merkaba.

The Merkaba realigns the density of our Cosmic Body. As the planet and Cosmos realigns their rotation of particle spin - or density of consciousness - so does the body realign to this less dense form.

NEUTRON CREATION FORMULA NEUTRON MEDITATION

Neutron Meditation creates the electromagnetic spin required to connect the Neutron to the Proton in order to become a Light Body. The seals from the Eye of Manifestation melt away and return the divine right of manifestation when the solar energy completely enters in to the eighth and ninth portals of the inner head area.

The Ascension Program of Eternal Life Programming

Learn how to transform energy into a Neutron and align every crystal cell in the body with the neutron that transforms the carbon based body into a silica based light body.

Begin the transformation of the body into an immortal temple of crystal light energy.

The LIQUID LIGHT CLEANSING continues over and over.

The IRRADESENT Body is shining brightly now. It has been charged fully with Krystic Templates from the Balancing Portals of streaming braids of light and sound that has been amplified by Dolphinoid Starry Brothers are preparing us to remember and return.

HEAR THE CRYSTAL CELLS BEGIN TO SING

Inhale from tail bone collect metallic sparks back into tail bone feel warm sensation.

Inhale from CRYSTAL HEART a light from tail bone comes up to CRYSTAL HEART and then light splits one light goes down to bottom of feet and one goes up 18" above head.

THE ASCENSION PROGRAM

crystalmagicorchestra.com

Each Individual has been on this five million year journey of performing the re-birth of a race line which was the most cherished and sought after raceline in the Universe because it contained the gateways to all of the Universes. We had our orbing ability, our telepathic ability and our Eternal Life Ability of our original Race line stollen from us, and now we are learning how to reclaim it.

The purpose of all of the Future Holographic Music at CrystalMagicOrchestra.com has been created through the Consciousness of the Guardians, the Cosmic Councils, the Akashic Keepers, the Makers of Light and Sound of the Fourteenth Dimension, the Sirian Council, the Oraphim Council, the Taran Council, and all others who have been working non stop to perfect our Divine Templates within each one of us for millions of years.

This Divine Plan only contains harmony and support and love of all others ideas. This is how the Kingdom of Heaven is formed. We braid and stream our individual frequencies of consciousness into complete harmony with all other streams of consciousness. Ideas are actually Frequencies. When those who have learned to speak in WORDS will begin to speak in FREQUENCIES.

The Angels Breathe their Consciousness of Light and Sound one idea at a time. They stream millions of beautiful harmonic ideas. Regardless of how many streams of light energy they exhale through our breath, they all blend together harmoniously. This is how we return to the ATTUNEMENT with our Grand Consciousness of Source.

The key to unlock mystical secrets of enlightenment. This key is a vibratory tool that allows the brain to secrete liquid light energy through the body. This liquid light is the key that unlocks the diamond doorway to the Future Self. It is the future self that is already lined with the iridescence of rainbow light of the fourteenth dimension, the spark of white light of Source Consciousness that ignited Oneness between the Co-Creation Consciousness of the 15th dimension and one step beyond into the 16th step or the step beyond the Earth's Matrix.

The Ascension Program of Eternal Life Programming

The ETERNAL LIFE ALBUM is a personal HEALING SESSION. It could be likened to what would be expected if one of you went to a Reiki Healer or Sound Healer for healing sessions. It could be likened to having eight hours of healing sessions per day for a week.

When I create the ETERNAL LIFE ALBUM I first go to Source Consciousness field and ask Source to hold the 12 coded divine blue print of the individual (the name of the person who ordered the ETERNAL LIFE ALBUM) inside the flame of eternal life creation that the idea was originally made from.

We are each made in the image and likeness of Source. That image and likeness is a negative of the picture of the idea that Source is creating. That idea is held within Source Consciousness and rebirth into creation every trillionth of a nano second. When the brand new image and likeness is imprinted on the idea, the idea is reborn as a brand new image with the new thoughts and ideas of the new experiences encoded within it.

I hold that idea within the Source Flame. That idea is already perfect and it contains the 12 coded divine blue print of angelic raceline.

That old idea that was created billions of years ago must go through a rebirth at this time. We are all being reborn into a new harmonic universe, a new space and time portal. Each time we are born we come into the planet through a stargate. Many of the stargates attached to Earth were destroyed and we were disconnected from many of them. Now, we are being placed in a different time portal where we are back in alignment with all 12 stargates, which allows us to obtain the 12 sub harmonics in each of our chakras.

These 12 sub harmonics comes from combining the spiritual coding from the chakras outside of the physical body with the chakras within the physical body. In order for an entity to return to a place in the universe, there must be an essence or a frequency signature of that entity left in that place from the time the entity left the place in the universe.

In order for our bodies to become realigned into the eternal life domain of the harmonic universe, I take the idea or the image that is within the Flame of Source and create a light body image of that idea. I place that idea within a flame. I use a candle flame. Within the flame is the complete spectrum of light, the entire rainbow. The flame includes the hertzian, infra red, visible light, invisible light, x ray light, and gamma waves. The idea is held within the complete spectrum of light of Source Consciousness.

That idea that is whole and complete walks through the candle to the other side and returns back with the connection of frequencies of the spiritual side- the blue body self. The idea becomes complete as it connects with the blue body.

The idea must also be taken in to the Inner Earth realms of the Cosmic Domain. I take the idea into the Etheric Core of the 13th dimension and then into the 14th dimensional of the Spiritual Etheric Heliotalic Light Domain of the Cities of Light, the Inner Earth, and then down into the Crystal Liquid Light, the Mirror light of heliotalic frequencies. This is the location of the Etheric Star Formation that was placed around the area where Earth is located now. That Star Formation is called Urtha.

This idea within the Source Flame must have its frequency signature implanted within the Cloud Cities, Cities of Light, the Star Formation, the Aquafarian Realm of Urtha. The idea does not exist there because most of us haven't been there before. This place was created by the Aquafarians from the Aquinos Matrix millions of years ago as a refuge and an escape chamber for this time. Since we were never there before, we must leave an imprint there so that in the future we can go there.

Crystalai and aDolphino went to Aquafaria to leave this seed of their frequencies. However, when they went there, they were met by a family who took them to a crystal palace. They were told that they built this palace for them long ago and it has waited for their return. So, there are in fact, a few of us who have been there before. That is why it is necessary to link frequencies of those who haven't been there before through the frequencies of those who have been there.

When the client is being put through the eight hour healing sessions, the old damaged codes within the chakras are transformed by having the frequency signatures of the individual returned to the original perfect divine imprints. This coding is imprinted in each of the chakras to align the 12 sub harmonics of the perfect raceline back into the individuals template.

Each cell in our body is supposed to contain this divine blueprint that was created in the image and likeness of Source. As the clients idea body is taken into the crystal liquid light of Inner Earth and into Urtha, the heliotalic frequencies emerge from the skin and the skin becomes the shining.

The healing takes place from the within, beginning with the blood crystals transformation, the bones turn into sound frequencies and the skin turns into light.

Each one of these steps of transformation takes a great deal of focus, alignment into the allness of

Source Consciousness, a continuous holding of the idea within the flame of transformation. Each time I focus on one specific aspect of the entire healing of the body, there is one tiny little breath involved. Each time I can feel and hear that the breath is perfect and the healing is complete, I record that breath.

I layer each of the breaths of transformation for that one specific individual into my recording mechanism. By the time I am finished, I usually have five hundred or more breaths. Next, I weave these breaths into the formulas and frequencies of codes of attunement that the Guardians and Source direct me to. Each individual is given a different set of codes and formulas. These codes come as frequencies and I breathe them. Some times they are heard as tones of God Language and sometimes they are pure breaths. Each recording comes out very different.

I am giving this guideline to help my readers understand why this item costs the price it does. I am sure that there are not any Reiki healers out there of any reputable nature that would give you eight hours of healing sessions for five to seven days in a row for this price.

Once a client returns from a Reiki or Sound Healing clinic, that healing will sometimes last a day or a week, if the client is lucky. That is because the old Reiki technologies are based on the Chi of an energy that has been blocked from Source for eons of lifetimes. Taking an energy that has been broken from Source at the Cosmic level and trying to do the repair work at the Planetary level just does not fix the problem.

This problem that is blocking our eternal life system happened billions of years ago, and the guardians have been working on fixing it for billions of years. There are many problems in each level of creation, far beyond the chakras within the body. The frequencies must be realigned clear out into the Universal Spheres, Cosmic Spheres, pre sound and light realms and the allness of Source's original idea of creation.

So, we are talking about a healing that would last as long as a band aid, or one that is complete and lasts for eternity.

Ascension -Connection between Consciousness and the body. Ascension isn't just about being a good person, going to church and getting forgiven by Christ and then going to heaven. It isn't that easy because there is a direct link between the consciousness of your spirit and the atomic structure of the body. The part of the spirit that is embedded into the atomic structure of the body is called the JARI. It is a part of the spirit body. If the JARI is trapped inside of the atomic structure at death, the body will not ascend. It will continue to be trapped on the Earth and will continue to return. This is what we did for the last ten million life times. Our JARI has been stuck inside of our atomic structure.

We must make sure our Jari is free from the atomic structure in order to ascend out of here.

We must transmute our spirit body out of the atomic structure in order to ascend. Once we have done that so many times that there is no quantum left in the body to ever ascend out of it, the person has entered the path of FALL. That person will need to return to Source through space dust return -ashes to ashes dust to dust. That is what would had happened to this planet and everyone on it if we hadn't been given the assistance of the AQUARI Matrix.

The path of Fall means the person just won't remember anything. They will return to Source and start over again.

Those on the path of fall have run out of energy. They are having to get energy from others. In a normal system that is not in Fall there is an eternal flow of energy giving an eternal source of eternal life.

The Ascension Program of Eternal Life Programming

So, we take this perfect formula of creation and rebirth that was given to us by the Guardian Races and we record it because it is made of Frequency Signatures. The breaths carry the frequency signatures and they are recorded in perfect harmonic convergence. Each of the frequencies transmutes into the highest frequency of Source Consciousness in order to hold that reality of the divine code for ever.

We began learning this process with the Meditations and God Language in the Complete Ascension Process Kit, The Ascension Portal Kit and the Pure in Heart Kit. These can be purchased at the website. Those workshops are over seven years old, however, they were the original foundations of the Frequencies, the Understanding and the Basic Tools needed for Ascension.

Each time I create an Album of Frequencies or a Set or Kit which also contain meditations, journeys and explanations, I am recording another nano second in the time frame of our Ascension.

The Ascension is being created through Specific Frequencies and Specific Frequencies Alignments within the Music of the Spheres.

If you really want to learn that complete process I recommend you spend fourteen years of study with the DVD kits titled the Freedom Teachings, the Sliders Series and all other Keylontic Science Teachings.

I already went through the teachings so that I could attune to the exact frequencies that were brought to Earth during this Ascension Time.

If you want to learn to do it your self, you should put aside about the next twenty years of your life.

I was trained how to do this by the Elohim Angels, the Ascension Teams, the Crystalai Council, the Sirian Council, the Akashic Light Teams, the Eka and EirA Light Teams, the Beloveds of my local families and guardians.

If you would like to read my Personal Ascension Process of activating 5 DNA by 2008 and imitating 12 more sub harmonics to consummate my 6th DNA strand by 2017, the new book titled 12 DNA - The Music of the Spheres Ascension Program from the Cosmic Twins Diary - with Keys to the Universe (this book!) contains the daily records of this process.

If you would like to begin your own ASCENSION PROCESS, it must begin with the Music of the Spheres, their Frequencies, their Attunement into the Atoms of the Body. It must begin with the morphogenetic fields of consciousness from the Six Avatar Children. It must begin with removing the Seals between the DNA with the Zero Point

ECSTAZEE. It must begin with filling the body with the Violet Flame Album of the 2008 Infusion of Sun Alcyone and the Ultra Violet Sun Album and the Cosmic Butterfly. It must begin with the Eternal Life Waters bringing the Hydrolaise and Trypolaise into the cells. It must begins with the emersion of the Frequencies of Consciousness that are INDIVIDUAL in NATURE to You and You alone.

Each Individual has been on this five million year journey of performing the re-birth of a race line which was the most cherished and sought after raceline in the Universe because it contained the gateways to all of the Universes. We had our orbing ability, our telepathic ability and our Eternal Life Ability of our original Raceline stollen from us, and now we are learning how to reclaim it.

The purpose of all of the Future Holographic Music at CrystalMagicOrchestra.com has been created through the Consciousness of the Guardians, the Cosmic Councils, the Akashic Keepers, the Makers of Light and Sound of the Fourteenth Dimension, the Sirian Council, the Oraphim Council, the Taran Council, and all others who have been working non stop to perfect our Divine Templates within each one of us for millions of years.

The Ascension Program of Eternal Life Programming

HOW TO USE THE ETERNAL LIFE ALBUM

Each time an order is placed for the ETERNAL LIFE ALBUM, the individual has individual questions because each INDIVIDUAL has an entirely different BACKGROUND KNOWLEDGE.

Some of you have backgrounds in New Age teachings, some have backgrounds in Indian Medicine Man or Shamanic Healing, some in Akashic Records readings, some in Metaphysical teachings.

That is why it is very difficult to give step by step listening instructions.

You see, it is always your BACKGROUND KNOWLEDGE that will over power whatever my words might actually mean.
If you have any background of any other teaching, you are always going to think I meant what your other teacher already told you, and you will automatically be transmuting away the information that I am giving you.

Please try to consider reading my explanations of what I am trying to teach you as something BRAND NEW that you have never heard before. Try not to use your old BACKGROUND KNOWLEDGE that is stuck in your old thinking brain.

The Ascension Program of Eternal Life Programming

warm Greetings to you Crystalai!
wow,,,i feel speechless,,your last newsletter "preparing to shift,,just literally
took my breath...today was and is magic i ask for help and the universe answers
today i received a most beautiful visualisation-meditation from Bashar,,and working
with Crystals,,,creating a new reality,,,now i received your teachings and my heart
did a double take on past present future
for me it is a pearl,,i feel so blessed,,for a flash of a second ,,i got it,,something
cracked,,i will read this over and over,
as for the" Eternal Life Album". i received another gift,,your trust in me..
i am deeply honored,,you see me,,and it brings tears of gratitude to my eyes
i learn so much from you in such short time and all i feel is resonance.,,as if
Heaven itself is spinning me in a cocoon to help me coming HOME,,,that is
how i feel.
Crystalai,,my profoundest
Thanks and Gratitude to you.
,i had some awesome experiences
in my life,,but i also so much struggle with myself
.
the record is stuck,,the needle is skipping and pattern repeating over and over
since childhood,,,and i just don't get it how to change a situation into something

other than what i see or live,,it is so frustrating,,

i am good with others,but when it comes to me,,,i feel lost. i really have a hart time

living in this 3 D,,,i never understood how to work it

today we did a matrix clearing, removing the shadow lair from those dark ones.

there will be changes very soon..Kartron spoke about the music of the spheres

and frequencies and it is all in the same line with your music and the teachings

you offer,,i am so thrilled to have the Best of the Best in my life. i am so grateful.

Crystalai,,i am so happy and thankful to have found you

your teachings and letters nourish my soul,,,and from the bottom

of my heart;;i love you   and i know what Love is.

thank you

IMAGINATION !!!!!

YOU MUST LEARN TO USE YOUR IMAGINATION

The Ascension Program of Eternal Life Programming

Your world will be transformed by using your imagination to create your PAST, PRESENT AND FUTURE

As long as you keep seeing your past as you remember it --your future will never change.

The key to changing your reality is by imagining your perfect past present and future.

Your wonderful reality where you see Fairies and Blue Spheres is the reality that you want to tune in to.

See that reality of magical possibilities as your past present and future.

You must begin simply by writing a list.
The list needs to say:

I have always been fabulously wealthy.
I am fabulously wealthy.
I will always be fabulously wealthy.

Create a list using that formula.

I have always had perfect health.
I have perfect Health.
I will always have perfect health.

I have always had 12 DNA.
I have 12 DNA.
I will always have 12 DNA.

GIVE ME SIMPLE STEPS IN LISTENING VISUALIZATION

First Visualize the Frequencies as a Light Portal that connects 36 inches above the head and down into the Crystal Heart of Mother Earth.

Draw a picture of this area. See your body standing on the Earth and draw a circle from 36 inches above the head of the body down into the center of the Earth. Realize that the place in the Earth is in the Cosmic Realm--not the Planetary.
See that Circle around your body and into the Earth's Cosmic Realm as the place where all of the Frequency activation takes place.

You are keeping your self wrapped inside of a COSMIC FIELD OF ENERGY.

This is the place where your Cosmic Merkaba would Lock you into At One Ment with the Source Field of Love.

The Ascension Program of Eternal Life Programming

Before you begin listening to the music, draw this picture, and visualize your self standing within this Cosmic Sphere. This is the Cosmic Sphere that the Music is LIFTING YOU INTO.

NEXT

Before you begin listening, create a mini me of your self, and send that mini me up to 36 inches above your head.

Become that mini me. See yourself sitting in a Lotus Blossom with your legs crossed, 36 inches above your head.

Stay there while you are listening to the music.

The music contains the frequencies to lift your physical body up to the Consciousness where your mini me self is sitting.
Focus on filling your body with the frequencies while you are sitting in the Lotus Blossom.

NEXT

Stay 36 inches above your head.

1. Listen and focus on the frequencies of light in the stomach area.

2. Listen and focus on the frequencies of light in the crystal heart.

3. Listen and focus on the frequencies of light in the tailbone.

4. Listen and focus on the frequencies of light in the back of the neck.

5. Listen and focus on the frequencies of light in the center of the head--pineal gland.

NEXT

Continue to remember to bring all of the light and sound into a ball of light energy and see it being breathed into the stomach, crystal heart, tailbone and pineal gland.

VISUALIZE this as ANGELS OF LOVE PLAYING HARPS inside of each of those Key Areas. They are connecting each cell in the body to the MUSIC OF THE SPHERES that sings us into PERFECT SPIRITUAL TRANSFORMATION.
NEXT

Stay 36 inches above.

Feel a crystal star two feet above the head. Allow all of the frequencies in the music to fill that crystal star until you see the star spinning and you see sparkling stardust flying from inside of it. Next, bring the star full of Christ Consciousness Star Dust into the head and the heart, and the tailbone and the feet.

See that crystal star spinning sparkling stardust into every cell in the body.

Feel each cell in the body filling with stardust, which contains the Divine Blue Print of the SOURCE template.

Repeat this while visualizing the stardust as an even more ETHERIC substance of a vapor like stardust.

Repeat this while visualizing the stardust as the the pre plasma vapor of Spiritual Water.

When the Body is filled with this pre light and sound Vapor called HYDROLAISE (Spirtual Water), the Body Transforms into the Light of Christ.

VISUALIZE your body becoming Full of Light until it is Glowing from the inside to the outside.

While absorbing and feeling the frequencies stream through every cell in the body, see or feel a white light portal connecting from the pineal to the crystal heart down through the feet and into the core of mother earth. Feel the angelic frequencies connecting you into the frequencies stored in Mother Earth that contain your cellular memory of your original spiritual self made in the image and likeness of the god self, Christ self and the spark of Source co-creative energy.

Feel the frequency of Divine Love, Divine Life, Divine Truth, Divine Mind, Soul, Spirit, Intelligence, Principle Victory Power Manifestation, Supply and the Divine Plan. These are the Frequencies stored in the Core of Mother Earth in the Cosmic Realm of the 13th Dimension.

Continue to connect the frequencies of consciousness into the Body Template areas and the vortex areas. This will progress the activation of the DNA.

VISUALIZE YOUR BODY

The body is standing deep within all 15 spheres of Consciousness or within all Five HARMONIC UNIVERSES.

Each Harmonic Universe has thousands of Suns containing tons of STARDUST- pre-stardust of that Crystalline Vapor called Hydrolaise.

Feel the frequencies of all of the millions of suns stream into the head, the heart and every cell in the body.

Feel the frequencies of the inter-dimensional angels, divas, and fairies singing and dancing into your cells and into your consciousness.

Collect all of these frequencies into your cells to activate the cellular memory of your original divine self -- your immortal self that has the ability to live for ever, create the heart's desires and heal instantly.

We can know that this field of Consciousness is Perfect, always has been perfect and always will be perfect.

When the EKA Body is being connected to within the Earth, take our Consciousness down into the Earth's Crystal Heart deep within her Vortex and then travel deep within into the 13.5 Cosmic Core of the Earth's Iron Core. Whereas the old Akashic Records were found in the Earth's Iron Core of a Fourth Dimensional Realtiy Field.

When the Akashic Reader helps the patient to find the Life time that has created a continuous problem in their life, the answer that is found is an answer that comes from the Astral Realm. When the practitioner attaches consciousness 8 inches above the head, they are moving into astral consciousness.

The Ascension Program of Eternal Life Programming

That Consciousness is only 4th dimensional substance that contains all of the problems that exist on Earth. So, or course it is easy to find the source of our problems in that layer of Consciousness.

In the method of using the ETERNAL LIFE Frequencies of Consciousness, we are not searching for the problem, we are returning the PERFECT SELF that we were created to be. The problems that were placed in the Astral Field were placed there to keep us locked inside of the Earth's Matrix.

The Frequencies in the 14th and 15th dimension were created to give us ETERNAL LIFE.

We are each made in the image and likeness of Source. That image and likeness is a negative of the picture of the idea that Source is creating. That idea is held within Source Consciousness and rebirthed into creation every trillionth of a nano second. When the brand new image and likeness is imprinted on the idea, the idea is reborn as a brand new image with the new thoughts and ideas of the new experiences encoded within it.

I hold that idea within the Source Flame. That idea is already perfect and it contains the 12 coded divine blue print of angelic raceline.

That old idea that was created billions of years ago must go through a rebirth at this time. We are all

The Ascension Program of Eternal Life Programming

being reborn into a new harmonic universe, a new space and time portal. Each time we are born we come into the planet through a stargate. Many of the stargates attached to Earth were destroyed and we were disconnected from many of them. Now, we are being placed in a different time portal where we are back in alignment with all 12 stargates, which allows us to obtain the 12 sub-harmonics in each of our chakras.

These 12 sub-harmonics comes from combining the spiritual coding from the chakras outside of the physical body with the chakras within the physical body. In order for an entity to return to a place in the universe, there must be an essence or a frequency signature of that entity left in that place from the time the entity left the place in the universe.

In order for our bodies to become realigned into the eternal life domain of the harmonic universe, I take the idea or the image that is within the Flame of Source and create a light body image of that idea. I place that idea within a flame. I use a candle flame. Within the flame is the complete spectrum of light, the entire rainbow. The flame includes the hertzian, infra red, visible light, invisible light, x ray light, and gamma waves. The idea is held within the complete spectrum of light of Source Consciousness.

References

Deane, Ashayana, The Voyagers: The Secrets of Amenti Volume 2, second edition, 2002, Wildflower Press, NC

Deane, Ashayana, The Sliders DVD Series 1-12, (2000-2012) Azurite Press

Doyle, Arthur Conan, The Coming of the Fairies (1922) Hodder & Stoughton. New York, Toronto and London

Eddy, Mary Baker, The Science and Health, with Keys to the Scriptures, Published by The First Church of Christ Scientist, Copyright 1971 The Christian Science Board of Directors

References

Goldsmith, Joel, Living Between Two Worlds, 1974, Acropolis Books, Santa Barbara, California, edited by Loraine Sinkler

Goldsmith, Joel, Conscious Union with God, Wilder Publications, VA, 2011

Henry, William, 2006, Mary Magdalene: The Illuminator, Adventures Unlimited Press; First Printing edition (September 1, 2006)

Index

Symbols

11:11 Frequency Fence 23
12 Coded Divine Blue Print 167
12 D Christos 128
12 DNA 189
12 DNA ACTIVATION 264
12 sub harmonic strands 263
12th Level Avatar 222
14th Dimension 156
14th Dimensional Frequencies 13
48 DNA 328
144,000 selves 62
2017 165

A

ADVANCED DNA ACTIVATION 264
Agartha 166
Akashic Records 18
AKASHIC RECORDS 314
Andromeda Consciousness 29
Andromeda Galaxy 173
Aquafarian 176
are all a necessary part of the process of melting 252
Ascension Path 27
ascension portal 135
Aton 152
ATON 152
Avatars 131

B

Base tones 26
base tones and over tones 285
bio fields 177
Bliss 15, 154
Blood of Christ 56
Blue Body 69
Blue Hue 156
Blue Maharaji 67
Braharama Raceline 167
Breath 154
bringing the highest frequencies 189

C

Candle Technique 156
carbon based body 172
catastrophic impact 65
Children of God 163
Christ body 175
Christic 12D 134
Christic Template 182
Cinderella 62
cloak that blocks the reality of Source Consciousness 171
Cloud Cities 135
code 127
cognition 131
Comet Ison 157
Cosmic Blanket 63
Cosmic Council 19
Cosmic Frequencies 328
cosmic liquid light energy 135

INDEX

Cosmic Massage 263
cosmic microphone 57
Cosmic Mystery School of the Omniverse 17
COSMIC TWINS 39
Crystalai Council 18
Crystal bodies 176
Crystal Gel 56
crystalmagicorchestra.com 61

D
D-5 Violet Wave Infusion 25
D-6 Stellar Wave Activation 25
Divine Blue Print 125
Divine Minds 181
Divine Science 231
DNA Activation 26
DNA consummation 29
DNA Consummation 213
DNA DOCTOR krystalaimagic@gmail.com 284
DNA initiation 29
DNA restoration 285
Doctorate in Education 286
dolphins 135
Dolphin Therapy 252

E
Earth's template 131
Edons of the Inner Earth 176
Elohim 165
Elohim Angels 189
Elohim of Hearing 29, 190
Emerald 166

INDEX

Emerald Covenant Nations 166
Eternal Harmony 260
ETERNAL LIFE ALBUM 314, 386
eternal life bodies 176
ETERNAL LIFE WATERS SET 263
evolutionary blueprint 27

F

fifth dimensional body 155
FREE CHOIC 259
Frequencies from the Universal Life Force 264
Frequency Fence 8
frequency signature 127
Frequency Signatures 10, 181
Frequency Specific Mid Brain 231
FUTURE GLOBAL MANAGEMENT 38

G

god 173
God Language 287
Golden Crystal Core 157
Guide 14

H

Harmomic Keys 24
HARMONIC CONVERGENCE 276
Harmonic Keys 10, 11
harp strings 161
HARVEST 217
Heart of Mother Earth 177
HEAVENLY BIRTH 276
hertzian frequency 183
hide the Soul 174

INDEX

High Context Communication 37
higher parts of ourselves 132
hologram 58, 65, 66
holographic beam 157
Holographic Beam 159
http://en.wikipedia.org/wiki/File:Cottingley_Fairies_1.jpg 15
Human Angelic Raceline 18

I
Illuminati 164
incorrect formula 176
Indigo Children 165
Infinite Love 260
Infinite Way 20
inorganic birth 172
instantaneous creation 175
International Communication Consultants 36
invisibility cloak 170, 174

J
Jehovah 173
Jesus and Mary 66
Joel Goldsmith 19
June, 2008 28

K
karma 64
Karma 180
Keylontic Science 231
Key Signatures 10
Knights of the Templar 56
Kuthumi 14

INDEX

L
Leviathan 128
Light Body 69
LIQUID LIGHT CLEANSING 378
locked into the hertzian field 171
Love 155
Luciferian Covenant 129

M
magnetizes 171
manifest 241
man made template 173
Mary Baker Eddy 19
Mary Magdalene 56, 152
Melt 252
Merkaba 11
Mind of God 190
Mother Earth's Crystal Heart 377
Music of the Spheres 9, 180

N
Natural Person 179
Near Death Experience 160
new babies 179
Nibiru 163
Normal Body 173
Normal Man 174
Normal Self 180

O
Omnipresence 260
Oraphim Cetacean 167
orb 155

Over tones 26

P

Parallel Universe Album 158
Photon Belt 158
Photon Belt of Sun Alcyone 297
Plasma Ships 156
Promise 188
Promise Album 191
Psychic 21

R

radiation fields 174
reborn 176
recombining 141
Red Dragons 140
resurrection 66

S

Scalar Grid mechanics 130
Seal 171
Second Harmonic Universe 11, 59
Silver Seed 170, 171
silver seed atom 175, 178
silver seed awakening 176
Sirian Council 25
Sirius B 59
Soul Families 161
sound and light technology 127
sound waves 186
Source Consciousness 170
Source Field ignited 177
Source Frequencies 156

INDEX

space ship 65
space ships from Sirius B 135
Spirit 152
Spirit Body 172
stairway to heaven 153
Stardust 283
Star Language 37
Sub harmonic 156
sub harmonics 285
Sun Alcyone 158
SYMPHONY OF LOVE 264

T

Teams of Consciousness 181
telepathic 287
THE MATRIX OF ILLUSIONS 38
THE MOTHER SHIP 255
Third Activation 28
Thoth 213
Three Crystal Spheres 38
three spheres 56
time acceleration shift 27
Time Matrix 10
true Christic baby 171
truth 174

U

ULTIMATE DNA ARCHETYPE 264
Universal Distortion 132
Universal Life Force Currents 63

V

violet flame 180

Violet Sun 24
vortex 186

Z

ZERO POINT BODY MEDITATION 376
Zetas 163

CPSIA information can be obtained at www.ICGtesting.com
Printed in the USA
LVOW10s1651210615

443296LV00031B/1107/P